WHAT OTHERS

KING C⊕TTON

"Big things happen in small towns, and sports matter in real life. Cotton Robinson's blend of inspiration, teamwork, preparation, and persistence provided for his players, both on and off the hardwood, a clear road map to success. Thanks to Fred B. McKinley and Charles Breithaupt, contemporary basketball fans can today glean similar wisdom from the late, great coach. The story of his life is told with such detail and warmth, you'll feel like you were there."

—ERIC ANGEVINE
College Basketball Insider at ESPN.com

"In a time when Texas high school basketball was trying to find its place, Cotton Robinson of Buna set the table for its future by winning seven state championships. A pioneer in his field, Robinson established a premier basketball program that provided a winning formula to be used by those who followed in his footsteps. In *King Cotton*, McKinley and Breithaupt share great insight into how Robinson put together all the pieces to become one of the most successful coaches that Texas, and perhaps the nation, has ever seen. This book is a must read for those who love sports or simply want to learn about how to win in life."

—LEON BLACK
Retired Head Basketball Coach
University of Texas

"A very good read and great insight into one of our state's true coaching legends."

—BILLY GILLESPIE
Head Basketball Coach
Texas Tech University

"*King Cotton* chronicles the life and career of one of the best coaches in Texas's long and storied sports history. Through this book, we all continue to learn from the master teacher, both on and off the court."

—RICK SHERLEY
Executive Director
Texas Association of Basketball Coaches

"A must read for all sports enthusiasts. *King Cotton* is a great book about legendary coach Cotton Robinson and the significant contributions that he made to the game of basketball. I still utilize the Buna Offense at the major college level."

—DOC SADLER
Head Basketball Coach
University of Nebraska

"Fred B. McKinley and Charles Breithaupt have given us a well-written, skillfully researched and documented tribute to Coach "Cotton" Robinson, a true Texas basketball legend. For those interested in the historical development and execution of the double post offense, still a staple of many coaching philosophies, *King Cotton* provides a step by step analysis. Without question, the authors have combined their talents to vividly capture and portray the true mystique of the Buna boys, their coach, and the famed "Buna Offense." *King Cotton* should be included in the library of every coach and fan of our great game of basketball."

—SAM TIPTON
Executive Director
Texas Girls Coaches Association

Also by Fred B. McKinley

A Plea for Justice:
The Timothy Cole Story

Black Gold to Bluegrass:
From the Oil Fields of Texas to Spindletop Farm of Kentucky

CHINQUA WHERE?
The Spirit of Rural America, 1947–1955

Devil's Pocket, a Novel

Also by Charles Breithaupt

"A Study of the Relationship between Students' Perceptions
and Characteristics and Their Participation in
Extracurricular Activities in High School."
Ed.D. Dissertation, University of Texas at Austin, 1996.

KING C TTON

Coach Cotton Robinson
and the Buna Boys' Basketball Legacy,
1948–1963

Fred B. McKinley
and
Charles Breithaupt

NORTEX PRESS   NORTEX   Waco, Texas

To those who dare to dream.

FIRST EDITION
Copyright © 2012 by Fred B. McKinley and Charles Breithaupt
Printed in the United States of America
By Nortex Press — A Division of Sunbelt Media, Inc.
P.O. Box 21235 🕮 Waco, Texas 76702
email: sales@eakinpress.com
💻 website: www.eakinpress.com 💻
ALL RIGHTS RESERVED.
1   2   3   4   5   6   7   8   9
ISBN 13: 978-1-935632-26-9
ISBN 10: 1-035632-26-4
Library of Congress Control Number 2012932143

Contents

Foreword

King Cotton describes how a small town coach in Texas captured seven state high school titles, a record that stands alone in the 90-year history of state tournament competition.

Fred B. McKinley and Charles Breithaupt, both of whom grew up where it all happened, present a beautifully written narrative that details the life of Marshall Neil Robinson and how he came to be regarded as one of the best coaches Texas high school basketball has ever seen. From austere beginnings, through tough times, unparalleled success on the hardwood, and eventually to the Texas Basketball Hall of Fame, the two reveal how Robinson achieved an incredible career record—538 wins and only 98 losses. Surprisingly, all this originated in a community with less than 1,600 residents and no more than 255 high school students enrolled at any given time.

The authors' words are crisp, the photographs are warm reminders of a bygone era, and the anecdotes expose the compassionate side of an otherwise stern and demanding coach who rarely compromised. Meticulously researched and documented, *King Cotton* is a story of inspiration that carries the reader on an extraordinary journey. And at the end, one comes away with what it feels like to be part of a basketball dynasty.

As for me, I got to witness up close and personal one of the events described in the book. Coach Robinson's Cougars beat my high school team, the Dimmitt Bobcats, 60 to 36 in the 1961 state championship, in a game that wasn't as close as the final score.

I was a senior guard on that team and to this day, I don't just remember that Buna beat us that night in Gregory Gym; I remember how they beat us. Never before had we come across a team as tenacious and fundamentally sound as were the Cougars. It wasn't they were that much bigger than us—their leading scorer that night stood all of five-foot-seven—it was their undying adherence to Coach Robinson's teaching that made them the better team.

I was struck by how well disciplined Buna was under Cotton Robinson. They were a well-oiled machine, utilizing a full court press and suffocating our offense. They not only outplayed us—they outworked us. It made me feel a little better that we weren't alone as Buna went 43–0 that year. They were as well coached of a team as I'd ever seen.

And so I became more than just an interested bystander watching the progression of the Buna program. They would go on to win two more championships under Coach Robinson, and they did it the right way. The Cougars were dogged on the court and sportsmen off the hardwood. Their coach instilled principles in his teams that were bigger than just results on the court, he taught them life lessons as well.

Cotton Robinson touched many lives. Numerous former players went on to coaching careers of their own, passing on his legacy to countless other players—and many of those players went on to coaching careers of their own, ensuring that Coach Robinson's philosophy lives on even to this day in Texas high school basketball. Long after he retired to a life of selling insurance, he would welcome both new and veteran coaches into his home to share his insight and wisdom.

Even though my team was on the losing end that night in Austin, I learned a few lessons myself. One of the great things about sports and competition is that it teaches you about life. There is always a winner and that means there is also a loser. But you win with class and you lose with dignity and know you gave it your best effort and live to fight another day. Those are philosophies that have served me well in my career in law, politics, and education.

It's hard to fathom the success that Coach Robinson had at Buna. It was a different time and place, and as you will read in these pages, the on court success eventually came to an end. But Cotton Robinson's legacy is far greater than the seven banners hanging in the gym in Buna and that is a flame that will never flicker.

—KENT HANCE
Chancellor
Texas Tech University System

Acknowledgments

The writing of *King Cotton* has been both an adventure and a labor of love, but we did not go it alone. From the outset, we had two major goals in mind: to ensure a finished narrative worthy of its namesake, and to guarantee historical accuracy by means of corroborating documentation. Therefore, we sought out the advice and assistance of varied sources, and the response was overwhelming. We remain deeply indebted to many individuals and organizations and so, we recognize the following.

First, we extend our heartfelt appreciation to the members of the Robinson family. Cotton's daughters, Lynda Robinson Sanford and Janice Robinson Black; sisters, Lyndall Robinson Hale and Lillian Robinson Pierce; and brother, Stanley Robinson, all of whom contributed in one way or another. However, without the strong backing of Mrs. Sanford, who went over and above, this work would probably have never seen the light of day. Lynda patiently endured the continued telephone calls and seemingly never-ending e-mails that requested additional information and clarifications about her famous father. And, too, during the interview process, she and her husband, Butch, opened their home and provided more photographs, documents, and information than we ever expected.

Although too numerous to list here, we acknowledge the many former Buna Cougar basketball players and team managers who responded with completed questionnaires and follow-ups that made this book more than a recitation of statistics. These personal accounts allowed us a peek into the soul of their revered coach, a man who commanded respect far and wide by the way he lived and likewise, groomed his players for the challenges that lay beyond sports. In this regard, J. C. Smith,

Jim Mellard, Lionel Reese, Delman Rogers, John Rich, Jim Richardson, and Jimmy Burke deserve special mention.

Furthermore, we are appreciative of Kent Hance, Chancellor of the Texas Tech University System in Lubbock, for taking time from a demanding schedule in order to read the original manuscript and then pen the foreword to this chronicle. Also, we wish to thank Kimberly Rogers, Chief of Staff, University Interscholastic League, Austin, Texas, for her valuable suggestions and editorial comments.

Others also provided in-depth research, among them Penny Clark, University Archivist, Lamar University, Beaumont, Texas; Charlotte Holliman, Special Collections, Mary and John Gray Library, Lamar University, Beaumont, Texas; I. Bruce Turner, Special Collections, Dupré Library, University of Louisiana, Lafayette, Louisiana; Vivica Pierre, Dupré Library, University of Louisiana, Lafayette, Louisiana; Sandra Uselton, Office of the Registrar, Sam Houston State University, Huntsville, Texas; Barbara Kievit-Mason, University Archivist, Sam Houston State University, Huntsville, Texas; Susan Doherty, Executive Assistant, University Interscholastic League, Austin, Texas; John Johnson, Jasper County Historical Commission, Jasper, Texas; Lena White, Librarian, Buna Public Library, Buna, Texas; Pam Davis, Librarian, Buna High School, Buna, Texas; William Grace, Library Manager, Tyrrell Historical Library, Beaumont, Texas; and Earl Moore, Leon County Genealogy Society, Centerville, Texas.

Many others also deserve a particular note of gratitude, specifically the following, who supplied support, information, photographs, and leads. To any whom we may inadvertently have left out, please accept our sincere apologies.

In alphabetical order by first name:

Allen Clegg, Buna, Texas
Anita Babineaux, Registrar's Office, University of Louisiana, Lafayette, Louisiana
Anthony "Pete" Hillin, Longview, Texas
Ardie Dixon, Lufkin, Texas
Ashlee Jordan Haefs, Buna, Texas
Ava Brown, Librarian, Big Sandy ISD, Dallardsville, Texas
Barbara Franklin McCann, Buna, Texas
Becky Cleveland, Justice of the Peace, Precinct 4, Buna, Texas
Benny Johnson, Orange, Texas

Bill Kirkpatrick, Wharton, Texas

Billie Gene Clark, Buna, Texas

Billy Gillespie, Head Basketball Coach, Texas Tech University, Lubbock, Texas

Bob Springer, Texas Basketball Hall of Fame, Carmine, Texas

Bobby and Melba Breithaupt, Buna, Texas

Bobby Guy Ener, Hemphill, Texas

Bobby Simmons, Leesville, Louisiana

Bobby Stratton, Sulphur, Louisiana

Buddy Bender, Baytown, Texas

Byron P. Terrier, Assistant Superintendent, Goose Creek Consolidated ISD, Baytown, Texas

Cade Sirmans, Athletic Media Relations, University of Louisiana, Lafayette, Louisiana

Carolyn Rauwerda, Buna, Texas

Cathy Capps, Director, Texas A&M Lettermen's Association, College Station, Texas

Charles Chesnutt, Houston, Texas

Charles Guillory, Buna, Texas

Charles Lindsey, Sugar Land, Texas

Charles Simmons, Buna, Texas

Charles Westbrook, Beaumont, Texas

Cherie Morgan, Sterling Municipal Library, Baytown, Texas

Chris Colletti, Executive Director, Young Men's Business League, Beaumont, Texas

Christi Fountain, Administration, Buna ISD, Buna, Texas

Cindy Menard, Office of the Registrar, University of Louisiana, Lafayette, Louisiana

Clinton Johnson, Orange, Texas

Coy Fletcher, Woodville, Texas

Deon Cummings Thornton, Buna, Texas

Derryl Stanley, Lumberton, Texas

Doc Sadler, Head Basketball Coach, University of Nebraska, Lincoln, Nebraska

Don Mathews, Sour Lake, Texas

Don Muckleroy, Principal, Buna High School, Buna, Texas

Don Skinner, Hideaway, Texas

Don and Roanne Stanley, Buna, Texas

Dot Smith, Buna, Texas

Doug Barclay, Wimberley, Texas

Doug Stanley, Bullard, Texas
Dwaine Reese, Richmond, Texas
Edwin Battise, Livingston, Texas
Eric Angevine, College Basketball Insider at ESPN.com
George Jones, Lumberton, Texas
Georgia Callier Spencer, Buna, Texas
Geraldine Hyden, Buna, Texas
Glen Stancil, Cypress, Texas
Glenn Cummings, Beaumont, Texas
Harold and Kay Simmons, Buna, Texas
Helene Hillin, Buna, Texas
Herbert Muckleroy, Silsbee, Texas
Herbert Ross, Buna, Texas
J. D. O'Keefe, Pasadena, Texas
Jackie Bond, Jasper, Texas
Jackie Swearingen, Village Mills, Texas
James Simmons, Victoria, Texas
James Withers, Tucson, Arizona
Jerry Buckner, Many, Louisiana
Jerry Goins, Buna, Texas
Jerry Smith, San Benito, Texas
Jerryl Stanley, Buna, Texas
Jo Nell Knight, Buna, Texas
Joan Smith, Orange, Texas
John A. Hatch, Longview, Texas
John McHugh, Vidor, Texas
John "Nickie" Meaux, Lake Conroe, Texas
Johnny Carter, Madisonville, Texas
Johnny and Nelda Sheppard, Buna, Texas
Kenneth and Bettye Champion, Buna, Texas
Kenneth Cobb, La Grange, Texas
Larry and Deneice Gerald, Buna, Texas
Laverne Bishop, Richards, Texas
Leon and Peggy Black, Austin, Texas
Lewine Germany Foster, Buna, Texas
Linda Franklin Monk, Troup, Texas
Linda Steele, Assistant to Chancellor, Texas Tech University System, Lubbock, Texas
Lonnie Lavender, Venus, Texas
Macarthur Gibson, Lafayette, Louisiana

Mark Durham, Port Arthur Public Library, Port Arthur, Texas

Mark Kimbrough Mosley, Austin, Texas

Matt Lucas, Deer Park ISD, Deer Park, Texas

Matt Simon, Media Relations, Texas A&M University, College Station, Texas

Melissa Swedoski, former Publisher and Editor, *Buna Beacon*, Buna, Texas

Melvin and Lori Ellison, Orange, Texas

Mike Barley, Detroit, Texas

Nancy Wegener Sealy, Houston, Texas

Odis Booker, Kirbyville, Texas

Orren Ray "Cotton" Whiddon, Nacogdoches, Texas

Pat and Mary Stanley, Buna, Texas

Pat Stom, Beaumont, Texas

Patricia Lannou, Secretary, Goose Creek Consolidated ISD, Baytown, Texas

Paul Swearingen, Buna, Texas

Peggy Walters, Buna, Texas

Peggy Whitehead, Buna, Texas

Phil and Vivian Rogers, Schulenburg, Texas

R. C. McFarland, Lumberton, Texas

Raymond Cleveland, Buna, Texas

Rebecca Drews, Navasota, Texas

Regina Bolton, Young Men's Business League, Beaumont, Texas

Revis Whitmire, Broaddus, Texas

Richard DeVore, Princeton, Texas

Richard Charles Simmons, Hemphill, Texas

Richard Whitaker, Port Arthur Public Library, Port Arthur, Texas

Rick Sherley, Texas Association of Basketball Coaches, Sugar Land, Texas

Rita Willis, Librarian, Cypress-Fairbanks High School, Houston, Texas

Robbie Muckleroy, Harper, Texas

Robert Dale Cummings, Buna, Texas

Robert Hargrove, Buna, Texas

Robert Lynn Muckleroy, Kirbyville, Texas

Rod Aydelotte, *Waco Tribune-Herald*, Waco, Texas

Roy Dale Adams, Assistant Principal, Deer Park High School North, Deer Park, Texas

Rusty Sowell, San Augustine, Texas

Sam Tipton, Executive Director, Texas Girls Coaches Association, Austin, Texas

Shannon Capps, Executive Director, Library Services, Troup High School, Troup, Texas
Sharon Stancil, Coppell, Texas
Steve Hyden, Buna, Texas
Sue Mellard, Boerne, Texas
Syble Reeves Franklin, Buna, Texas
Terry Maillet-Jones, Librarian, *Beaumont Enterprise*, Beaumont, Texas
Thomas Foster, Village Mills, Texas
Thomas Richard Walters, Pasadena, Texas
Tom Westbrook, Buna, Texas
Tommy G. Clark, Wildwood Resort City, Texas
Tommy and Judy Richbourg, Buna, Texas
Victor Rogers, Pearland, Texas
Wanda Orton, Fredericksburg, Texas
William P. Bond, Assistant Principal, Buna Junior High School, Buna, Texas
William Withers, Buna, Texas

And lastly, we commend Kris Gholson, publisher at Eakin Press, for his usual support; Pat Molenaar, book designer and typesetter; and Kim Williams, cover designer, because without their combined efforts, none of this would have been possible.

—THE AUTHORS

Introduction

"Every sport pretends to a literature, but people don't believe it of any other sport but their own."
—ALISTAIR COOK

Americans love their basketball, and as with all sports, we admire those teams that rise to the top, and in spite of all odds, remain there year after year. But given the state of intense competition, parity, and our inherent desire to pull for the underdog, so-called dynasties are hard to come by. Even so, at least two come to mind.

The Boston Celtics, with the likes of John Havlicek, Bob Cousy, and K. C. Jones, ruled the professional circuit during the 1960s; while on the college scene, there may never be another to equal the record accumulated by the UCLA Bruins. Between 1963 and 1975, the legendary John Wooden's Bruins captured the NCAA championship ten out of twelve years. With such dominating players as Lew Alcindor a.k.a. Kareem Abdul-Jabbar, Gail Goodrich, and Bill Walton, the Bruins' winning streak reached an incredible eighty-eight games.[1]

Most teams may never experience such success on the hardwood. Yet, the classic tale of David and Goliath is the stuff of American dreams. For those who've seen the movie *Hoosiers*, it's quite easy to understand the tug at the heartstrings when watching a small-time, rural school go up against a much larger rival—and in an amazing display of human will, come away with a state championship.[2]

As in Indiana, Texas high school boys' basketball runs deep in tradition, and in March of each year, the University Interscholastic League sponsors a state tournament in Austin that showcases the very best, the crème de la crème. Whether they're from the smallest school district or the largest, teams take to the courts with high hopes, while those who cheer them on either gather in the stands, or in front of their televisions

Courtesy of the UIL, which currently governs extracurricular activities for over 1,400 high schools in Texas with nearly two million participants, and with full permission to reprint, the following represents historical data on that organization. The information, in its entirety, is quoted directly from page 9 of the Basketball Pressbook *of the 42nd Annual University Interscholastic League Boys' Basketball State Championship Tournament, Austin, Texas, March 1–3, 1962. The Pressbook was compiled for sportswriters and sportscasters by Max R. Haddick, then UIL Director of Journalism.*

The University Interscholastic League, organized in December, 1910, sponsored its first State Meet in May, 1911. Only speech, track and field contests were sponsored at first. In 1915, football, basketball, baseball and tennis were included as League events, but only tennis was played to a State Championship. The others were played on a county championship basis, with the State divided into a number of "districts," following county lines. A minimum of four games was required for a team to lay claim to a county championship.

The first State Championship basketball tournament was conducted in 1921. El Paso defeated San Antonio 25–11 in the final game. Sixteen teams, bi-district winners from 32 districts, played in the tournament. No accurate data are available on total participation in that first year, because organization was loose, with many tiny country schools fielding teams recruited from an afternoon's game from among the boys in the school. If the game was lost, the team might never be reassembled for another game. If the game was won, the team might continue playing until it could claim a county championship, and then might or might not enter the district tournament. Only at this point did records begin to reflect the number participating. The estimate for that year was 300 teams.

The first tournament was played March 11 and 12, 1921, on the 90x50 court in the old Men's Gymnasium on the University campus. Cups were presented to the winning and runner-up teams by the University of Texas President, Dr. Robert E. Vinson. Gold medals went to members of the All-State Team, which was chosen by an appointed committee during the early years of League tournaments, and had official standing in League records.

In 1922, estimates on participation placed the figure at slightly more than 500 teams. Winner of the second State Championship was Lindale High School, but later disqualification gave the title to runner-up El Paso. Governor Pat Neff presented cups to both teams, and, in a shift to the current practice, medals were given to individual members of the two top teams. No All-State awards were given, although an official team was named. A Sportsmanship Medal was presented officially to Bennie Strickland of Waco.

Estimated participation in 1923 was 1,300 teams and in 1924 around 1,400 participated. The 4th annual tournament (1924) was marked by the addition of a consolation tournament for teams eliminated in the first round. Judge O. S. Lattimore of the Court of Criminal Appeals presented the cups and medals. Medals went to All-State players, and a sportsmanship medal to Joines of Houston.

In 1942, basketball was split into conferences — AA, A and B. It was further divided in 1948 by the addition of the City Conference. A complete restyling in 1952 brought the present five conferences — AAAA, AAA, AA, A and B.*

*In 1980–1981, Conference B was eliminated, and a new conference, 5A was added.

and radios, to lend encouragement for their favorite. The charged atmosphere proves that hometown pride reigns supreme.

While discussing the fact that "many families had standing reservations in Austin for state tournament weekend," Joan Smith, who played basketball at Buna, cited an excellent example of this community spirit. "The last one out of town, turn out the lights," she wrote. "No one is left in Buna but Grannie Mixson."[3]

Regardless of how loyal or demonstrative the fan base, one championship game never produces two victors, leaving the loser to cope and regroup. As the vanquished arrive in the dressing room, each member displays the natural emotion of letting down friends and family, teammates, and most of all, the coach who brought them to the big dance. An outstanding coach tries hard not to reveal personal disappointment. Instead, he seizes the opportunity to build for the future, and rather than chastising everyone for the loss, he props up the confidence of his dejected players. "We'll get 'em next year, boys," he says—and surprisingly, on occasion, the script seems to be pre-written in that exact fashion.

Sportswriters, sportscasters, and pundits alike have long argued how it is possible for some teams to excel, while others fall far short of expectations. All sorts of generic answers reveal themselves. The other guys were just too fast, too strong, too tall and had better training facilities, maybe a newer gymnasium. They had a better coach, some say, and besides, they had the experience factor on their side. Furthermore, ours are young; they're too green to handle the pressure. Perhaps, others speculate, it's nothing more than blind luck, the way the ball bounces, the referees' call, or from a religious viewpoint—it might be divine intervention.

Those who enter the ranks of head coaching at the high school level do so at great peril. Boosters and school officials will accept losing seasons for just so long, and eventually for the helmsman, it's either the road to victory or the highway out of town. And in Buna, Texas, if one is fortunate enough to succeed beyond his wildest dreams, district, bi-district, regional, and state championships came to be expected. Cotton Robinson knew the pitfalls. This is the story of how he met the challenge.

CHAPTER ONE

Buna's Place in Americana

"Enjoy the little things in life, for one day you may look back and realize they were the big things."
—ANTONIO SMITH

Buna, Texas, was beaming with pride in 1964, and it had higher aspirations for the years to follow. Notwithstanding the school's tremendous success in both the boys' and girls' basketball programs, guided by the tandem of Cotton Robinson and R. C. Hyden, respectively, the town was booming economically. With new business and home construction at an all-time high, the local Chamber of Commerce held a contest in March to see who could best describe Buna's place in the region.

H. C. "Bill" Williams, a local realtor, submitted the winning slogan: *Buna, Texas "The Hub of the Golden Wheel,"* which some simply interpreted as a reflection of the chamber's forward vision by merely pointing out that Buna, with a population of about 1,600 and plenty of room to grow, was a great spot to relocate. For others, however, especially the movers and shakers of the much larger Beaumont, Port Arthur, and Orange—long referred to as the *Golden Triangle*—the logo must have appeared peculiar, because it encircled their entire cities, built on oil production that began with the great 1901 Spindletop oil strike.[1]

Growing up in pre-1964 Buna also made quite an impression on John Rich, one of Cotton's protégés. "I left home at the end of my senior year in 1957, spent four years in college, and then began my professional life," he said. "Although I no longer live there, I still am very proud to tell people, 'I am from Buna.' My wife teases me by telling friends that I face the East when I pray and that Buna is the next best thing to Jerusalem. I love that town!"[2]

What about Buna's past, and how did it get to this point?[3]

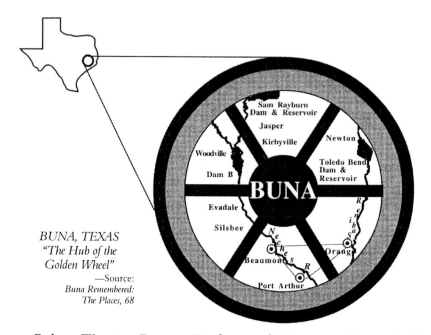

BUNA, TEXAS
"The Hub of the
Golden Wheel"
—Source:
*Buna Remembered:
The Places, 68*

Robert Wooster, Regents Professor of History at Texas A&M-Corpus Christi, pinpoints Buna's location "at the junction of Farm Roads 253 and 1004, U.S. Highway 96, and State Highway 62, thirty-six miles north of Beaumont in south central Jasper County." The community, originally called Carrolla, received its name from the well-heeled Carroll family of Beaumont, who made a fortune in the East Texas pineywoods. Later on, the name was changed to Buna in honor of one of the Carroll relatives, Bunah Corley.[4]

In order to support logging, the principal industry of the area, lumber magnates built spur lines to link Buna with nearby Orange and Newton, and on July 21, 1916, a townsite was established. By 1944, the *Texas Almanac* put Buna's citizen count at 650 and the number of businesses at twenty-three, all served by one post office. Four years later, the population had increased by 130, and three new merchants were added to the roll. Buna was then, as it remains today, unincorporated. The total land area of the community is still less than six square miles.[5]

Prior to 1920, the Buna Independent School District was formed, and in 1931, when Robert "Bob" Cummings joined the staff as a teacher, the entire student enrollment numbered 300. From then until the early 1940s when he was elevated to school superintendent, Mr. Cummings coached, drove school busses, managed the business office, and served as high school principal.[6]

For those who grew up in Buna in the 1940s, '50s, and early '60s, most everyone would probably agree that it provided many advantages, compared to present times. There was virtually no crime, unless you include the shenanigans of youngsters stealing watermelons from a neighboring farmer. For more serious violators, Deputy Sheriff Leonard Franklin and Constable Allen Garsee dealt with them. No one heard of teens using drugs or abusing alcohol, and marijuana was just a strange word uttered by a screen actor. Of course, there were no cellphones or any of the electronic devices on which we depend today. Youths entertained

Robert Cummings
—Courtesy *The Cougar,* 1959

themselves at sock hops, social gatherings at churches, and special events held at the old gymnasium. They listened to radio stations in Beaumont and Port Arthur and danced to the music of forty-five rpm records. Televisions did not make their way into mainstream Buna society until the mid-1950s, so Guy and Beatrice Thomson, who opened the Roden movie theater in late 1949, could expect a full house on the weekends.[7]

Teenage boys took their dates to the picture show on Friday or Saturday nights. Afterward, for those who could afford it, they treated their girlfriends to hamburgers, cherry cokes, and other snacks at places like the City Café, Fea's Café, Jim's Drive-In, and Monte's Dairy-D-Lite, before perhaps winding up at the usual parking spots near Antioch Cemetery.[8]

As time permitted, many teenagers met up at Higginbotham's Drug Store after school and especially on Saturdays to enjoy each other's company, hang around the soda fountain, play the jukebox, and partake of banana splits, various soft drink concoctions, and thick, chocolate malts. Rock and roll music was in its infancy, and when Elvis Presley burst onto the scene, he quickly became the heartthrob of teenage girls. Plymouth Belvederes and Ford Fairlanes of the 1956 and 1957 model years were really popular, and if one owned a 1957 black Chevrolet two-door Bel Air hardtop, like the one driven by Johnie Paul Spencer, this was way past "cool."[9]

Citizens of the community could obtain from various local merchants just about everything essential to meet their daily needs: butane from Noble-Sowell Company and insurance from Lillie Walters. Men and boys got their hair cut at Allie Richardson's Barber Shop, and women and girls could get their "hairdos" at Jean's Beauty Shop. Other establishments included Mixson Brothers, Scurlock's Hotel, Buna Motor Company (the Ford dealership), M & M Chevrolet, Dock Davis's Service Station, Skinner's Texaco, Tony's Gulf Service Station, Ellison's Minimax, Kaine's Grocery, Western Auto, Buna Medical Hospital, and East Texas State Bank.[10]

At one point, it seemed that Buna had a dairy at every turn. Those owners with children, however, expected them to contribute to production, both before and after school hours. Basketball practice, no matter how important, was tolerated as long as the chores were done.[11]

As some might put it, these were the best of times that represented a special innocence that will never return to America. For the most part, students paid attention in class and minded their teachers. For the unfortunate few who didn't, they will now tell you that licks of corporal punishment at school resulted in more of the same at home.[12]

While men worked at local businesses, on small farms, at jobs associated with the timber and oil industries, or whether they pipelined in other states, most wives were stay-at-home moms. Therefore, they were able to greet their children at the end of the school day, and lend much-needed guidance to ensure they stayed out of trouble. During that era, Buna represented a cross section of Americana, and it's no surprise that so much attention was given to sports.[13]

Basketball came to Buna High School during the 1910–11 season, but the first football team was not assembled until some nineteen years later, November 1929. Even from the beginning, it appeared that the latter would never match the popularity generated by the former, yet the two managed to coexist until 1943. That year, school trustees conferred with Bob Cummings and together, they decided to eliminate the football program. There were several reasons, according to Robert Hargrove, a Buna resident who played on the last squad. World War II had taken a tremendous toll on the daily lives of most Americans, including the school districts that served their children. Widespread shortages, especially in gasoline required to transport athletes to participate in competition, forced school administrators to make serious choices on how to survive the crisis. By hook or by crook, priorities had to be reshuffled. "Thus," Hargrove said, "it was felt that the school would be best served by conserving funds for purely educational purposes—and to maintain basketball."[14]

In addition to his duties as school superintendent, Bob Cummings also served as basketball coach, and his 1945–46 players brought home the 15-B district title. But when Coach T. L. "Syrup" Jones's 1947–48 team lost out to district winner Bronson, Cummings began to look elsewhere for a spark to revamp the program.[15]

Exactly how and when he heard about Marshall Neil Robinson has been lost to the ages, but regardless, Cummings made contact with the recent graduate of Sam Houston State Teachers College in Huntsville, Texas to see if he had any interest in the head coaching job. During the interview process, Robinson hedged his bets. He had his alma mater send out three transcripts: one to Buna, another to himself, and the third to Dumas, located in the Texas Panhandle. The application that he submitted to the Dumas Demons begs for further discussion. Charlie Lamb, one of Cotton's closest friends, had moved there right after high school, and apparently Cotton had visited him and liked the area. Unfortunately, it is unknown whether the Demons offered a job to Robinson, but if they had, and it had been accepted, perhaps—and more than likely—the vaunted Buna Dynasty, under the reins of another's leadership, would have never taken shape.[16]

Cotton Robinson on grounds of Sam Houston State, circa 1948
—Courtesy Lynda Robinson Sanford

CHAPTER TWO

Hard Times

"Four steps to achievement: Plan purposefully. Prepare prayerfully. Proceed positively. Pursue persistently."

—WILLIAM WARD

The marriage of William Bryan Robinson and Ouida Pearl Ward, both native Texans, produced nine children, with four of them preceding the birth of Marshall Neil on March 14, 1925. And between August 23, 1927 and May 25, 1935, there were four more additions to the family.[1]

Marshall Neil Robinson was born at home in Pleasant Ridge, a small settlement located in Leon County, Texas, about 118 miles north of Houston. Lyndall Robinson Hale, one of Marshall's sisters, said that

William Bryan and Ouida Pearl Robinson
—Courtesy Lynda Robinson Sanford

Pleasant Ridge "consisted of a general store, a Baptist church, a school (first to ninth grades), and a mill where we took corn to have it made into meal."[2]

Early on, kinfolk began to refer to Marshall as "Cotton," because his hair resembled the color of the same-named cash crop that was grown widely in the region. He started school in the "ridge," but before the second grade, he transferred to Centerville, where his father served on the school's board of trustees. During these years, William Bryan "Willie" made his living working for Leon County, operating a road grader pulled behind a tractor driven by a fellow employee.[3]

Sometime before Cotton began the seventh or eighth grade, his dad decided to leave his county job and concentrate on farming a rather large parcel of land owned by his brother-in-law, Elmer Ward. Willie moved his family to the "flat woods" and into an unfinished house located two miles from the bus stop, where Cotton and his siblings had to walk each day to catch a ride to their school in Leona. At first, Ouida Pearl hesitated to relocate to a new house without a bathroom and kitchen cabinets, but Willie promised to quickly complete the project, so she gave in. Mrs. Hale fondly remembered her mother. "She was a wonderful Christian, always willing to help others," she said. "She saw to it that we attended Sunday school and worship services. Everyone living on the 'ridge' would call for her to come when there was sickness in their family."[4]

An unfortunate set of circumstances occurred when Ouida Pearl reached her mid-30s. She fell ill to a malady that plagued her for the rest of her life, and about the same time, her older sons who had tired of farm life became scattered to the four winds. Jack joined the Navy, and both Ersell and Elton enlisted in the Air Force. Their parting meant that Lyndall and Cotton had to take on adult responsibilities.[5]

In a change intended to ease the family's financial burden, Willie went to work for Elmer hauling logs to a sawmill in Centerville. At home, Lyndall did the cooking, and Cotton chipped in with the clothes' washing. As a child, Cotton was relatively healthy, although every summer, he came down with malaria. In the Robinson household, thankfully, he was the only one to ever contract it.[6]

To say that Cotton Robinson grew up in harsh times is an understatement. While still in his youth, he witnessed the devastating, one-two punch of the Great Depression and World War II, which produced extreme shortages on the home front. Allocation became necessary in order to keep the armed forces fully supplied, so the government limited most products for individual consumption. Items like cheese, tea, milk, sugar, eggs, cooking oil, and fuel could only be purchased with ration stamps.

For the Robinsons, there was one bright spot. Since Willie's family either raised or produced much of what they ate, no one in the household went to bed hungry. Life went on, regardless. While school was in session, and only after completing their household duties, were Cotton and Lyndall allowed to drive the Model-A Ford to attend their afternoon classes in Leona.[7]

Lyndall graduated in 1940, and she left for nursing school in Houston. She had received assurances in advance that her paternal grandmother would move in and care for the family during her absence, but the arrangement fell apart after a few days, forcing Willie and his children to fend for themselves.[8]

Coach Bill Bitner of Leona High School, arguably the most influential person in Cotton's life, saw firsthand the hardship that the youngster faced daily, but he also recognized his potential, if only given a fighting chance. Even though Cotton was still a student, Bitner got him a job driving a school bus. Two other families in town also pitched in and let Cotton stay with them during the week so that he wouldn't have to make the long trip each morning to begin his route.[9]

Cotton Robinson
Leona School Days, 1941–42
—Courtesy Lynda Robinson Sanford

Coach Bitner took Robinson under his wing, and taught him how to play basketball. It was soon evident that the young man's stocky frame lent itself to the center position, and while Cotton continued to improve his shooting, rebounding, and defensive techniques, he came to truly love the game. He also developed a keen sense of competitiveness on the basketball court that could only be quenched by winning. He played for the Leona Lions for three years, but the last season, that of 1943, was by far his best.[10]

In accordance with the Texas University Interscholastic League Rules of the day, playoff systems were used to determine one district winner that would move on to regional competition. Therefore, in order to earn a trip to Houston, Leona had to win two local tournaments comprised of eleven other teams in District 43. In the first event held on January 23, 1943, in the Centerville gym, Bitner's boys beat Lone Star, 38–16, and then followed up by trouncing Buffalo, 38–10. They met College Station's A&M Consolidated in the final. The Leona "Five" had little trouble dispensing with a less-talented opponent by a lopsided score of 59–26, with Cotton contributing twenty-eight points to the winning cause. All told, Robinson scored fifty-two combined points in those three games to make him the most productive player of the first tournament.[11]

By winning the second district tournament on February 6, the Lions qualified for a first-round bye in the Regional V, Conference-B championship games. They beat League City, 40–23, in the semifinals, and then took the title, the first in school history, by smothering Sugar Land, 43–28. Cotton, this time with nineteen points, outpaced his teammates, represented by J. D. O'Keefe, L. D. Thompson, Durard Lamb, and Thomas Rogers. Afterward, Cotton was unanimously chosen as the center for the All-Regional Team.[12]

Standing tall and exuding confidence, Bill Bitner drove himself and only six players to the state tournament in Austin. When the coach and his small squad arrived, they hoped to return with a first-ever state championship trophy to their tiny school. After all, things couldn't have looked better for the Leona entry; they had just chalked up their thirtieth win of the season to remain undefeated.[13]

On Friday, March 5, at 9:00 in

Bill Bitner
—Courtesy Lynda Robinson Sanford

the morning, the Lions took the floor in the first round against Slidell. Although reports show that the game was hard fought, the day would belong to Slidell who scored twenty-nine points to Leona's twenty-six. Cotton accounted for ten of those against the eventual winner of the Conference-B championship, and for his effort, he was named to the All-State Tournament Team. But given his fierce competitive nature, such recognition was of little consolation, and the fact that his team lost by only three points made matters all the worse.[14]

Almost three months later, on May 26, 1943, Robinson, who'd been voted by his senior class as most popular boy, best in athletics, and prophet, graduated from high school. Prior to that, however, on March 13, one day before he celebrated his eighteenth birthday, he had enlisted in the U.S. Navy and applied for entry into the new college V-5 Program, designed to provide training for naval aviation cadets. In the interim, he was allowed to remain at home, until he was called into active service, or upon acceptance into college.[15]

In either case, Cotton determined that he needed additional funds, so he wisely used his time. Another of his sisters, Lillian Robinson Pierce, described how. "Cotton bought peas from farmers in Centerville, and he would separate and then place them into bags," she said. "Often, it would be 10:00 in the evening before he left for Houston to sell them at the Farmers' Market. It was a good money-maker for him."[16]

By his actions, Cotton Robinson demonstrated at an early age that he had already learned one of the key ingredients of success. *Preparation* would serve him well in his future endeavors.

CHAPTER THREE

College, the Navy, and a Fresh Start

"Nothing is predestined. The obstacles of your past can become the gateways that lead to new beginnings."
—RALPH BLUM

Prior to October 4, 1943, Cotton Robinson received the eagerly awaited word that he had been accepted into the Naval V-12 Unit at Southwestern Louisiana Institute in Lafayette, Louisiana (now the University of Louisiana at Lafayette). He was put here, rather than the V-5, because at the time, there were too many enlistees to train as pilots.

Generally speaking, the Navy had set up its V-12 Program at selected colleges and universities to guarantee within its ranks a steady stream of qualified officer material, earlier depleted by the demands of World War II. Moreover, it allowed many high school graduates from lower-income families a chance to earn an education that otherwise would have only been a pipe dream. Cotton definitely fell into this category.[1]

Author James G. Schneider further described the curriculum as follows:

It left with each school the authority to select its own textbooks, determine course content (within some broad outlines), and establish the level of academic achievement necessary for a trainee to remain in the program. Although

Cotton Robinson in uniform
—Courtesy Lynda Robinson Sanford

the Navy urged that full academic credit be given for the courses, that determination remained with the schools, as did each institution's criteria for the awarding of degrees.[2]

But there were unexpected benefits as well. The locations offering this great opportunity were scattered all over the country. Thus, many young men from large urban areas wound up in smaller colleges, while those from rural settings found themselves mixed in with others from big cities. Because V-12 participants were able to take classes alongside civilians, both geographic distribution and diversity were achieved.[3]

Documents of the University of Louisiana at Lafayette reflect that Cotton enrolled in November 1943. He moved into Stadium Dormitory, registered for a full load of classes, and tried out for the basketball team, then coached by J. C. "Dutch" Reinhardt. He made the squad, but nothing within the school's athletic history reflects how much playing time he got. Even though Reinhardt's SLI Bulldogs posted a dismal 4–13 record for the 1945 season, Cotton received a letter for being on the team.[4]

Navy V-12 Unit, Company D, Southwestern Louisiana Institute, October 1944
(arrow points to Cotton Robinson)
—Courtesy Lynda Robinson Sanford

SLI Bulldogs, 1944
Cotton Robinson, No. 44, back row, center
—Courtesy Lynda Robinson Sanford

162nd Unit vs. Southwestern Louisiana Institute, January 17, 1945
Cotton Robinson in center frame, Number 44, (arrow points to his location)
—Courtesy Lynda Robinson Sanford

In February 1945, Cotton left SLI and proceeded to Notre Dame, Indiana, for further training, then to Great Lakes, Illinois, and finally to Pearl Harbor, where he attended a signalman's school before being assigned to the USS *Winooski*, a fuel transport vessel. At his discharge on May 6, 1946, he had reached the rank of Signalman, Third Class, and

Signal School, 1945 (arrow points to Cotton Robinson)
—Courtesy Lynda Robinson Sanford

Navy Buddies Horsing Around. Cotton Robinson in white uniform with SP on sleeve
(arrow points to his location)
—Courtesy Lynda Robinson Sanford

Cotton Robinson at Sam Houston State Teachers College
—Courtesy Lynda Robinson Sanford

Cotton Robinson at Sam Houston State Teachers College
—Courtesy Lynda Robinson Sanford

during those three years, one month, and twenty-four days of service to his country, he received a Victory Medal, an American Campaign Medal, and an Asiatic-Pacific Campaign Medal. After Cotton picked up his separation pay of $85.17 and discharge papers at Norman, Oklahoma, he pointed himself in the direction of Leon County, Texas—and home.[5]

By September of the same year, he took advantage of the GI Bill (signed into law on June 22, 1944, by President Franklin D. Roosevelt) and enrolled at Sam Houston State Teachers College in Huntsville, Texas, to continue his education. He had already decided to become a coach, so he chose as majors physical education and social science with a minor in industrial arts. He also made the basketball team.[6]

One article dated February 7, 1947, from *The Houstonian*, Sam Houston's campus newspaper, described a recent game held at Stephen F. Austin in Nacogdoches, Texas, in which the Sam Houston Bearkats trailed by ten points with about nine minutes left on the clock. When the Bearkats clawed their way back to win by a score of 62–57, a reporter wrote, "Substitute Marshall Robinson and Murray Mitchell got hot at this stage to spark a Kat rally that virtually ran the Lumberjacks out of Axeman gym."[7]

That same year, the university presented Cotton with a "T" award. Barbara Kievit-Mason, archivist for

The 1947 Sam Houston Bearkats— from left, front row: Marshall Robinson, Larry Elkins, Holmes Ellisor; top row: Jim "Bubba" Linack, Murray Mitchell, D. H. "Cotton" Watkins
—Courtesy
Sam Houston State
University

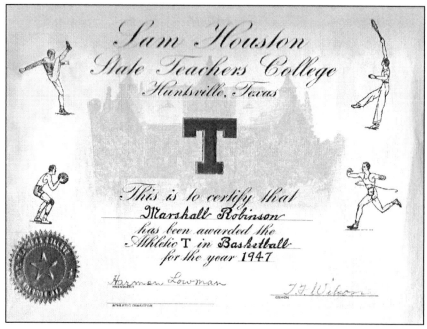

Cotton Robinson's Gold T Award
—Courtesy Lynda Robinson Sanford

Sam Houston, explained the significance. "The 'T' was for men who earned their 'best of the best' in letters in the different branches of college sports," she said. "The gold 'T' was started in 1923 when the Sam Houston Normal Institute became the Sam Houston State Teachers College, and it represents the 'Teachers' colleges we had in the Texas State University System at the time."[8]

Cotton graduated on August 27, 1948, with a Bachelor of Science degree and a two-year certification to teach high school, and that's when Bob Cummings, Buna superintendent, hired him to coach both the boys' and girls' basketball teams. This was not exactly what Cotton had in mind—coaching the girls—but he had to start somewhere.[9]

At Sam Houston, Cotton had met and befriended J. L. "Smokey" Withers, who lived in Buna, and as luck would have it, Smokey's parents, J. W. and Vera, offered room and board to the new Cougars' coach. This ready-made home environment must have helped Robinson make an easy transition, especially with the way that he, an ole farm boy himself, loved to eat. William, Smokey's younger brother, told about the many times that Cotton consumed at breakfast his ample share of Vera's two pans of large biscuits. There was another instance, too, when Cotton and Smokey came in and found a note from Vera advising them that she had prepared a lemon ice box pie that could be found in the refrigerator. Cotton removed it and finished off the whole thing by himself. Afterward, he issued a full apology to his landlady who had already determined that the pie must have been one of her best yet.[10]

As a youngster back in Leona, Cotton spent much of his spare time hunting and fishing, so naturally, he brought with him to Buna the love of these activities. Once, finding himself without a proper pointer-retriever, Cotton sent William, a small boy, amongst the cornstalks in the snow-covered field with instructions to flush out a covey of quail. William obeyed the directive, and soon Cotton was blasting away. When William's dad found out about the incident, he failed to appreciate the rationale behind the episode and so, he scolded his tenant. Cotton expressed remorse, and the entire matter was forgiven. No one could long stay mad at Cotton Robinson; there was just something unique about his personality.[11]

William Withers also recalled another occasion that displayed the humorous side of his parents' boarder. One morning when Cotton and William were fishing, a thick mist rolled in. "You know, William," Robinson said, "this kinda reminds me of a time back in Centerville when it was so foggy, the catfish walked out of the water onto the bank. Dad and I would drive them into a pen, and then I'd shut the gate."[12]

When the twenty-three-year-old first arrived within the boundaries of Cougarland and stepped on the Buna school grounds to begin his new assignment as head basketball coach, he focused on the two most imposing structures on campus. Facing Highway 62, the brick school building had been constructed in 1926 at a staggering cost of $40,000, but eight years later, it had become overcrowded. To solve the problem, a wing was added to each end to accommodate the growth in student population.[13]

Cotton Robinson
—Courtesy Lynda Robinson Sanford

Buna High School
—Courtesy Ashlee Jordan Haefs

Behind the school building, he saw the log gym, erected in the 1930s by WPA (Works Project Administration) labor. As he toured the facility, he noted a depressed look about it. The interior plank walls needed a coat of paint, as did the rough-hewn bleachers—actually, there were so many needed improvements that he didn't know where to begin. He vowed to eventually complete everything on the repair list, but for now, he had more important matters to deal with. In spite of its ragged condition, this gym would be his new workshop, and the place where he would either fail, become an average coach, or be cast into the role of town hero. Cotton Robinson had to put together, not one, but two competitive basketball teams, one for the boys and the other for the girls.[14]

Through the years, the old gym's mystique became so interwoven with the fabric of school spirit, those in Buna who grew up during its three decades of use found it hard to imagine one without the other. Proms were held there, as well as all sorts of community functions. Of course, it was home to the Buna boys' and girls' basketball teams during some of the glory days, but as the ravages of time began to take a toll on the landmark, amusing stories began to circulate.

Buna Log Gymnasium

—Courtesy Lionel Reese

The small Buna School District received minimal funds from local tax revenues; therefore, it was virtually dependent on the state for its daily operations. Since money was tight, Robinson was forced to personally perform much of the work in the gym, and whether he was qualified or not really didn't enter into the picture. After the first electrical scoreboard had been installed for a while, problems developed. Faulty relays kept some of the lights burning when they shouldn't have. Cotton diagnosed the cause as a simple quick fix—he thought that by oiling the components, he'd stop them from sticking.[15]

With the power turned back on, it became clear that Cotton had overdone it. The scoreboard shorted out and literally went up in smoke. Embarrassed, the coach had no choice but to confront Mr. Cummings, a true watchdog of all unnecessary expenditures, and advise him of the recent blunder. The superintendent, though obviously agitated, yet showing great restraint, ordered a replacement.[16]

J. C. Smith, who played for Cotton from 1950 through 1954, provided a personal experience in the gym. "Once when I was a freshman, we were playing South Park [Beaumont], and it was flooding outside. Water leaked through the roof and began to accumulate in the dips of the flooring," he explained. "Benny Johnson was dribbling the ball down the right side toward our end, but when he reached the forward position, he started to slip on a wet spot. He was afraid that the referee might call a 'walking' violation so he just threw the ball toward the goal. Much to his and our amazement, it went in. In disbelief, the South Park guys just shook their heads."[17]

Joan Smith, another veteran Buna basketball player, added one of her favorites. "A team from a very large school in Houston arrived to play Robinson's Cougars," she said. "Upon entering the old log gym, one player glanced up . . . and realized he could see stars twinkling through a hole in the roof. He then belted out the beginning verse of a popular song of the time, 'Don't let the Stars Get in Your Eyes.'"[18]

Geraldine Hyden, a former teacher at Buna High School, described an episode that she'll not soon forget. "When the South Park Greenies visited us one night, many of their fans in the bleachers opened their umbrellas and began to snicker," she said. "But after the Cougars won the game, the joke was on them."[19]

"Opponents who played in the gym," Joan Smith continued, "began to think the Buna players had such well developed ball handling skills because they had to practice maneuvering water puddles on the floor during the rainy winter season."[20]

Buna Log Gymnasium, May 1955
Delman Rogers, standing in front of left door
—Courtesy Delman Rogers

With such testimonies, it's understandable how the log gym, though impossible to heat, with its barn-like and rustic appeal, complete with leaky roof and scarred, uneven flooring, became an integral member of Buna's basketball teams. But as progress dictates, the old must yield to the new.

Another facility—The Bob Cummings Gymnasium—was opened for basketball play in January 1957. Although many activities were still held in the old standby, its rapid deterioration posed a concern for individual safety. School administrators conducted a visual inspection which revealed that several roof trusses had shifted and were in danger of falling. Given the age and condition, repairs were not an option. After the condemnation, Bill Anderson got the contract for the demolition. He thought it was going to be an easy matter to take down the old building, but when he asked Raymond Doyle Walters to tie onto the outer members of the structure with his bulldozer and pull, nothing budged but the heavy equipment. Several more attempts failed, so Anderson and his crew dismantled it piece by piece.[21]

CHAPTER FOUR

Building Years

"When you aim for perfection, you discover it's a moving target."
—GEORGE FISHER

Scant records reflect that Cotton's first boys' team, the one of 1948–49, finished as runner-up to Hemphill in District 55, Conference-B competition. While Buna's overall record of 22–15 didn't represent any real improvement over that of the previous year's ball club, it highlighted the fact that Cotton had his work cut out for him.[1]

Robinson also found time to keep playing basketball on a personal level. A local Buna Humble (Exxon) dealer named E. C. "Ham" Hargrove had for the last four years sponsored an independent basketball team named the Hams, and Cotton was on the squad that, as of January 1949, had won twenty games with no losses. Basically, the Hams played all comers, including professional organizations like the Whiskered Wizards out of St. Augustine, Florida. During their years of operation, Hargrove's teams provided the citizens of Buna with a lot of entertainment.[2]

On the high school front, the Cougars of the following season began to jell under Robinson's leadership. In December 1949 and January 1950, they took consecutive consolation (third place) trophies at tournaments held in Kirbyville and Jasper, in which Edwin "Ed" Whitehead and Richard Charles Simmons, respectively, were named to the All-Tournament Team. But in early February, they suffered a setback as Bronson ousted them from the Burkeville Invitational.[3]

As district playoffs began on February 11, Cotton's team bounced back. They defeated Bleakwood (near Kirbyville) and then won three of the next four games—two against Burkeville, and one over Pineland—to take the championship in District 59. For his outstanding play, Richard Charles Simmons received another honor when he was se-

The Cougars of 1948–49. From left, front row: Lynn Richardson, Ed Whitehead, James Clyde "Blackie" Withers, Richard Charles Simmons; top row: M. N. "Cotton" Robinson, Charles Guillory, Lonnie Lavender, Milton Coyle, Kenneth Westbrook, Charles Lindsey.

—Courtesy Lynda Robinson Sanford

The Hams of 1949. From left, front row: Pete Sanford, Earl Ellison, Ham Hargrove, Fuzzy Knight, Glenn Snell; back row: Bubba Kaine, Howard Hargrove, Rufus Tanant, Truman Gaskin, Cotton Robinson

—Courtesy *Humble Sales Lubricator*, Jan. 27, 1949

Action in the old Buna gym, circa 1949
Hams vs. Navy—Cotton Robinson, No. 24, left of center (arrow points to his location)
—Courtesy Lynda Robinson Sanford

Action in the old Buna gym, circa 1949
Hams vs. Navy—Cotton Robinson, third from right (arrow points to his location)
—Courtesy Lynda Robinson Sanford

Cotton Robinson, 1949–50
—Courtesy Lynda Robinson Sanford

lected as Buna's lone representative on the All-District Team.[4]

The coveted district title meant that for the first time, Cotton would take his boys to bi-district, the first rung in the ladder of state playoffs. J. C. Smith, then an eighth-grade student at Buna Junior High, well "remembers seeing the new trophy from winning district, and all the excitement at school." In fact, the entire community got into the spirit, and as game day drew closer, a virtual parade of vehicles could be seen leaving town, including Bob Cummings's pickup truck packed to the limit with luggage. Although the Cougars lost the

The Cougars of 1949–50. From left, front row: Dale Cummings, Dalton Crocker, Raymond Doyle Walters, Harold Simmons (student manager); top row: M. N. "Cotton" Robinson, James Clyde "Blackie" Withers, Clinton "Radar" Johnson, Benny Johnson, Lynn Richardson, Andy Mosley, Thomas Richard Walters, Ed Whitehead, Kenneth Westbrook, Richard Charles Simmons, Norman Knight
—Courtesy *The Cougar,* 1950

playoff game, which sent them back home to tend their bruised egos, things were looking up, considering that according to the 1950 Buna Schools' yearbook, the overall season record stood at "twenty-nine wins in thirty-seven starts."[5]

Cotton used the summer to continue his education at Sam Houston State Teachers College. When he'd graduated from there in 1948, the school had granted to him a two-year teaching certificate, and in order to lift that provision, he took four additional courses, including the "Coaching of Basketball," in which he made a grade of B. It is ironic that perhaps the greatest coach in the history of Texas high school basketball didn't make an A in his specialty. All the same, at the end of the period extending from June 6 to August 25, 1950, Robinson received a four-year high school teaching certificate.[6]

Also during this time, another important event occurred in Coach's life. On July 1, 1950, A. M. Jenkins, a justice of the peace in Huntsville, united in marriage Cotton and Monte Sybil Smith, a raven-haired beauty and the daughter of Luther and Ruthie Smith of Buna. Cotton was twenty-five years old, and Monte Sybil was just shy of her nineteenth birthday.[7]

The new bride, who'd graduated from Buna High School on May 21, 1948, met her future husband at the Baby Galvez Resort, located near Honey Island, on the banks of Village Creek in Hardin County, Texas. The retreat, whose name means Little Galveston, attracted visitors and their families from all over the state, including scores from Jasper and Jefferson counties. Some came to swim and relax, but other young folks like Monte Sybil and Cotton flocked to the pavilion to dance and listen to the music played by a live band.[8]

After basketball season started for the 1950–51 school term, the Cougars were hampered by the tragic loss of teammate Andy Mosley, who in March had died of an accidental gunshot wound incurred during an overnight camping trip with friends. But Robinson's boys put this terrible incident behind them, and once again kept up the pace by winning the Vidor Tournament. In so doing, they surprised most everyone in the second game held on December 8 by beating a much larger school, French High from Beaumont, in a close one, 31–30. The next day, they had no trouble putting away Rosenberg, 48–32, and Nederland, 39–32, in the semifinals and final, respectively. For their performances, Clinton Johnson and Norman Knight were named to the All-Tournament Team.[9]

However, at the Huntsville Tournament held in mid-January 1951,

Norman Edward Knight, 1950
—Courtesy Jo Nell Knight

the Cougars barely squeaked past Wells, 22–19, and Sweeny, 43–41. They came back strong against Sugar Land, 54–39, before falling, 38–32, to host Huntsville in the semifinals. For the first time that season, Buna had tasted defeat.[10]

In the Huntsville game, Clinton "Radar" Johnson of Buna recalled that he received four fouls in the first five minutes. According to Clinton, that sparked both anger and suspicion from the fans who had driven a long way to see their Cougars shine. "Cotton and the whole Buna crowd were very upset," he said, "because they thought the referees were favoring the home team." For J. C. Smith, then a freshman on Robinson's squad, his stay during the tournament in an old and very cold military barracks made the most lasting impression.[11]

The Cougars of 1950–51. *From left, front row: J. C. Smith, Clinton "Radar" Johnson, Norman Knight, James Clyde "Blackie" Withers, Benny Johnson; top row: Harold Simmons (student manager), Robert McGaughey, Bobby Stratton, Kimbrough Mosley, Thomas Richard Walters, Dalton Crocker, Bobby Guy Ener, Dale Cummings, Raymond Doyle Walters, M. N. "Cotton" Robinson*
—Courtesy *The Cougar, 1951*

The Cougars' perfect record in District 62 competition earned for them another shot at perhaps getting past the first round of playoffs. They returned once more to Huntsville, on February 23, 1951, this time to face the China Lions, winner in District 63. Regrettably, no records exist as to the score of this bi-district game; nevertheless, Buna's win sent them to the regional tournament, where they were beaten in the semifinals by the Big Sandy Wildcats out of Dallardsville. Once again, Robinson's team had made an early exit from postseason competition, and while this trend unsettled the Buna head coach, he had reason to feel confident. For this, his third season, his boys had posted a great record of 41–3.[12]

Coach had another reason to be thankful. His wife, Monte Sybil, presented him with a new baby girl, Lynda Nell, born on March 31, 1951, at a small clinic in Silsbee.[13]

In order to meet new alignment criteria established by the UIL (University Interscholastic League of Texas) for the 1951–52 school year, the Cougars were placed in Conference A, District 20, which included towns to their west, Anahuac, Cedar Bayou, Crosby, Dayton, Hull-Daisetta, Liberty, and Sour Lake. Oddly enough, Cotton soon got

The Cougars of 1951–52. From left, front row: Clinton "Radar" Johnson, James Clyde "Blackie" Withers, Bobby Stratton, Robert Goins, Dalton Crocker, J. C. Smith, Tommy D. Clark, Bobby Guy Ener; top row: M. N. "Cotton" Robinson, Velton Worsham, Thomas Richard Walters, Robert McGaughey, Raymond Doyle Walters, Kimbrough Mosley, Lionel Reese, Delman Rogers, Dale Cummings

—Courtesy Lynda Robinson Sanford

word that some of the other coaches in his new district didn't necessarily look forward to the addition of the Cougars into their mix. The most vocal criticism apparently came from none other than Coach David "Cotton" Watkins of Cedar Bayou, an old teammate of Robinson's at Sam Houston State Teachers College. The Cedar Bayou Bears had done extremely well as of late and now, perhaps Watkins thought that he might be in for a real slugfest to retain that standing.[14]

The 1951–52 Cougars won the Vidor Tournament, with Blackie Withers and Clinton Johnson receiving All-Tournament Team honors. But in the Junior Chamber of Commerce Tournament held in Houston on January 4–5, 1952, Buna managed only a fourth place finish, disappointing at the least. Soon, though, the tide shifted. The big showdown with Cedar Bayou over which team would take the district title never materialized, and Buna won handily. Now, the Cougars were going back to postseason playoffs. Before they left for College Station to take on the Luling Eagles in the first leg of Regional III-A competition, Cotton's boys beat the Lamar Tech College freshmen, 40–33, in a warm-up game.[15]

Buna swamped Luling 49–17, and Troup squeezed by Burnet, 50–49. Thus, the next round's matchup had been determined; two big cats—the Buna Cougars and the Troup Tigers—would vie for the right to meet either Lovelady or Joaquin in the regional championship.[16]

Bobby Guy Ener, who played on that Cougar team, described the 27–23 loss to the Tigers as the worst defeat ever experienced by Cotton Robinson. The natural question: how did it happen? Ener and his teammates, J. C. Smith and Bobby Stratton, explained that the game started around noon in DeWare Arena, the Texas A&M gymnasium used prior to the opening of G. Rollie White in 1954. "The east end of the old gym was layered with all glass windows," said Smith, "and the sun was horrific."[17]

"Furthermore, the glass backboards let the glare right through to the rim, and we couldn't see very well. Also the backboards seemed to bother our shooting, because they were much more solid than the metal ones we were used to."[18]

So, for the third consecutive season, Robinson's team retreated early. Around Cougarland, folks wondered if Cotton, with a record that year of 37–6, could ever win the big one. Sportswriters began asking similar questions.[19]

As Buna began its fifth season under Coach Robinson, 1952–53, some thought this could possibly be the year that the Cougars would go all the way. But even though the team was shored up by eight veterans, a hard reality lay underneath the surface. Most who'd returned lacked extensive experience playing on the A-Team, made up by the starting five, and perhaps a sixth man brought in from the bench. Cotton rarely deviated from this approach to who played and who didn't, and only when a starter fouled out, or his team was so far ahead in a game—there was no danger of losing—did he substitute backups.[20]

Experience aside, Thomas Richard Walters had returned for the fourth time; J. C. Smith, Bobby Guy Ener, and Kimbrough Mosley for their third; and for Lionel Reese, Delman Rogers, Tommy D. Clark, and Velton Worsham, this would be their second. In hindsight, the notion of bringing home a state title should have been suspect from the very beginning.

On December 4, 1952, Buna had the privilege of meeting Orange Stark High School to kick off the inaugural YMBL (Young Men's Business League) Tournament in Beaumont. Toward the end of the game, the Cougars had a comfortable lead, and Cotton signaled for a

The Cougars of 1952–53. From left, front row: Lionel Reese, J. C. Smith, Tommy D. Clark, Bobby Guy Ener, Kimbrough Mosley, Delman Rogers; top row: Velton Worsham, Jackie Swearingen, John Ed Hargroves (also known as John Ed Lester), R. C. McFarland, Billy Holland, Tommy Gene Clark, Thomas Richard Walters, Donald Hillin, Victor Rogers, Richard DeVore, M. N. "Cotton" Robinson. (Adrian Brown, not shown.)
—Courtesy Lynda Robinson Sanford

timeout. "Boys, we're pretty far ahead," he said, "so let's stall. We don't want to give these fellows a chance to tie it up." When play resumed, Lionel Reese had an open shot, and he took it. Jerry Roach, the center from Stark, tried to block the jumper, but he couldn't. Lionel's shot went through the net, and Buna won the game 44–36.[21]

"That didn't stop Cotton from chewing me out," Lionel said. "He kept telling me that anything could have happened if I'd missed. To him, the real issue wasn't whether I scored or not, but the fact that I went against his direct order."[22]

In the second round, at six o'clock in the evening on December 5, the Cougars squared off against the powerful South Park Greenies and Jerry Mallett, their six-foot-four senior center, who squashed Buna's chances of taking home the YMBL title. Cotton had lost to an excellent team, because South Park would eventually go on to become the next Conference 3-A state champion.[23]

Eight days later, the Cougars had much better luck. They won the fourth annual Vidor High School Invitational by defeating French High of Beaumont, 61–49. At Buna right before Christmas, Cotton's team barely beat Orangefield, 45–43, but in Nederland, the Bulldogs posed no problem as the Cougars came out on top, 63–47. At the start of district competition, Cotton had his team in top form. They breezed over Liberty, 60–44, Dayton, 45–39, Hull-Daisetta, 71–33, Sour Lake, 41–25, and Dayton for a second time, 52–39.[24]

In January 1953, Buna entered a tournament held at Huntsville, and they went as far as the semifinals before losing to Cedar Bayou, 47–36. In the finals, however, Big Sandy took the championship.[25]

Although the Cougars were finishing with yet another fairly good season, they came up short in the two games that counted most. On their home court, with center, J. C. Smith, out sick and battling a high fever, Buna met the Cedar Bayou Bears on January 23. This was the first of two scheduled games between the two, and a lot rested on the outcome. Whoever won on this night would go one-up in the District 20-A race.[26]

Even with Smith's absence, the Cougars were out front during the first three periods. The leads had been narrow, though, and Cedar Bayou never trailed by more than six points. With less than five minutes on the clock, the Cougars were still in the driver's seat, 39–36, but that's when the cornered Bears reared up and fought back. The Bishop twins, Herbert and Hebert, nicknamed "Hit," ignited a Cedar Bayou rally. Herbert scored with two long shots and a lay-up, and Hit followed with four free throws. When the buzzer sounded, the Bears took home a 46–43 victory and a one-game lead in district competition.[27]

Regardless, Buna still had a slim chance to make the playoffs, but it was akin to drawing to an inside straight. If they could win over the

Buna Cougars, Warm-Up Action, Huntsville Tournament, January 1953— left to right: Tommy D. Clark, Jackie Swearingen, unknown
—Courtesy Mark Mosley

The Cedar Bayou Bears of 1952–53. *From left, Robbie Muckleroy, Freddie Cochran, Herbert Bishop, Coach David "Cotton" Watkins, Aiden Forsythe, Buddy Bender, (Hebert "Hit" Bishop, not shown)*
—Courtesy Laverne Bishop and Buddy Bender

Bears in their second game, they would force a one game playoff to determine a district champion.[28]

The second meeting with Cedar Bayou that occurred on February 17 exposed the Achilles' heel of the Cougars. Robinson was simply outcoached by Cotton Watkins, his former teammate at Sam Houston, who closely watched Buna's offense and concluded, rightly, that Coach's game plan relied on a heavy dose of feeding the basketball to the post (center) position. Even though Robbie Muckleroy, one of the Bears' defensive spark plugs, didn't suit up because of the flu bug, his other teammates, including Buddy Bender, filled the gap.[29]

From Buna's first possession through their last, the Bears' relentless defense sagged (pulled back), and by blocking one pass after the other intended for J. C. Smith at center, they effectively took him out of the game. No one on the Buna squad could make up the difference, and the Cougars again went down by three points, 40–37.[30]

This second loss to the Bears ended the Cougars' season; they'd finished with a record of 38–7. There would be no trip to regionals this year, because at that time, only one team, the district winner, Cedar Bayou, would move on. The Buna players and their coach took the defeat very hard, but there would be a time for redemption, hopefully. "Although things looked bleak," said J. C. Smith, "I think this fired us up for the next year, making us more determined to do well." And, too, before next season rolled around, Cotton had plenty of time to retool his offense—and long before the calendar page turned to September 1953, he had come up with a stroke of genius.[31]

As history shows, this was to be the last district defeat that any team coached by Cotton Robinson would endure. Jimmy Cobb, one of Coach's all-time clutch players, later revealed part of the reason why. "After the winning streak began," he said, "none of Cotton's players wanted to explain to him and the people of Buna why his team didn't take district."[32]

The central theme of Cobb's quote is quite obvious. As both external and self-induced pressure increased on Robinson to produce winners every season, the same intensity fell proportionately on the shoulders of his players.

CHAPTER FIVE

The Austin Debut

"If you can find a path with no obstacles, it probably doesn't lead any-where."

—FRANK CLARK

After two heartbreaking district losses to Cedar Bayou that pre-vented Buna from participating in last season's playoffs, Cotton Robinson vowed not to let this happen again. Improvements were needed, certainly, but what would he do with an offense that had long since grown stale. Four starters were back, and that would help. Still, the dilemma remained. How would he counter a sagging defense? If he did nothing, he ran the risk of once again losing district, because other coaches would probably copy what Cedar Bayou had already used so efficiently.

Cotton went to the drawing board. He began to tinker, and before the end of summer, he demonstrated why he was usually ahead of the pack. He came up with an innovation, so simple in concept, that when imple-mented led to the complete frustration of most coaches who faced it.

"We were always looking to feed the post," said J. C. Smith, a sen-ior on the 1953–54 squad, "but we also moved the ball continuously to the open man for an outside shot if the defense didn't cover. It was a perpetual offense that started in one set and ended in the same, so we just ran it repeatedly."[1]

"We also had a special play, Number 10, which called for the post to clear to the corner," he said. "That allowed for two possibilities: the guards could drive the lane, or if the post was now open on the outside, he would be free to take the shot."[2]

Without saying as much, J. C. Smith had just described the basic elements of Coach's new offensive strategy, which called for slow, de-liberate ball control—and above all, patience. In an era before the game had shot clocks, the Cougars took whatever time they needed to score. The methodical and surgical precision of taking only high-percentage shots wore down many an opponent and completely threw defenses off balance. "People used to say," quipped John Rich, also on the 1953–54 team, "Buna never works up a sweat on offense."[3]

Bound by a new attitude, a new offensive playbook, a stingy man-to-man defense, and an aggressive half- or sometimes full-court press—all backed up by a recently created high school pep squad—the Cougars cut a wide swath through the eastern zone of District 20, scoring an average of seventy-six points a game and limiting the opposition to thirty-six. The team also walked away with first-place tournament victories at nearby Jasper and Vidor and went as far as the semifinals in the second annual YMBL Tournament in Beaumont, where it took a much larger school, the Milby Buffaloes out of Houston, to oust them, 49–41.[4]

On February 5, 1954, the Cougars mauled the Hull-Daisetta Bobcats, 82–43, to take the eastern zone title in District 20. Before they could go any further, though, they had to go up against Cotton Watkins's Cedar Bayou Bears, their nemesis from last season, who'd just wrapped up the western zone title in the same district. But this year

The Cougars of 1953–54. From left, front row: J. C. Smith, Kimbrough Mosley, Tommy D. Clark, Lionel Reese, Delman Rogers; center row: Jackie Swearingen, R. C. McFarland, John Rich, Robert Goins; top row—M. N. "Cotton" Robinson, Jerry Smith, Donald Hillin
—Courtesy Lionel Reese

would be very different in outcome, as Cedar Bayou's sagging defense, so dominant against Buna in their last meeting, crumbled. In a best two out of three series to determine the district championship, the Cougars won the first game on February 12 by 52–42, and then on February 16, the second, 59–40. Though far at this time from receiving statewide recognition, Cotton Robinson had clearly asserted his dominance as "King Cotton of District 20."[5]

The Cougars met District 19 champion Centerville in the first round of playoffs, winning that bi-district game by a score of 63–41. Then at the Region III-A Tournament held in College Station, Buna trounced Burnet, 56–46, but in the finals on February 27, they teetered on the brink of disaster. Troup, with a tenacious zone defense, put up quite a fight, before losing to the Cougars, 46–44. Kimbrough Mosley's two free throws in the last seconds of the game had saved the day. Thereafter, J. C. Smith was named as best player of the regional tournament.[6]

The wins over Burnet and Troup entitled Cotton's boys to make their initial trip to the state tournament in Austin, where they would face the Sweeny Bulldogs in the first round on Thursday, March 4. Robinson hoped that Lionel Reese, one of his playmakers, would be able to go the distance. In a workout the previous Monday, Lionel had slightly sprained his ankle, but he now appeared fine. As he and the Cougars departed for Austin on Wednesday, March 3, sportswriters had already established them as tournament favorites. Dreams hung in the balance, because neither the Cougars nor the Bulldogs had ever won a state basketball title.[7]

Cotton was excited. Yet he was hesitant to get his hopes up too high. He well remembered that almost eleven years ago, he had been at another state tournament. Because Coach was an extremely private individual, none of the Buna boys knew much about his playing days, or that he had gained acclaim at Leona. Immediately before the regional tournament they'd just gone through, Robinson sat down with his Cougars and issued a challenge. "We really need to get to state," he said. "Remember that we've been to the playoffs before and lost. So if you boys could pull it off this time, they'll probably put your pictures in the trophy case."[8]

In reality, no one on Cotton's team could fully comprehend that he wanted the trip to Austin far more than they did. In fact, he sought desperately to replace the bitter memory of losing by only three points to Slidell over a decade ago.[9]

The State Semifinal Game of 1954

THE TEAMS

Buna Cougars Coached by M. N. "Cotton" Robinson	Sweeny Bulldogs Coached by Jack Crawley
Players	**Players**
Clark, Tommy D.	Alford, William
Goins, Robert	Allen, Frank
Hillin, Donald	Allen, Johnel
McFarland, R. C.	Bland, Glynn
Mosley, Kimbrough	Boone, Russell
Reese, Lionel	Finley, Charles
Rich, John	Hall, Dennis
Rogers, Delman	Harvey, Gerald
Smith, J. C.	Sanders, Billy
Smith, Jerry	Surber, William
Swearingen, Jackie	Thomas, Bobby
	Ward, Bobby
	Wells, Gary

Participating Teams, First Round, Conference A
—Courtesy UIL, Austin

Coach Robinson was never one for rousing pre-game speeches and as usual, he didn't say much in the locker room or on the floor before the buzzer sounded for jump ball at center court. Time and again, he had gone over every play in practice with his starters: senior guards, Kimbrough Mosley and Tommy D. Clark; senior center, J. C. Smith; and the two forwards, senior Lionel Reese and junior Delman Rogers. Each one of these guys knew what he was supposed to do, almost without thinking about the next move. Although everyone had heard about Russell Boone, the six-foot-four phenom from Sweeny who wore jersey number 45, nothing had prepared the Cougars for what happened next.

In his own words, Delman Rogers recalled the event. "Cotton usually assigned me to guard the other team's best shooter, because I had kept their scoring low," he said. "With Russell Boone, however, it was a different story. As he came from the right forward position, he would catch a pass near the free-throw line, and follow through with a high jump fade-away that I could not block."[10]

Delman was not alone that late March afternoon; no one could stop

Russell Boone. But the Cougars hung in, and at the end of the first quarter, they led 22–21. At the end of the half, the Sweeny Bulldogs had tied the score at forty-three. Cotton knew they were in for a rough finish and once more, he told his boys to do their best, protect the ball, take only the open shots, crash the boards, and try and limit Boone to less than his usual thirty points per game.[11]

By the end of the first half, the lead had changed hands several times, but J. C. Smith, Tommy Clark, and Kimbrough Mosley of Buna kept the scoring close. While the Bulldogs pulled away in the third quarter, Buna rallied, and then jumped ahead by two near the end of the fourth. When Tommy Clark, the Cougar guard, put his team once more in position to add to the lead, the unthinkable occurred. A Sweeny player stole the ball, took it the length of the court and scored, tying the game at seventy apiece. So with a mere six seconds left on the clock, the pressure shifted to the Cougars. With time running out, J. C. Smith got the ball, dribbled to Buna's free-throw line, and got off a jump shot. Everyone in Gregory Gymnasium—the home of the Texas state basketball tournament—held their collective breath as the ball first hit the rim, rolled around for what seemed an eternity—and then miraculously, went through. Buna had won the game![12]

The large crowd that had accompanied the Cougars to Austin finally had something to boast about. Their team would now play in the finals. They stormed the floor, mugged their players, and near pandemonium broke out. Along the sidelines, Cotton appeared uneasy—he had a terrible feeling in the pit of his stomach.[13]

Watchful eyes soon turned to the referees, huddled at the scorer's table. Did J. C. Smith's goal count? Everything hinged on the opinion of an elderly timekeeper, said to have been also a janitor at Gregory Gym. Under intense pressure to make the controversial call, he finally declared that Smith's shot should not be allowed. Geraldine Hyden, who'd attended the game with her husband, R. C. Hyden, the Buna High School principal, had found the nip and tuck action so distressful, she left briefly to collect her wits. She had just returned to her seat, but not in time to see Smith's last shot. "I thought that the Buna fans were going to riot," she said. Eventually, cooler heads prevailed, and order was restored. Buna and Sweeny were headed into the first overtime period in state tournament history.[14]

Not a single player on Buna's team, or any of their supporters, could quite believe it. The refs must be blind, they argued, and what about that timekeeper? What's his story? Even today, Delman Rogers and Lionel Reese contend without hesitation that the ball was in the air a split second before the buzzer sounded, and J. C. Smith continues to relive the shot that almost was—the one that should have made all the difference.[15]

Nevertheless, in overtime, Russell Boone scored two quick buckets. The Cougars began to foul out one by one, and soon the team had lost most of their starters. Though they tried hard, the substitutes couldn't keep up—and when overtime ended, so did Buna's hopes of going to the next round. The final score read Sweeny 74, Buna 72.[16]

Russell Boone led his team with thirty-nine points or 53 percent of the total output and along the way, he established a new individual play-off record by erasing one previously set in 1947 by Gordon "Junior" Carrington of East Mountain. Too, the 146 total point production of both teams set records in both state and Conference-A competition. Added to that, Sweeny's seventy-four points created a new mark for a Conference-A team. For Buna, the high scorers were: Smith with twenty-six, Mosley-sixteen, and Clark-fourteen. In a *Beaumont Enterprise* article, reporter Bo Byers wrote, "Records fell like autumn leaves."[17]

Sweeny went on to defeat Sundown in the final by a score of 92–67 to take the championship, and for Russell Boone, this meant another milestone. He broke his own record that was set in the Buna game by demolishing Sundown's defenses with a spectacular fifty points, and en route, he helped his school put into place more state and Conference-A records.[18]

Buna faced off against New Boston in a consolation (third place) contest on Friday, and the Cougars won the lackluster affair, 49–37, with Kimbrough Mosley and J. C. Smith putting in seventeen and fifteen points, respectively. According to Dr. Billy Wilbanks, sports historian, "The All State Tournament Team included Russell Boone of Sweeny; Don Waygood and Dave Hogue of Sundown; and J. C. Smith and Kimbrough Mosley of Buna."[19]

Even though the Cougars were returning home with a third-place trophy in their first trip to a state tournament, they hung their heads. We came so close, they said, only to be robbed. The starters loaded in Cotton's old Mercury, and the rest of the team got on the bus. During the long trip back to Buna that took over five hours, Robinson admitted to his players that they weren't to blame for the loss to Sweeny. He blew the team's chances, he explained. If only he had made timely adjustments, the game would have been won long before J. C. Smith's last-second shot that ended in controversy. While the players understood their coach's motives, his statements did little to ease the pain, especially for the four seniors: Mosley, Clark, Reese, and Smith, who'd let their last chance of claiming the Conference-A title slip through their fingers.[20]

Years later, Cotton reflected on the Sweeny game. "That was a tough way to debut in the state tourney," he said. "They breezed to the state title after beating us. Those kind of losses cut deep."[21]

But the people of Buna, who'd traveled to Austin to see the game, and those back home that couldn't, expressed only gratitude—and pride in what their team had done this season. Aside from the overall record of 44–4, there were many other reasons. Until the Cougars met Sweeny, they had lost only three games, one each to Houston's Milby, Fenton, Louisiana, and Big Sandy, a perennial powerhouse that came in as runner-up to Conference-B champion Cayuga in the most recent state tournament. Buna avenged two of these losses, by beating Big Sandy and then Fenton in a rematch by eleven points.[22]

The Cougars had put up a gallant effort in a two-point loss to the eventual Conference-A champion. They had fought the Sweeny Bulldogs tooth and nail, playing their hearts out in a game in which the lead changed hands eleven times, and neither team ever led by more than five points. This is one they should have won, the players agreed, if not for a pitiful call at the end of the second half.[23]

Although they were few to begin with, the Sweeny game silenced most of Coach's critics around Buna, those who voiced opinions while in barbershops, on the street, or at neighborhood gatherings. Now, these same folks believed as others long did. Cotton Robinson had the ability to field a team capable of competing toe-to-toe with just about any other high school in Texas, no matter how large. Cougar fans began speaking with a ramped-up bravado and walking with a new swagger. The value of Coach's stock had taken an amazing bump; and without wavering, Cougarland proclaimed faith that a state championship was just around the corner.

CHAPTER SIX

Evolution of a Winner

"Practice does not make perfect. Only perfect practice makes perfect."
—VINCE LOMBARDI

Cotton Robinson was a large man, standing about six-foot-one and weighing well over 200 pounds. He had a booming voice, a huge grin to match an infectious smile, a fair complexion, steel blue eyes, and typically had his sandy colored hair cut in a flat-top style that became his trademark. Due to his hands-on personality, everyone he came into contact with admired and considered him a friend. Outside the gym, Cotton was laid back, patient, and affable. But on the basketball court, he took on a different facade. Hardnosed, dedicated, passionate, and driven to win are some of the terms that best describe his approach to coaching.

As discussed in the Introduction, sports enthusiasts everywhere say that it's a difficult task for any team to reach the pinnacle of success, much less repeat year after year. What sets these teams apart from their competitors? Some propose that it's just a matter of being in the right place at the right time—and having the better defensive and offensive weapons, while others argue that champions are forged in the crucible of hard work, grit, and determination.

In the case of the Buna Cougars, Cotton Robinson had access to some talented players, yet there's no question that he made them even better. After graduating from high school, more than thirty received athletic scholarships, but none of them showed up on prospect lists of big-time, out-of-state colleges and universities or on their recruiters' radars. Why? Texas was not then thought of as a place worthy of producing outstanding basketball players. Besides, back in that time and age—and claimed by a great many—the Lone Star State had just two sports: football and spring football.

That said, did Robinson have a secret formula? There is no easy answer to this question. Player motivation to sign up for Cotton's rigid program laced with unusually high expectations, his interaction with members of his team, and how he maintained discipline, all are part and parcel of the Buna success story.

As a devoted disciple of the game, Robinson was totally committed to the art of coaching, and he never stopped teaching and learning about the sport he dearly loved. To gain even the smallest advantage over the opposition, he often consulted two of his favorite books on basketball, *The Science of Coaching*

Cotton Robinson, circa 1964
—Courtesy Lynda Robinson Sanford

and *Man-To-Man Defense and Attack*, both authored by Clair Bee, a famous coach who was later inducted into the Basketball Hall of Fame.[1]

Cotton was meticulous, never leaving much to chance. He scouted opponents whenever possible, but in some cases, he had no other option but to improvise. Those times, he'd call his players around at the start of a game. "Boys, I don't know a thing about this team, so go out there and do the best you can," he said in a slow Texas drawl. "I'll have them figured out in a few minutes and when I do, I'll call a timeout and tell you how to play them." And, according to Pat Stanley, one of the many whom Robinson coached to All-State honors, this fallback plan worked most of the time.[2]

On the sidelines during a game, Coach kept a clipboard close at hand. He jotted down notes on plays that needed improving, new ones that just came to mind, and every mistake that he would cover during the next practice.[3]

As Buna's teams reached the level where winning became routine, other coaches began to take notice. They wanted to know what made

Cotton Robinson tick. One such coach from Beaumont's South Park High School came to Cougar Gym, and he soon detected Cotton's clipboard. This gave him the idea that maybe if he also used one, his team might fare better in a future game with Buna. Sure enough, when the next meeting occurred, the South Park coach carried his own clipboard, and he began taking copious notes. But when the Cougars pulled ahead by an impressive score—and stayed there—the South Park coach disgustedly threw his clipboard to the floor, proving that this one tool does not in itself make a brilliant coaching career.[4]

Cotton's greatest accomplishment was convincing his players to be better on the hardwood than they actually were. In teaching them to overachieve, the Buna coach melded the great, the good, and the average by crafting specific roles to showcase individual ability. In turn, he expected every member of his team to listen and follow the dictates of one voice—his.

And chances are if one played for the Buna Cougars between 1955 and 1963 and heeded his advice, he heard what Jimmy Richardson, a member of two Buna state championship teams, did before a final game at the state tournament. "Don't win this one for me, don't win it for Buna High—win it for yourself," Cotton said. "If you do, you will own the championship forever."[5]

Motivation

What made these youngsters, many from poor families and the majority with a rural community background, want to live and breathe the sport of basketball? Why did the following boys want to play first for Buna, and then for Cotton Robinson? Or was it the other way around?

For James "Jimmy" Burke, he recalled that his "first awareness of basketball came while watching some of Coach's early aces, such as Delman Rogers, Blackie Withers, Clinton 'Radar' Johnson, and J. C. Smith." Furthermore as a child, he witnessed the play of a semi-pro team called the Whiskered Wizards that barnstormed the area. He marveled at how one of its key members, Bubba Kaine, who played at Buna High School in the middle 1940s, was able to connect from beyond what is now the three-point arc. Burke also explained that a player named Donald Troutman from Fenton, Louisiana, was the smoothest and best he'd ever seen. "I remember sitting beside one of the poles in the old gym and being mesmerized by him," said Jimmy. "That's when I fell in love with the game and knew that I wanted to be a basketball player."[6]

Victor Lee Rogers, Sr., a member of the first basketball teams organized at Buna High School in 1910 and then at Texas A&M in 1913, passed the love of the game on to his sons, Delman, Vic, and Phil, all players of Cotton's. Pat Stanley viewed the sport as an avenue to college, and J. C. Smith sought to emulate former players like Johnnie Richardson. Others, including Billy Kirkpatrick, Don Stanley, Melvin Ellison, and Jerry Smith, wanted to compete simply because their friends did. "Basketball was the sport the community emphasized," said John Rich. "Since there was no football played at the time, my enthusiasm for basketball developed from my participation with all my friends, and it eventually became our main interest."[7]

Raymond Cleveland's inspiration came from a totally unexpected source. "J. R. Graves [teacher and elementary school principal at Buna] stopped me on campus one morning, and asked why I didn't play basketball," Raymond said. "I told him it was because I had asthma, and that I could not keep up with the other kids. He explained to me that Betty Sue Stark had the same ailment, and she played in order to develop her lungs. So, I started playing for that reason."[8]

James "Jimmy" Richardson never considered any alternative but basketball. Jimmy explained that he and his older brother, John, "hoed out a court at home and maintained it fairly well until we started playing at the school gym. We had a farm system of sorts [on campus]," he said. "The seventh grade coach, Mr. Stark, taught us exactly the things that Cotton wanted us to know."[9]

High Expectations

Basketball became a year-round affair in Buna, but it was done strictly by the book—UIL guidelines—that prohibited a coach from being on the premises at certain times giving directions. But that never deterred Cotton Robinson from strongly encouraging his players to practice wherever and whenever they could during the summer break.

If they didn't have a basketball goal installed at their residence, he helped them put up one, as in the case of Raymond Cleveland. Delman and Vic Rogers, however, took matters into their own hands. The two boys "found an old barrel, took off one of its hoops, and nailed it onto a long post." Then for a net, Delman said they confiscated "one of their father's burlap bags and sewed it around the hoop." They used this makeshift contraption for about two years, until Victor, Sr., finally put up a real one for them, complete with backboard.[10]

Billy Kirkpatrick lived on a dirt road about eight miles outside town. When he was in the eighth grade, Coach presented him with "a goal, a net, and a ball." He fully expected Billy to enlist his father's assistance in getting everything up in short order, a week at most. If not, Cotton said he'd be out to help. The next time Robinson drove by Billy's house on the way to one of his favorite fishing spots, the goal was not only up, it was being used. "It was a thrill," said Kirkpatrick, "for an 8th grader to be out shooting baskets when Coach would drive by."[11]

Even though Cotton didn't personally observe the efforts of each player during the off-season, he never gave up total control. To cover this contingency, he kept a sign-in sheet at the gym to see how long and who practiced during the summers. Over the years, these sessions became legendary. Current team members and those who aspired to make the team gathered at the gym on Monday, Tuesday, and Thursday evenings and then again on Sunday afternoons to scrimmage for two full hours under the tutorship of former standouts who believed in carrying on the winning tradition. "There would be anywhere from ten to twenty-five people in the gym, and the ages ranged from fourteen to forty-five, with many players from early years participating," said Jimmy Burke. "This was tough physical play that really helped develop our skills in every aspect."[12]

During summer sessions such as these, James Mellard honed his craft under the guidance of J. C. Smith. "J. C. was almost my personal mentor," Mellard explained. "He'd played the post position for the Cougars and knew what Coach wanted of players at that spot."[13]

"And because he was about my height, though outweighing me by thirty or forty pounds," James continued, "J. C. was really a handful for me to deal with. By example, he taught me to play good position, to block out on the boards, and perhaps most important, he created a situation that encouraged me out of desperation to invent what became my signature, the 'fade-away' jump shot."[14]

Most days, except during school hours and church on Wednesdays and Sundays, the gym was pretty much open twelve months out of the year. However, home games and other school functions took precedent. Players knew the routine; simply knock on coach's door, reach inside and retrieve a key—but before leaving the gym, put everything back like you found it.[15]

The real work began after school started. Various members of Cotton's teams provided flashbacks of these marathon two and a half to three hour practices that ran the gamut. Some described them as brutal, intense, focused, structured, hard, and well organized, but to Herbert Ross, he said the whole thing reminded him of boot camp. Pat Stanley viewed them as HELL! "I never once considered quitting the team," admitted Delman Rogers, "but I often thought about dying."[16]

"I am certain that 98 percent of all the other teams in the state had the same degree of grueling workouts," said Jimmy Richardson. "The difference between Buna and the others was that we actually practiced to win. My recollection is that we spent an inordinate amount of time playing the last two minutes of a ball game. Cotton unam-

Cotton Robinson, circa 1968
—Courtesy Lynda Robinson Sanford

biguously suggested that if we could be within two or three points with two minutes to go, we would usually win."[17]

"Drills on post defense, getting the ball to the post, defense on an opponent's guard play, blocking out on the boards, whatever—we did them all," James Mellard said. "We played a very physical brand of defense and ball control, so the drills often got really personal, almost a test of your manhood."[18]

"Day in and day out, Coach insisted that we each practice the shots we would typically take in games," James continued. "It was fun to shoot but, still, we knew that we had to work at it or he would get on our cases."[19]

Interaction with Players

During practice, Coach had no problem correcting those who weren't giving their all—and he could be very vocal about it. When J. C. Smith had a bad game, Coach didn't hesitate to tell him that he was playing on reputation, not effort. He told Jimmy Cobb, "You can't jump high enough to land on a piece of toilet paper." Once, Cotton took Dan Stancil to task. "Son, if you'd get out of bed on Saturday mornings and mow the grass instead of letting your dad do it," Robinson shouted, "you might have the strength to hold on to a ball and not let the other guys steal it from you."[20]

After sloppy plays in practice, some of Cotton's favorite phrases were used to create within his team members work ethics comparable to his. "Son, that's not worth a continental," he'd say. If a defensive player tried to block a shot by slapping at the ball, he'd be greeted with, "Son, you're just chopping wood. Keep your hand up in his face and make him shoot over it." To teach better defense, he'd say, "It's just like sitting down in a rocking chair; bend your knees until you can reach down and touch the floor."[21]

John Rich stated that while he was growing up, he often heard, "You can't play for Cotton unless you are willing to get splinters under your fingernails."[22]

If a player took the ball down on a fast break and missed a lay-up, Coach said, "Son, you're missing it because you need to jump up. You're broad jumping instead of high jumping." Or if one asked him how to do something repeatedly, he'd answer, "Even an old fat man like me can do that." Then Cotton demonstrated. But if he wasn't successful, no one dared to speak out. When someone passed the ball, and it was blocked, he'd say, "Any grandma in the stands could have seen that coming." Of all mistakes, J. C. Smith said, Cotton hated turnovers the most. He allowed just four lost balls a game, Don Stanley reiterated, but if that number was exceeded, there would be hell to pay at the next practice.[23]

"Stay low, and move your feet," Robinson told his players on defense.[24]

James Mellard said that Coach often would compare bad plays to his little daughter's ability to do them correctly. But he also knew when to temper harsh critiques with compassion, because at times, he'd simply put his arm around the fellows' shoulders and gently tell them what he wanted. To accomplish the desired result, Robinson used an array of techniques to motivate his players and shape them into a cohesive unit bound together by a winning attitude.[25]

Coaches have long considered fraternization with members of their team as taboo, because it tends to denigrate authority. One should maintain distance, they say, or your players will walk all over you. Cotton was different in that respect. He was one of those rare individuals who knew how to go from being a stern coach to a hunting and fishing buddy who let many of his players tag along.

One cold morning, Cotton took Delman and Vic Rogers, both Cougars, on a hunting trip. Coach parked his vehicle, and the three scattered out in different directions, each standing quietly beside a tree waiting to bag a squirrel or two. After a while, though, Vic got bored and cold, so he returned to the car. He crawled on top of the hood, hoping that it would generate some heat, but no such luck. So he began looking around for something to help pass the time. That's when he saw some 12-guage shotgun shells on the dashboard. A great idea soon followed.[26]

Vic took one of them, walked a few paces, and jammed it in the fork of a tree. He stepped back, took steady aim with his .22 rifle, and fired. When he hit the shell's primer and it went off, he was really proud of his marksmanship.[27]

About twenty minutes later, Cotton walked up and said, "I thought I heard someone shoot." The boy admitted that he had fired only once. Cotton responded, "No, there were two shots." Vic, who would go on to become a supervisor/trainer with the FBI, said that he was always amazed at Cotton's ability to discern between those two individual shots that occurred a split second apart.[28]

Charles Simmons, another of Cotton's Cougars, and Delman Rogers provided accounts of two separate fishing trips, one not so noteworthy, and the other so much so, it bordered on the implausible.

"Coach took me and some of the guys fishing on the Sabine River," said Simmons, "and before we left, he told us not to worry about food. He'd take care of that."[29]

Herman Davis, who played for Cotton from 1957 through 1959, was a tall, lanky kid with a flat-top haircut and a good disposition. Added to that, he was quite a character. In truth, the term "jokester" best applied. But Herman came by that naturally; his parents owned the purple polka dot house on Highway 62 in downtown Buna.

Anyway, Herman joined Cotton, Charles, and the others that afternoon, and all had visions of a big haul. These lofty goals weren't without merit, however, because Robinson usually caught a lot of fish wherever he went. But what some of the fellows may have forgotten is that Coach planned this trip no differently than countless ones before.

"After we arrived," Charles continued, "we set two or three short trotlines, ran them a few times, but we didn't catch anything big enough to cook. About midnight or so, Herman could stand it no longer. He

Cotton Robinson, circa 1984
—Courtesy Lynda Robinson Sanford

asked Cotton if we could have some of the food he'd brought along."[30]

As it turned out, the provisions, on which Herman depended to relieve his hunger pains, consisted of nothing more that one loaf of bread and a bottle of ketchup. Suffice to say, he had not yet learned the austere lesson of living off the land, and Coach must have been somewhat troubled by not considering a worst-case scenario. Shortly thereafter, everyone returned home, still hungry, but equipped with another priceless memory.[31]

In the summer of 1954, the dam at Steinhagen Reservoir near Jasper, Texas, developed a crack, but before it could be repaired, the Army Corps of Engineers dropped the water level to historic lows. Cotton had heard of some good fishing below the dam, so he invited a few of his players, including Delman Rogers, J. C. Smith, and Lionel Reese, to accompany him on a trip that might last upwards to three or four days.[32]

Before long, three trotlines, each with thirty-three baited hooks, were strung across a creek bed, and the waiting began. At midnight, Delman and his buddies went out to check and see if they'd caught anything, never expecting what they actually found. Even now, Delman swears that every hook yielded a catfish. As they prepared to leave with their amazing bounty of ninety-nine, someone shined a light into the water, revealing that shad had started to jump in an attempt to elude the big bass that followed closely behind. And before the boys reached shore, seven bass had accidentally landed in the boat with them, bringing the total to 106. "I stayed up all night cleaning fish," Delman said.[33]

When the group returned to Buna, Delman willingly shared this adventure with anyone who cared to listen. Although a few expressed a sharp interest in hearing the complete details, most poked fun at this perceived exaggeration and walked away, dismissing it as another fantastic fish tale. Even an avid fisherman like Cotton urged discretion. When he found out about what his player was saying, he called him aside. "Delman, don't tell that story," he said. "People don't believe it, and besides, it makes me look bad."[34]

Though everyone thoroughly enjoyed themselves on this latest fishing trip, by the next practice each player knew his place in the pecking order. Cotton was in charge, and more times than not, he did what Coach told him to do.

Because Cotton Robinson had grown up in hard times, he had a soft spot for those who shared comparable circumstances. Bobby Guy Ener, who played for Coach between 1950 and 1953, recalled a touching example. "At times, I had to miss days of school to work at anything I could get to help buy food for my family," he said. "But Cotton and Mr. Cummings would not penalize me as long as I made team practices."[35]

"When we stopped for hamburgers and such while traveling to and from out-of-town games, I rarely joined my teammates, because I was usually flat broke. So, to keep me from being embarrassed, Coach slipped a little money my way when no one was watching."[36]

Similarly, Anthony "Pete" Hillin found himself in almost the identical setting. Pete, who played on Cotton's last three championship teams, came from a large family that included six boys and two girls. "There was no extra money," he said, "so when we stopped at Dairy Queens and places like that when we played out of town, I didn't have any money to buy anything with." Again, as with Bobby Ener, Coach didn't want the boy to be humiliated, so he gave him three or four dollars on the sly. Hillin said this became standard fare throughout his junior and senior years.[37]

Cotton had high hopes for all of his boys, and his teachings went far beyond sports. He stressed the importance of how they'd later contribute to society—and whether they'd be hardworking, have civic responsibility, and possess a general sense of compassion for other people. These were the three attributes he considered as the most significant. Furthermore, he encouraged those who wore the blue and white Cougar uniforms to stay in school, study hard, and go to college. Unfortunately, most of them came from families that found it difficult enough just trying to make ends meet, much less paying for their son's higher education. That's why Robinson pushed so intently to get athletic scholarships for his players. John Rich, a Cougar veteran, provided another instance of Cotton's generosity.[38]

"Toward the end of my senior year, I wasn't sure whether I'd receive a scholarship offer or not," John said. "I desperately wanted to continue my education but frankly, I didn't know if that would ever happen. One Sunday afternoon, Cotton came to our house and offered to help if my parents agreed. He promised to pay my tuition to college, and I could reimburse him at a later date."[39]

"As things worked out," John continued, "I didn't need his loan, because I received an athletic scholarship to Kilgore Junior College and, thereafter, another to East Texas Baptist University. It's no doubt that Cotton's name and influence helped me in both situations."[40]

Discipline

During games, Cotton Robinson never screamed at his players. If he thought someone was doing something wrong, he'd call a timeout and have them sit on the bench. A simple explanation and an acknowledgment about how to correct the error usually did the trick. He didn't want to hear excuses. A straightforward "Yes, Sir" or "No, Sir" met the obligation, but he wanted the offender to look him directly in the eye when he said it.[41]

No one reported ever hearing Cotton use a curse word. Instead, he used mild substitutes, such as "aw, shaw." Likewise, he never tolerated foul language from any team member, either on or off the court. Nor did he allow anyone, except himself, to challenge a referee. In this regard, Cotton said, "I'll do the talking when it needs to be done, and that probably will be a mistake."[42]

"Virtually, every single thing Coach did had to do with reinforcing good habits and eliminating the poor ones," said Jimmy Richardson. "I believe that his highest priority was that we listen to what he was saying and clearly indicate that we understood."[43]

Richardson colorfully described the time when as a ninth grader, he played offensive post position in a scrimmage against another school's A-Team. Cotton became irritated with Jimmy, because he constantly allowed himself to be "blocked out." "He came over to me discreetly, looked into my eyes, and while my head was suggesting 'Yes, sir,' my eyes must have indicated that I was not really hearing or absorbing," Richardson said. "Then, he put his hands on my shoulders and popped them back and forth—just two very short movements. I was never nonattentive again."[44]

The bottom line was, while on the basketball court the team came first, and those who refused to follow his commands, and especially ones engaged in the practice of showboating, would find punishment a bitter pill. In Cotton's application of the law, the bench served as the best cure-all for wayward habits. And if that didn't work, his stern glare took care of the rest.

Every Cougar that ever suited up for Coach knew his creed of life. "Put God first, family second, academics third," he said, "and after that basketball and social life."[45]

For those who knew Cotton for any length of time, there's no denying that he lived by these words. Although a devout Christian and a member of the First Baptist Church of Buna, where he taught Sunday school, he believed in separating religion and the sport he coached. Once a player asked him why the team never prayed before the start of a game. Cotton responded, "God has more important things to do than be concerned about who wins a basketball game."[46]

He demanded that his team members eat in the school cafeteria; that way, he said, they'd get a balanced diet. Under his watchful eye, Cotton never allowed them to smoke cigarettes or consume carbonated

Left to right: Delman Rogers, J. C. Smith, Kimbrough Mosley. Old gym in background, circa 1954

—Courtesy Mark Mosley

drinks. Milk and juices were the preferred beverages. If he had ever caught anyone drinking beer, such an infraction would result in expulsion from the team. Curfews were no problem in those days; the parents took care of that. Relative to dress codes, Coach didn't worry about that either. "We tried to look our best," said J. C. Smith.[47]

The smoking and drinking issues made sense to the players, and these restrictions were usually followed. But some of the guys drew the line at another of more serious nature—not all agreed with or abided by the last rule of Cotton's Law, the one that pertained to dating during basketball season. Both Pat and Don Stanley repeated Coach's philosophy: "Girls and basketball don't mix!"[48]

To Robinson, social life disrupted concentration; it interfered with practice and how his boys performed during games. "Girling," as he put it, should wait until later. Once he even tried having his players first go home after a game, and then return to pick up their steadies. "But hormones have a powerful effect on a bunch of teenagers," said James Mellard, "so Coach's battle against romance was always going to lose."[49]

The question remains. Why would anyone put himself through the rigors of Cotton Robinson's training program—or attempt at such a young age to measure up to his noble expectations? Some might assume that the Cougars merely tolerated Coach because of the ultimate reward of glory. But, truthfully, they revered and respected him as a father figure. Above all, they wanted to please him the only way they knew how, and that was to win.

CHAPTER SEVEN

The 1954–55 Season

"What looks like a loss may be the very event which is subsequently responsible for helping to produce the major achievement of your life."
—SRULLY BLOTNICK

Sports lingo says that in order to learn how to win, one has to first learn how to lose. From the 1948–49 season through 1953–54, Coach had tried everything he knew to bring home a state championship. Although he'd failed to deliver the ultimate prize, he deserved special praise because in his first six years at Buna, his teams were four-time district champions and two-time district runners-up. The Cougars had been involved four times in postseason playoffs, but they were beaten in three of those before they finally reached the state tournament at Austin.

In March 1954, they bucked the trend and managed not only a trip to the state tournament, but returned with a third-place trophy in Conference-A competition. There's no disputing that Cotton Robinson had learned valuable lessons in each and every agonizing loss along the way, and if the words of the old sports adage bore a shred of truth, the 1954–55 Buna Cougars stood knocking on the door of greatness.

Before Cotton could begin thinking about playoffs and state trophies, he had to first win district. Only then could his team advance. With that behind them, maybe they'd be fortunate enough to surpass last season's performance. The pressure was on.

Robinson took a long look at what he had to work with. Delman Rogers, five-foot-eleven, the reliable veteran at the forward position, was back for his senior year. But who would replace J. C. Smith at center, Lionel Reese as the other forward, and the two guards, Tommy Clark and Kimbrough Mosley? These four recent graduates had scored all the points in last season's final game, except eight: six by Rogers and two by substitute R. C. McFarland.[1]

For one of the guard slots, Coach selected John Rich, a five-foot-nine sophomore, who had become quite a shooter and really adept on defense. Jackie Swearingen, a five-foot-eight senior, won the second guard position due to his passing ability and shooting accuracy on what would now be classified as a three-pointer. Donald Hillin, also a senior, who stood five-foot-eleven and weighed about 200 pounds, took the other forward spot. Donald was a strong rebounder and lined up opposite Delman Rogers. Coach selected John Ed Hargroves, another junior, five-foot-ten, as the sixth man in the lineup. John Ed might have been a starter, but he and Robinson shared a serious difference of opinion.[2]

Cotton had a disdain for show-offs. John Ed, known for his quickness and ball hawking, liked being the center of attention—to put it bluntly, Hargroves was a clown. As polar opposites, the two often butted heads, but John Ed was so talented, Coach couldn't bring himself to throw the young man off the team. This became the only documented example of Robinson's willingness to compromise on a player's attitude. He did so, however, with limitations. Jimmy Burke, a former standout for the Cougars, said Cotton told him that "John Ed was probably the best pure athlete he ever coached, but he could not play him regularly, because if he did, John Ed would not understand that he [Cotton] was still in charge."[3]

With the roster filled, except for the center, Cotton had two candidates to choose from. Robert Goins, a junior, was not just a great rebounder; his offensive repertoire included a turnaround scoop shot, a hook shot, and a jump shot. Robert had to compete with James Mellard, whose family had moved from Kirbyville to Buna in March 1954. James was still in the tenth grade when he enrolled in Buna High to finish out the year, and he was put in a physical education class with some of Cotton's ball players.[4]

That's where Cotton spotted Mellard, and he liked what he saw, particularly when the young man effortlessly jumped up in his street shoes and retrieved a basketball that had been wedged in between the goal and the backboard. That's when Coach swung into action. He and R. C. Hyden, the high school principal, checked the boy's record and found that he had plenty of eligibility left. Luckily for Buna, Mellard only played intramural ball while in Kirbyville.[5]

A. I. Tipton, a coach at Kirbyville, once suggested that James compete in a B-Team basketball game against Jasper. Mellard wrestled with the decision. He had second thoughts about whether he should or not and if he did, might that affect his future eligibility? He knew that his family planned a move to Buna, and once in school there, he really wanted to play for the Cougars, a team that he had long idolized. James wanted nothing to hinder his objective, so he went to Tipton and explained the circumstances. He asked what he should do. When the coach heard about the Mellards' planned relocation, he gave James some sound advice—it's not worth the risk. Stay out of organized competition, he said. Wait until you get to Buna.[6]

Mellard already had considerable experience; he'd played in Mauriceville from 6th-8th grade, and then in the ninth, at Carr Junior High in Orange. Now at Buna High, Cotton Robinson believed that he was talented enough to train with J. C. Smith, the starting center for the previous season's Cougars.[7]

J. C. Smith, large and aggressive on the basketball court, forced James to develop his fadeaway jump shot. "I'd fall back and even kick up my trailing leg to use that as a way to keep him off me, Mellard said, "and to give me space to shoot."[8]

These workouts continued the remainder of the 1953–54 school year and throughout the summer. After each one was finished, James found his own means of transportation to get home, which was quite a distance from the school. On occasion, though, Cotton came to his rescue.[9]

"In my first season of ball," James said, "as the fall turned into winter, there were times after practice that Coach would find me out on Highway 62, with my thumb out trying to hitch a ride home. Coach lived in town, and had no reason to be heading down 62, but he'd give me a ride and talk some with me about my game, what I needed to do to get better, and what my opportunities might become if I continued to improve."[10]

"He often spoke about how basketball, as it had for J. C. Smith and others, could give us a chance to go to college, even at a time when kids like us would rarely even imagine that college could be in our future," James continued. "The talk was kind and fatherly, but Coach knew the ride was important, especially when the weather was cold or wet."[11]

So, either by walking, hitching a ride along Hwy 62, or Cotton taking him, Mellard had to arrive home in time to help milk about fifty head of cows at the family dairy. He knew that it was only possible for him to continue playing basketball, as long as he kept up with these duties. Somehow, he, his sister Mary, and his dad found a way to make it happen.[12]

But James Mellard was no different than many Buna players who were in the same predicament. Usually there was only one car in the family, and their dads depended on it to get back and forth to work.[13]

Before the first game of the season, Mellard, then about six-foot-one, thought that he was ready. Coach Robinson did, too, and James became the starting center for the 1954–55 Buna Cougars.[14]

With the new season underway, the Cougars rolled. In Buna, they met the Spurger Pirates and blew them out by over forty points. However, when the two played on Spurger's home court, the result was utter devastation. The Pirates derailed a lethargic Robinson team who had begun to think of themselves as invincible. "Clearly, we had gotten too big for our britches," said James Mellard. "For that one game, we were a bunch of egotists on the floor, and we paid the price."[15]

Cotton used the latest loss as a great teaching tool. Afterward, the entire team understood what he had been saying all along: "Play hard, play smart, and use the best resources you have." There would be other

The Cougars of 1954–55. From left, front row: Revis Whitmire, Jerry Smith, Donald Hillin, John Ed Hargroves (also known as John Ed Lester), Jackie Swearingen, John Rich, Delman Rogers; top row: M. N. "Cotton" Robinson, Robert Goins, Pat Stanley, Don Stanley, Billy Holland, James Lamb, Jerry Buckner, James Mellard, Victor Rogers (student manager)
—Courtesy Lynda Robinson Sanford

losses this year, three more in fact, but the Cougars never forgot how they felt when Spurger took them down a couple of pegs.[16]

By December 1954, the Robinson Express had gotten back on track. They entered the Third Annual YMBL Tournament in Beaumont and defeated Pasadena in the first round. In the second game, though, Jeff Davis of Houston handed them a setback in a close one, 59–54.[17]

At the Vidor Invitational Tournament, which began on December 10, the Cougars beat the Port Arthur B-Team, Silsbee, Orangefield, and Little Cypress to win the meet for the fourth time in a row. James Mellard and Delman Rogers of Buna received individual honors by being named to the All–Tournament Team.[18]

On January 13, Buna blasted the Houston Smiley Golden Eagles by 74–31, with twenty-three Cougar points coming in the final quarter. In that game, Donald Hillin of Buna led with seventeen; teammates Delman Rogers and James Mellard contributed thirteen each. Even John Ed Hargroves, sometimes on the outs with Coach, got into the action and put in another thirteen. At this stage, the Cougars' record in District 20 was 4–0, and overall, it stood at a respectable 22–4.[19]

Buna cruised to another perfect season in district play. On February 22, they met the Woodville Eagles in a bi-district tilt, held at a neutral court in Kountze. The Cougars completely overpowered the Woodville squad, crushing them 67–37. James Mellard led Buna with sixteen points; teammate Delman Rogers followed close behind with twelve. Cotton let fourteen of his boys suit up for that game, eleven of which played and added to the point total. Coach never liked to run up the score on anyone, and before he allowed that to happen, he'd empty the bench. Sometimes, though, the B-Team got caught up in the moment, and they continued to pour it on.[20]

The Cougars' bi-district win against Woodville put them once more in the Region III-A playoff hunt. This time, they'd meet another Eagles outfit, the latest from Newton in District 17. On February 26 in College Station, as the semifinal game began, it was clear from the get-go that Newton wasn't going to lie down for anybody. The Eagles led 13–12 at the end of the first period, but by halftime, trailed 28–24. Newton dug in, and late in the third quarter, they'd regained the lead, 32–31.[21]

Cotton took a timeout. At the Cougar bench, he knelt in front of his team, scribbled plays on his clipboard, and urged his players to do what they had practiced for. Robinson told them that they deserved to win— so go out there, and make Buna proud.

The talk worked. The Cougars mounted a strong comeback, and

when the third quarter ended, they were in front 38–33. In the fourth frame, Newton collapsed under a full-court press defense and managed just four points, while Buna poured in twelve. The Cougars won the game decisively, 50–37, and two of their members, Delman Rogers and James Mellard, scored sixteen and fourteen, respectively.[22]

With the impressive win, the Llano Yellow Jackets were all that stood between the Cougars and a second consecutive appearance in the state tournament. In the regional final, Llano started fast and led 13–10 early in the first quarter. By the end of the half, the Cougars were down by one, 20–19. After that, Robinson's charges put on a great defensive effort. They clamped down hard, holding the Yellow Jackets to only five points in the first fourteen minutes of the second half.[23]

Meanwhile, the Cougars took full control on offense. With the accuracy of Mellard's fadeaway jumper and Rogers's sharpshooting from the outside, Buna led 31–22 at the end of the third quarter. When the final buzzer sounded, the Cougars had won 47–29. The duo of Mellard and Rogers of Buna led all scoring with twenty-one and thirteen points, respectively. James Mellard also received a Region III-A award for being the high scorer in his conference.[24]

By winning over Llano, Buna gained another shot at the Conference-A crown. But what about last year's rival, the one that knocked the Cougars out of the previous state tournament? The Sweeny Bulldogs, without Russell Boone, who'd graduated, didn't even qualify for the playoffs. Also absent from the state tournament scene were the other finalists from last year: New Boston and Sundown.[25]

Would Buna go all the way? That was the question of many. Yes, according to the conventional wisdom of Texas sportswriters. Never mind that last season, this same prediction had missed the mark. That was then, and this is now, they argued. Barring game-changing controversial calls, Buna should reign supreme over Sudan, Plano, and Dickinson, their counterparts in the Conference-A bracket. When asked about the Cougars' prospects of taking their first title, Cotton responded diplomatically. "The teams are all good when they get into the state meet," he said, "but we believe we've got as good a chance to win as anyone else."[26]

With the exception of a few minor bumps and scrapes, the Cougars were in great physical condition. Donald Hillin, one of the starting forwards, and Jerry Smith, a sophomore guard, had been recently sidelined by the flu, but both had recuperated in time to rejoin the team. Early Wednesday morning, March 2, Robinson and his boys loaded into private automobiles and set out for Austin and the state tournament. Upon arrival, they checked into the Lamar Motel. The Cougars had drawn Plano in the semifinals the following afternoon, and all were anxious.[27]

The State Semifinal Game of 1955

THE TEAMS

Buna Cougars Coached by M. N. "Cotton" Robinson	Plano Wildcats Coached by Carter E. Massey
Players Buckner, Jerry Goins, Robert Hargroves, John Ed Hillin, Donald Holland, Billy Lamb, James Mellard, James Rich, John Rogers, Delman Smith, Jerry Stanley, Don Stanley, Pat Swearingen, Jackie Whitmire, Revis	**Players** Allman, Lewis Braden, Doyle Dunn, Larry Fuller, Glenn Gentry, Paul Gordon, Jim Gunn, Don Harrington, Jimmy Pannell, David Rogers, Doyle Shields, Sam Shields, Tom

Participating Teams, First Round, Conference A
—Courtesy UIL, Austin

In a stunning upset in the early Conference-A semifinal game on Thursday afternoon, the Dickinson Gators defeated the Sudan Hornets, led by six-foot-five center, Leon "Pod" Hill, and six-foot-two forward, Charles Lynch. Coach knew who his opponent would be in the final on Saturday afternoon, but first Buna had to get by the Plano Wildcats.[28]

When Cotton's team began their warm-ups, they held a slight height advantage over Plano from the Dallas area. The won-loss record favored the Cougars as well. They'd lost only four games, while the Wildcats posted nine. But statistics do not win ball games; that was up to the players and their respective coaches.[29]

Buna started strong with Mellard chipping in eight points. Plano seemed to be in a trance as it took them over three minutes and twenty seconds to finally get on the board. At the end of the first quarter, the Cougars dominated, 17–4. Mellard continued to score, Delman Rogers got into the act, and midway through the second quarter, Buna was ahead 27–11. Just when it seemed that the Cougars were going to walk away with an easy win, Plano came to life. By the end of the first half, Wildcats Doyle Rogers, Lewis Allman, and David Pannell had cut Buna's lead to nine, 33–24.[30]

In the third quarter, Doyle Braden of Plano added seven more, and the Cougars' lead dwindled to only six, 42–36. Buna's Mellard and Rogers were off their game, and as things were beginning to seem uncertain for the Cougars, Cotton looked to his bench for a playmaker to help right the ship. He inserted John Ed Hargroves into the lineup. The irrepressible forward went to work, making his presence known immediately. Before the fourth period ended, John Ed had stepped up with three field goals and two free throws. The hustle that he showed, not to mention his eight points, rejuvenated his teammates. They took control of the backboards with strong rebounding, keeping the ball out of the Wildcats' hands.[31]

Plano coach, Carter Massey, could do little but sit by and watch the clock tick away. When the buzzer sounded, the Cougars had won by a final score of 56–48. Remarkably, the seven players who saw action accomplished what no other Buna team ever had. They would play in their first state championship game against Coach Ray McLerran's Dickinson Gators, the team that beat Sweeny twice during their district competition, keeping them out of the playoffs.[32]

As a member of the 1954–55 Cougars, James Mellard provided many details of what happened prior to the title game with Dickinson. After the victory over Plano, Robinson took his boys to supper. "In Austin, this was a real experience for most of us," said James. "With our expenses paid, we could eat in nice places and order meals that generally we could not afford in 'real' life."[33]

Soon thereafter, the Cougars returned to the motel for some much-needed rest. They had an early curfew that night, but most of them found it difficult to sleep. On Friday morning after breakfast, the team returned to the tournament and saw some other games. In between, Coach allowed them some personal time, free of his supervision. The boys gathered outside on the grass and in the shade of Gregory Gym, where Jackie Swearingen presided over some old fashioned bull sessions with his compadres, who could now totally relax and just be themselves. "All the jokes and storytelling kept us loose, kept our minds off the game with Dickinson," Mellard said. "That was probably a good thing."[34]

Finally—on Saturday, with the big event at hand, the Cougars suited up. Cotton reiterated that his players should do what they were taught. He told them to expect a tough, physical effort from Coach McLerran's Gators, but mostly, he delivered the same message that he always did: "Play your game. Do it right. It will work out eventually."[35]

None of the Cougars noticed any change in Cotton's mood. "He was like a law of gravity," James observed. "He seemed to me in total control of his emotions."[36]

The State Final Game of 1955

THE TEAMS

Buna Cougars Coached by M. N. "Cotton" Robinson	Dickinson Gators Coached by Ray McLerran
Players Buckner, Jerry Goins, Robert Hargroves, John Ed Hillin, Donald Holland, Billy Lamb, James Mellard, James Rich, John Rogers, Delman Stanley, Don Stanley, Pat Smith, Jerry Swearingen, Jackie Whitmire, Revis	**Players** Brown, David High, Johnny Lee Hughes, Hershel Hughes, Lloyd Mitchiner, Jerry Neill, Allen Thomas, Leon Tidwell, Johnny Ray Williams, Wayne Wolston, Clint

Participating Teams, Final Round, Conference A
—Courtesy UIL, Austin

From the tip-off at about 2:25 P.M. that afternoon, until late in the championship game, the Dickinson Gators picked apart the Cougar defenses on the strong shooting of guards Wayne Williams and Johnny Lee High, and forward Leon Thomas. Consequently, the Cougars lagged behind at the end of the first quarter, 13–11, and at the half, 34–24.[37]

In the dressing room, Cotton tried his best to fire up his players who seemed disheartened by the tempo of the game, and the fact that their shooting percentage was far below par. Though the Cougars didn't express it verbally, their appearances did. *We're so far behind*, they thought, *we'll never catch up*. Frankly, the situation also ripped through Coach's insides, but he held it all together, conveying nothing but encouragement. As his team walked back to the court, John Ed Hargroves spoke up—loudly. "Don't worry boys," he said, "I'll pull it out for you." Cotton's nerves were already frayed from being behind by ten points, and hearing John Ed's smart aleck remark just added more to the strain.[38]

At the end of the third quarter, Dickinson still led by 48–41, and it seemed that the Gators were poised to take home the title. For the majority of those sitting inside Gregory Gym, they suspected that Cotton and his Cougars had reached the end of the road. Maybe the win over Plano in the semifinals was pure luck. This became more of a possibility when James Mellard fouled out. But James had been rather ineffective, considering his high standards; he'd scored only ten points. And, too, Delman Rogers, the other kingpin for Buna, had the same tally.[39]

In the fourth period, Cotton needed a shake-up. He pulled Donald Hillin from the lineup. And that meant John Rich, Delman Rogers, Jackie Swearingen, Robert Goins, Jerry Smith—and John Ed Hargroves would have to play out the hand. Coach held out hope, but deep down, he had some serious misgivings about the result.[40]

With eight minutes to go in the game, the Cougars, trailing by seven, had to make a move, or else it was all over. Buna went into a serious ball control offense. The Gators twice sent John Rich to the foul line, where he connected on three free throws, and then Delman Rogers followed with two of his own. Suddenly, the game narrowed to 48–46 with 2:25 on the clock. Both teams scored, but Dickinson still led, 50–48. With Buna back on offense, Jerry Smith passed the ball to Delman Rogers who sank a long one. Delman's father, Victor Rogers, Sr., said that near where he sat, a lady, obviously a Dickinson fan, fainted when his son tied the score at fifty.[41]

The Gators responded, and they regained the lead, 52–50. It was still anyone's game, and neither side seemed to gain much of an edge, until Buna once again tied the score at fifty-two. Dickinson missed their shot, and the Cougars' unlikely hero, Hargroves, hit with only forty seconds left. Buna went ahead, 54–52.[42]

Dickinson now had the ball. John Ed was too strong off the board, and he fouled the Gators' Leon Thomas, who promptly sank two free throws. The score was knotted at 54 each. Buna's offense sputtered, so with the clock winding down, Dickinson controlled their own destiny.[43]

But one Cougar in particular was dead set against a Gators' coronation. In a shocking turn at the 25-second mark, John Ed planted his feet and took a hard charge by Clint Wolston of Dickinson. Hargroves calmly walked to his free-throw line, bounced the ball a couple of times, turned his head toward the Buna bench—and then smiled, as if to indicate *I told you so!* He made the first, *swish*, and then the second, *swish*, sending the crowd into a frenzy.[44]

With Buna up by two, 56–54, Dickinson was on the ropes. Five seconds later, John Ed stole the ball. The Cougars went on a fast break, Delman Rogers streaked toward his basket, and about the time he arrived, so did the ball. His easy lay-up ensured Buna's amazing come-from-behind victory of 58–54.[45]

"Mr. Robinson just laughed, laughed, and laughed," said Delman. "He could hardly believe it. We picked him up, took him, clothes and all, and put him in the showers. He was still laughing."[46]

Dr. Billy Wilbanks, author of *Texas Basketball Champs-Team Narratives*, said, "1955 was a watershed moment . . . as Dickinson would never again reach the state final . . ."[47]

Though somewhat improbable how the game unfolded—and ended, Cotton Robinson had won his first championship trophy, and he did it in a manner that would define his style. Regardless of how far behind, his Cougars stood more of a chance of winning than losing. Coach usually knew when and whom to put in a game to guarantee Buna's coming out on top. And in the 1955 state tournament, he demonstrated the latter quality by twice going to Hargroves.

John Ed Hargroves, who went on to become a successful professional rodeo clown, had reached center stage—and he excelled by making good on a promise to pull it out for the team. Two of his former teammates, James Mellard and Delman Rogers, give him all the credit for helping the Cougars win their first state title. Justifiably so.[48]

CHAPTER EIGHT

The 1955–56 Season

"Never underestimate the power of dreams and the influence of the human spirit. We are all the same in this notion: The potential for greatness lives within each of us."
—WILMA RUDOLPH

The March 1955 *Basketball Pressbook of the 35th Annual UIL State Championship Tournament* listed Cougars Pat and Don Stanley as five-foot-ten guards. "What I remember best about them is that in the spring I moved to Buna," said James Mellard, their All-State teammate, "they were so small, the basketball appeared like a medicine ball in their hands."[1]

"Though small, they were already really good, really smart players," James added. "When we chose up sides, they were the ones you always wanted on your team."[2]

Cotton Robinson saw a lot of promise in the Stanley twins, but he believed they had much more to offer—if only they'd grow a few more inches. The extra height combined with their speed and agility, he concluded, would make them powers to be reckoned with. For his current project, Cotton reverted to his own childhood, to a time when folks looked no further than the natural product of milk to provide their youngsters with strong bones and healthy bodies.[3]

"Cotton came out to our house one day and told my mother to pour a quart of milk every morning for my brothers to drink," said Dot Smith, the twins' sister. "We had our own cows, so it was whole milk. He said he wanted it gone by the end of the day. Mother did, and before long, Pat and Don were drinking more and more, and they were growing like weeds."[4]

That summer as the Stanley brothers grew in stature, Robinson planned for the new season, wondering what he'd have to do to match the previous record as Conference-A champion. When the season started, the Cougars struggled to get past their rival, Big Sandy, 42–41, and in the second and third games, they were throttled by Lamar Tech's "B" Team, 66–65, and then Milby, 61–52. Losing the first two out of three didn't bode well with the Buna coach, and he challenged his players to do better.[5]

Prior to beginning district competition, the Cougars won two tournaments, the Fourth Annual YMBL in Beaumont and the Jasper Invitational. At the Houston Jaycee Tournament, though, Buna was eliminated in overtime by Jacksonville's Fighting Indians. Jacksonville won that particular tournament on their way to becoming the 1956 Conference 2-A champion. On a positive note, the Cougars had lost but one more start, their second to Milby, 41–40. Later, however, they came back to offset two of the earlier defeats, downing Milby, 63–54, and the Lamar Tech "B" Team, 45–25. Cotton would have liked another shot at Jacksonville, but the schedule would not permit it.[6]

Regardless, the Cougars were ready to make a run at another title. In succession, Spurger, Hemphill, Zavalla, Jasper, Little Cypress, Kountze, Sour Lake, and Winnie fell—some of them twice—to the

The Cougars of 1955–56. From left, front row: Don Stanley, James Mellard, Revis Whitmire, John Rich, Pat Stanley, Robert Goins, Jerry Smith; top row: M. N. "Cotton" Robinson, Robert "Bull" Muckleroy, William Withers, Jerry Goins, George Jones, Dan Stancil, Jerry Buckner, Kenneth Cobb, Paul Swearingen, Victor Rogers (student manager)
—Courtesy *The Cougar, 1956*

Buna juggernaut led by a coach with an all-in mentality. In their last twelve games, the Cougars scored an average of sixty-six points to their opponents' thirty-four, during which they maintained another perfect record in district.[7]

In the bi-district round against the Woodville Eagles, Buna reeled off another devastating blow to the same team they'd beaten in the identical venue last year. After thumping the Eagles, 88–34, the Cougars went on to the Region III-A Tournament in College Station, where they followed up with wins over Joaquin, 58–34, and Bastrop, 49–41. Robinson now found himself in the enviable position of having his team qualify in three straight seasons for the state tournament.[8]

Cotton and his players arrived in Austin on Wednesday, February 29, 1956, and immediately checked into the Oak Motel at 2901 East Avenue. Dr. Rhea Williams, the State Athletic Director, had made reservations for fifteen—Cotton and his team of fourteen—at a cost of $2.00 per person. Everyone rested a bit before going out to eat. But they were back at the motel early, because their semifinal game against the Deer Park Deer was scheduled for the next afternoon.[9]

When Cotton heard whom he'd first lock horns with in the 1956 state tournament, he knew that his boys would be up against a team worthy of note, if for no other reason than their head coach, David "Cotton" Watkins. He and Robinson had been teammates at Sam Houston State Teachers College, and they'd been adversaries back in the day when Watkins's Cedar Bayou Bears handed Buna its last two losses in district. Now at Deer Park, Watkins had organized one of the four best A-bracket teams in Texas that had amassed a string of ten straight wins going into the game with Buna. On the season, they had lost just twice, once to Vidor and the other to Smiley, both very familiar to the Cougars.[10]

Four of the starting five of the maroon and white clad Deer were big men. The center, Wilbert Bigott, stood at six-foot-five, forwards Johnny Scheer and Jimmy Philpot were both six-foot-three, and guard Herbert Laake followed close behind at six-foot-one. The other guard, Franklin "Bubba" McLean measured five-foot-eleven.[11]

The Cougars were somewhat shorter. At six-foot-one, James Mellard started at center, Pat and Don Stanley, who'd grown three inches since last year, were now also six-foot-one, and they filled the forward positions, with John Rich and Jerry Smith, both five-foot-nine, as the two guards. All things considered, the contest to determine who'd progress to the finals seemed to be one too close to call.[12]

The State Semifinal Game of 1956

THE TEAMS

Buna Cougars Coached by M. N. "Cotton" Robinson	Deer Park Deer Coached by David "Cotton Watkins
Players	**Players**
Buckner, Jerry	Barclay, Maurice
Goins, Jerry	Bigott, Wilbert
Goins, Robert	Burke, Jimmy
Jones, George	Carpenter, Jerry
Mellard, James	Clanton, Wayne
Muckleroy, Robert	Harman, Roy
Rich, John	Henderson, William
Smith, Jerry	Laake, Herbert
Stanley, Don	McLean, Franklin
Stanley, Pat	Philpot, Jimmy
Stancil, Dan	Reeves, Wilburn
Swearingen, Paul	Scheer, Johnny
Whitmire, Revis	Smith, Marshall
Withers, William	Tunstall, Wayne
	Ussery, James

Participating Teams, First Round, Conference A
—Courtesy UIL, Austin

Bob Price, who attended the game, reported for the *Beaumont Enterprise*. "Mellard did the shooting and Rich the ball handling, hawking and rebounding," he wrote. "Lanky James [Mellard], who was named to the state Class A team, hit for twenty points and fourteen of them came in the second half. Rich was all over the court throughout the game, but especially . . . after Deer Park had threatened by coming within one point of the lead at the end of the third quarter."[13]

"The Stanley brothers, Don and Pat, had plenty to say about the outcome for Buna," Price continued. "Don was at his rebounding best and picked off thirteen from the boards while contributing six points. Pat came up with fourteen tallies, excelling on a jump shot from the right side about twelve feet out."[14]

The Deer stayed close in the first three quarters, but they caved in the fourth to a superior defense. While Watkins's team was scoring just four points—all free throws—the Cougars chipped in nineteen to pull away.[15]

"It was an ironman's game," Price concluded, "and neither side . . . [substituted] until only 2:35 remained in the game. The Deer sent in the first reserve and then with 1:20 left, Robinson benched his starters for a fresh unit."[16]

With the twenty and fourteen points put in by Mellard and Pat Stanley, respectively, Don Stanley and Jerry Smith added six apiece, Rich eight, and Revis Whitmire hit one free throw to seal the Cougars' 55–39 victory. Wilbert Bigott led the Deer with fourteen points.[17]

In his statistical summary, Price provided the following details. "Buna hit eighteen of its forty-two field attempts for a 41.9 average while the Deer Park team made fourteen of thirty-nine for a 35.9 figure," he wrote. "In the rebounding department, Buna collected thirty-five with the Deer getting twenty-four."[18]

After the game, Watkins and Robinson met up at center court, shook hands, and exchanged a few pleasantries. But soon the Deer Park coach turned and walked off the floor, defeated yet again by his old Sam Houston Bearkat teammate. Buna had amazed just about everyone in Gregory Gym, and they asked the inevitable. How do they continue to win like this? Cougar fans had long known the answer, but for the others who didn't, Bob Price, the *Beaumont Enterprise* sportswriter, provided the best response. "It was the Cougars' all-around polish that made the difference."[19]

The win ensured Buna a finalist berth with another old-time rival. The Troup Tigers and the Cougars had previously met twice in critical playoff games, both in regionals. In 1952, the Tigers had handed Cotton the worst defeat in his career, 27–23, but in 1954, Buna, on the road to their first state tournament appearance, reciprocated by ousting the Tigers, 46–44. The Conference-A state final of 1956, set for Saturday, March 3, would be the rubber match.[20]

James Mellard, the Cougar center, drew first blood with free throws, but Troup's Mike Johnson and Doyle Laney tied it up with charity shots of their own. Buna's Pat Stanley answered with a jump shot, and from that point on, his team never trailed.[21]

At the end of the first quarter, Buna led 14–7, the second, 26–19, and the third by seven, 39–32. Troup might have fared better, but the Cougar guards, Jerry Smith and John Rich, constantly applied defensive pressure. Moreover, Don Stanley, the other half of Buna's twin-brother forward unit, made numerous steals that brought the crowd of packed Gregory Gym to their feet.[22]

Meanwhile, "Mellard was still making the Southwest Conference

The State Final Game of 1956

THE TEAMS

Buna Cougars Coached by M. N. "Cotton" Robinson	Troup Tigers Coached by John H. Reagan
Players	**Players**
Buckner, Jerry	Blanton, Otho
Goins, Jerry	Gurney, Gerald
Goins, Robert	Johnson, Mike
Jones, George	Laney, Doyle
Mellard, James	Ledford, Buster
Muckleroy, Robert	Simmons, Robert
Rich, John	Smith, Ralph
Smith, Jerry	Smith, Robert
Stanley, Don	Toole, John
Stanley, Pat	Welch, Harlond
Stancil, Dan	
Swearingen, Paul	
Whitmire, Revis	
Withers, William	

Participating Teams, Final Round, Conference A
—Courtesy UIL, Austin

coaches drool on his fadeaway specialty," wrote Bob Price, once again reporting for the *Beaumont Enterprise*. By intermission, the Buna center had sixteen points, and in the third, he put in two more to lead all scorers. "Troup's hopes rose when with 2:20 left in the game, the Tigers pulled within three points of the Cougars," Price continued. "But Mellard and . . . the Stanleys went to work again, got the Cougars out in front by a comfortable margin, [and] then held the ball for the last minute." Buna went on to win by a final score of 52–42.[23]

There were several keys to the Cougars' victory over a demoralized Troup: Mellard's fadeaway jumper that contributed to his 26-point total, Pat and Don Stanley's extraordinary rebounding effort, the defensive play of Smith and Rich, and Don Stanley's sensational blocked shots. Pat Stanley finished with seventeen points, his brother Don had three, and John Rich followed with six. Troup's John Toole and Ralph Smith led their team with twelve each.[24]

For many, basketball championships and intoxicants have a lot in common. Soon, the folks of Buna turned their attention to next season.

"Coach, how about next year?" they'd often ask. "What do you think of our prospects?"[25]

Cotton simply answered, "We'll see." As he smiled and issued vague responses, Robinson was fully aware of the sobering fact that as a coach, he had built quite a reputation as a winner. The two-edged sword cut both ways. He knew that in the days to follow, much more would be expected of him. In private, he, too, expressed concerns. *What am I going to do*, he thought, *and how will I keep everyone happy?*[26]

Next season, he'd be without the services of James Mellard, his artist on the court with the fadeaway jump shot, who'd graduate, as would his backup, Robert Goins. Nor would John Rich return as a player, because he was ineligible in his senior year. John would serve in another capacity, however, as the team's student manager. But all was not total doom and gloom. Cotton had lost key starters before, and he'd bounced back with a vengeance.[27]

For the present, everyone would have to be content, considering that Buna had just won the Conference-A title, and they had broken a record in the process. The 1955–56 Cougars were the first Conference-A team to ever win a state title on two occasions, much less back to back. And, too, they were the only state championship team to repeat in 1956. John Rich and James Mellard were chosen to represent the Cougars on the 20-A All District Team, and when the Conference-A State Team was announced, Mellard and Pat Stanley were named as starters, with Rich and Don Stanley receiving honorable mention. Plus, the Cougars ended the year with a fine record of 38–4. All were sterling achievements of which to be proud.[28]

CHAPTER NINE

The 1956–57 Season

"We had just about everything in '57, good reserves, rebounding, shooting, defense. You don't often get boys like we had that year."
—COTTON ROBINSON

Another UIL realignment, based on enrollment figures, took effect the beginning of the 1956–57 school year. Even though Buna's total hovered around the 214 mark, the high school was moved into Conference AA with 164 others ranging between 200 and 370 students. This action intensified the level of competition for the Cougars.[1]

Some coaches may have possibly looked upon this restructuring as too much of a challenge, but for Cotton Robinson, it was an opportunity. He welcomed strong opposition, regardless of how large the school or reputation of its players. As a prelude, he used these forums to sharpen the skills of the Cougars, and get them geared up for district competition and hopefully, the playoffs and state finals.

"We schedule every type team, ones which use man-to-man and zone [defenses], and all kinds of offense," Cotton said. "You have to get the kids used to playing against these different types of teams, or later on when it counts, they don't know what to do." Coach always said that his boys couldn't learn a thing from someone they could beat by forty points, so why bother.[2]

That's why he pushed hard on Conference AAA and AAAA schools to include Buna on their schedules. Powerhouses like Houston's Milby, Smiley, Spring Branch, and Jeff Davis; Beaumont's South Park, French, Beaumont High; and the ever-dangerous Port Arthur Yellow Jackets were always prospective opponents.

But in a time before integration came to Buna, what was Cotton's stance on competing with all-black schools? Of course, there were none in his district, but there were plenty available locally, especially those

African-American teams in and near Kirbyville, just up the road about seventeen miles from Cougarland. In fact, there are various accounts that the concept of interracial competition intrigued him—and he wanted to follow through, but someone, whether parents or school administrators, nixed the idea.[3]

Odis Booker, a former great basketball player with the West Kirbyville Bulldogs, an all-black school, said that he has personal knowledge that his coach, Brady Beauregard, approached Cotton in 1963 and suggested that the two teams meet. Both agreed to it, pending a final decision by the superintendents of their respective schools. What happened next in the negotiation process is unclear, other than the game never occurred.[4]

It would have been very interesting, however, if the two had played, given that the Bulldogs went on that year to win the Conference 1-A state basketball championship in the Prairie View Interscholastic League (PVIL) when they beat Smithville Brown by a score of 64–45. From 1941 to 1967, the PVIL governed all extracurricular activities for black high schools in a comparable manner as did the UIL for segregated whites.[5]

Robinson also wanted to take on the first stringers of Lamar State

The Cougars of 1956–57. From left, front row: Jerry Smith, Jimmy Cobb, Jerry Goins, Paul Swearingen, William Withers, Robert "Bull" Muckleroy, Herman Davis; top row: Charles Simmons, Revis Whitmire, Dan Stancil, Pat Stanley, Don Stanley, Jerry Buckner, John Rich (student manager)
—Courtesy *The Cougar, 1957*

College of Technology in Beaumont, but in a game situation, the best he ever got was the "B" Team, probably because Tech's head coach Jack Martin and his staff didn't want to run the risk of embarrassment, trying to explain away a possible loss. But Cotton never shied away either from playing a smaller school with a great program, especially one with whom for so long he had a fierce rivalry. The Big Sandy Wildcats, who made numerous state tournament appearances in Conference B, is a great example.

Cotton often referred to outstanding players as "hosses," and the description well suited the starters of his 1956–57 team. Senior Jerry Smith, five-foot-ten, and junior Bull Muckleroy, five-foot-six, had returned as guards. Dan Stancil, a six-foot-three junior, was placed at forward, leaving the twins, seniors Pat and Don Stanley, both six-foot-two, to be used interchangeably at the other forward position and post.

When the season started, the Cougars picked up where the previous year's team left off. They racked up one victory after the other, winning a tournament in Lake Charles, Louisiana, and the Fifth Annual YMBL Tournament in Beaumont. In a wake of destruction comparable to that inflicted by a powerful Roman legion, the Cougars' trail was strewn with carnage of Port Neches, Galena Park, French, and Milby. Along the way, others fell twice, including the Lamar Tech "B" Team, Port Arthur, South Park, Big Sandy, Little Cypress of Orange, and Central out of Pollok. The Cougars also beat Milby for a total of three times on the year.[6]

By the February 5, 1957, district meeting with the last-place Dayton Broncos, Cotton's boys had amassed a string of thirty consecutive wins. When they crushed the Broncos, 85–28, they had thirty-one. In that game, Pat Stanley scored twenty-four, Don Stanley chipped in twenty-two, Dan Stancil had eleven, Jerry Smith-ten, William Withers-twelve, with the other six points shared by Revis Whitmire and Charles Simmons. To keep from running up the score, Cotton had inserted substitutes in the fourth quarter, but that didn't help. The backups kept adding to the total.[7]

Buna then beat Livingston, Cleveland, Liberty, and Port Neches to close out the regular season and another perfect record in district. Afterward, Cougars Jerry Smith, Pat Stanley, and Don Stanley were chosen as members of the All-District Team. And in the playoffs, it was business as usual; at bi-district, Buna destroyed Cypress-Fairbanks by thirty-two, 56–24. They bombed Rockdale, 72–39, in the opening round of the Region III-AA Tournament in College Station, before taking the title by downing Marlin, 53–26. Next stop: the 37th Annual Boys Basketball State Championship Tournament.[8]

As the Cougars arrived in Austin to try for their third straight state title—their first in Conference AA—Cotton sat atop a 64-game winning streak, dating back to last season. On March 7, 1957, when the state tournament began, his current team was considered the best high school basketball club in Texas. Period.[9]

The State Semifinal Game of 1957

THE TEAMS

Buna Cougars Coached by M. N. "Cotton" Robinson	Clear Creek Wildcats Coached by George Carlisle
Players	**Players**
Buckner, Jerry	Brizendine, Gary
Cobb, Jimmy	Brown, Robert
Davis, Herman	Counts, Richard
Goins, Jerry	Davis, Edward
Muckleroy, Robert	Davis, James
Simmons, Charles	Frost, William
Smith, Jerry	Goodman, Tom
Stancil, Dan	Hancock, John
Stanley, Don	Hardin, Butch
Stanley, Pat	Magee, Stanley
Swearingen, Paul	Milligan, Charles
Whitmire, Revis	Pell, Bob
Withers, William	Trcka, Chuck
	Taylor, Hugh
	Witte, Buddy

Participating Teams, First Round, Conference AA
—Courtesy UIL, Austin

On Thursday night, the Cougars were ready to go on the prowl. But near the other bench, Coach George Carlisle paced the floor. He worried that he had not prepared his boys well enough to repel the expected, withering barrage laid down by Cotton and his gifted troops.

Very early in the game, it became apparent that the Clear Creek Wildcats of Webster were going to concentrate on blocking out Pat Stanley, who played in the post position. Three Wildcats sank back on defense trying to keep the ball away from him, but his twin brother

Don, and Dan Stancil made them pay from the outside. Basically, Clear Creek had no idea which of the three big men to cover, and their game plan completely disintegrated. Buna led 20–12 at the end of the first quarter, 37–24 at the half, and 51–32 as the third drew to a close.[10]

Coach pulled Don Stanley because of foul trouble, but Pat took up the slack. He answered by scoring thirty-six points, breaking a Conference-AA record of thirty-five set the previous year by Carl Mitchell of Phillips in a state semifinal game against none other than this same Clear Creek. Late in the fourth quarter, Cotton put in his backup players so they could get some valuable playoff experience. By the time the final buzzer sounded, all but three of the Cougars' points were made by Pat Stanley, Dan Stancil, and Don Stanley with thirty-six, fourteen, and eleven, respectively. Bull Muckleroy scored two, and Jerry Smith, one. Robert Brown of Clear Creek chipped in twenty-two for his team's high-point honors.[11]

The Cougars had made this one look easy. With a strong rebounding effort and good shooting, they'd annihilated the Wildcats, 64–40. In the dressing room, Cotton reminded his boys: there's one more to go, and he warned them not to get cocky.[12]

Shortly after Buna had dispensed with Clear Creek, the Bowie Jackrabbits and the Seminole Indians met in the second semifinal AA action of the night. Because Seminole had lost six games during the season, the Jackrabbits were highly favored. But the Indians finished with an upset of 47–45, thereby gaining the right to face the Cougars in the final.[13]

The following night, Clear Creek's James Davis led his team to the AA consolation crown by defeating Bowie, 78–62, and in the process, he scored thirty-eight points, besting by two the record just set by Pat Stanley of Buna. With the way records were being set and broken, a few wondered just how long Davis's would stand. Perhaps, they said, we might see another one established in the upcoming clash between Seminole and Buna.[14]

Even with two returning regulars who played on Seminole's 1955 state championship team, very few observers gave the Indians little chance against the powerful Cougars. The stage was set for the Saturday evening duel, but would there be another upset in the making? Anything could happen in a championship game.[15]

Expectations are sometimes exceeded; other times not, especially in crucial playoff games, where players' emotions and adrenaline run amok. But Cotton Robinson had well taught his boys not to get rattled, and they soon demonstrated the value of his leadership. In the early

The State Final Game of 1957

THE TEAMS

Buna Cougars Coached by M. N. "Cotton" Robinson	Seminole Indians Coached by Metz LaFollette
Players	**Players**
Buckner, Jerry	Anderson, Bobby
Cobb, Jimmy	Bingham, Bobby
Davis, Herman	Caffey, Leland
Goins, Jerry	Cobb, Dan
Muckleroy, Robert	Doyle, Harold
Simmons, Charles	Doyle, Stanley
Smith, Jerry	English, Archie
Stancil, Dan	McLaughlin, Billy Bob
Stanley, Don	Teston, Darwyn
Stanley, Pat	Williamson, John
Swearingen, Paul	Wilson, Donnie
Whitmire, Revis	
Withers, William	

Participating Teams, Final Round, Conference AA
—Courtesy UIL, Austin

going, Don Stanley of Buna scored, as did his teammate, Bull Muckleroy. Seminole managed to stay close because of free throws, but the Cougars were up 10–6. By the end of the first quarter, Buna was ahead 19–13 with Don Stanley accounting for all of Buna's points except four by Muckleroy.[16]

It was more of the same in the second quarter. Don Stanley continued to connect from the post position, and the Cougars soon built up a 20-point lead, helped along by Pat Stanley, Muckleroy, and Jerry Smith. Seminole was completely befuddled by the Buna defense, and they only managed seven points in the entire second frame. It looked for all in attendance that the Don Stanley show had begun.[17]

Back for the second half, Don Stanley already had twenty-seven points to his credit. Coach asked his team to gather around. "Boys," he said, "we've got a chance if we just let Don do the shooting." In the brief meeting, Cotton never mentioned the word "record," but everybody knew what he was implying. Don Stanley had a legitimate chance of exceeding Russell Boone's 50-point total, still a record set in a tournament final of 1954 (Sweeny vs. Sundown).[18]

Don recalled Coach's doctrine of team over individual, and he voiced an objection. His teammates sided with Cotton, and all held firm. The plan was put into motion. But the Indians, too, had a plan of their own. They would put three men on the Cougar post, and surely, they thought, this would keep his scoring in check. In the third quarter that did temporarily seem to work, as Don only put in eight points, but in the fourth, he would break out and tally another sixteen.[19]

One particular referee in that game was also extremely interested in whether the Cougar would snap the old record, namely Earl Wray, who kept up with Don's total at any given time. With each of Don's first free throws, Wray handed him the basketball and sounded out how many points he had thus far. For example, at one interval, the referee chimed out in his normal high-pitched voice, "Well, Don, you have forty-eight now, and it's looking good."[20]

As he neared the magic number of fifty-one, Stanley began to experience leg cramps, and it appeared that his attempt at breaking Boone's record was in jeopardy. Cotton had no other choice but to rest him and hope that the cramps would let up some. Luckily for Buna, they did, and Don went back in long enough to break the record. That's when Cotton took him out for good. There was no need for more. With such a bold exclamation point, the *coup de grâce*, Coach, Don Stanley, and his Cougar teammates had put the Seminole Indians out of their misery.[21]

"Most of [Don] Stanley's field goals were scored on the same pattern—a high lob pass to the baseline to the right of the basket," George Breazeale of *The Austin American-Statesman* wrote. "Stanley then would go high for a lay-up, or would fake his defender, then drive in for a crip."[22]

Buna had completely manhandled Seminole with a final score of 74–45, behind their 62 percent shooting from the field and Don Stanley's record setting 51-point showing. Relative to the other Cougars, Dan Stancil posted an unselfish one point, Pat Stanley scored six, Muckleroy-twelve, and Jerry Smith-four. A 29-point margin in a state championship game was an amazing feat, considering that Buna had blasted Clear Creek by twenty-four in the semifinals. Twenty-four sportswriters, who participated in a poll, unanimously selected Don and Pat Stanley of Buna as members of the All-State Tournament Team. They were joined by James Davis and Robert Brown of Clear Creek, and Donnie Wilson of Seminole. Cougars Jerry Smith and Bull Muckleroy received honorable mention.[23]

Don Stanley would acquire even more tributes. He made the All-

Star Team for the East, and he became recipient of the highest award that a high school athlete can get, that of All-American. His brother, Pat, would play in the Texas North-South All-Star game.[24]

The scribes, who had suggested all along that Buna was the best boys' high school basketball team in Texas, were arguably correct. The 1956–57 Cougars had won a third straight state title for their school, finishing the season with an unblemished 40–0 record—and adding to a win streak that now totaled sixty-six. In other 37th Annual State Tournament action, Port Arthur claimed the championship in Conference AAAA, Smiley in AAA, and Big Sandy in B. Earlier in the season, the Cougars had twice beaten both Port Arthur by scores of 51–42 and 50–45 and Big Sandy by 52–35 and 86–64. Some sources go so far as to state that Buna had also defeated Smiley; however, the two teams never met in 1956–57.[25]

For Cotton Robinson, his team, and Buna fans everywhere, this was a spectacular ending to a remarkable season—one that many thought would never be duplicated. When writing about Buna in the future, sportswriters began to bandy about the "D" word. DYNASTY.[26]

H. S. R. No. 256

RESOLUTION

WHEREAS, In the Piney Woods of East Texas, boys learn their basketball by shooting at bushel basket rims on pine trees; and ———

WHEREAS, These boys become the best basketball players in the State of Texas; and ———

WHEREAS, During regular season play Buna defeated the State champions of class 4A twice; and ———

WHEREAS, The Buna Cougars have won the State Championship in class AA; now, therefore, be it ———

RESOLVED by the Texas House of Representatives, That congratulations be extended to the winningest team in the State of Texas--the Buna Cougars who have won sixty-six consecutive games; and, be it further ———

RESOLVED, That a copy of this Resolution be sent to each member of the team, and one to their fine coach, Cotton Robinson.

Shackelford

Waggoner
Speaker of the House

I hereby certify that H. S. R. No. 256 was adopted by the House on March 13, 1957. ———

Dorothy Hallman
Chief Clerk of the House

Resolution Number 256, March 13, 1957, honoring 1957 Cougars, originated in the Texas House of Representatives.

—Courtesy Lynda Robinson Sanford

SENATE RESOLUTION NO. 244

Lock

WHEREAS, The Buna Cougars recently won their third State Basketball Championship; and

WHEREAS, The faculty and student body of the Buna High School should be commended for this high accomplishment; and

WHEREAS, Coach Cotton Robinson has taught this team the finest in basketball skill, and in addition the highest principles of sportsmanship; and

WHEREAS, The Cougars have won sixty-six (66) consecutive games to become the State Championship Team; now, therefore, be it

RESOLVED, By the Senate of the State of Texas, that congratulations be extended to each member of the team; and, be it further

RESOLVED, That copies of this Resolution be sent to each of the players and to Coach Robinson.

Ben T Ramsey
President of the Senate

I hereby certify that the above Resolution was adopted by the Senate on March 19, 1957.

Charles Schnabel
Secretary of the Senate

Resolution Number 244, March 19, 1957, honoring 1957 Cougars, originated in the Texas Senate.

—Courtesy Lynda Robinson Sanford

CHAPTER TEN

The Harder They Fall

"Everybody pulls for David; nobody roots for Goliath."
—WILT CHAMBERLAIN

With three straight basketball championships under their belt, Buna Cougar fans had become too reliant on past accomplishments, and they fully expected a repeat in next March's state tournament. Diehards had already made their hotel reservations in Austin, and why not? Cotton's current team of 1957–58 showed real potential. Big six-foot-three Dan Stancil, who played such a pivotal role in last year's title run, was set at center, and he was joined by seniors William Withers, five-foot-nine, and Robert "Bull" Muckleroy, five-foot-six, at guard. Two five-foot-eleven juniors, Jerry Goins and Jimmy Cobb, filled the spots at forward. With these guys, a fourth consecutive title definitely seemed within reach.

On the reverse side, however, a few folks with a more practical outlook recognized the difficulty in filling Pat and Don Stanley's shoes, and to match the 1957 record of 40–0 would be certain impossibility. How would the scales tip?

That summer, as always, the practice sessions continued, and the players worked as hard as ever. Frequently, Cotton reminded each and everyone to never take winning for granted, and that only by complete dedication and a little luck, can champions remain on top.

Dark clouds were gathering in the direction of Dallardsville, and the severity of the storm that followed became evident in the Cougars' Friday night season opener at home. Old rivals, Coach Ford King and his Big Sandy Wildcats, who'd grown weary of all the shellackings they had taken from Buna in recent years, fought the Cougars to a tie through two overtimes. In "sudden death," Ford King, Jr., got the tip, and for the next minute or so, he and Edwin "Little Chief" Battise dribbled a few times and then passed off to one another. Buna's William Withers and Jimmy Cobb were guarding Battise and King, respectively.[1]

When Battise and King crossed in the middle of the court, Little Chief had the ball. The two Buna defenders switched, so that left Cobb on Battise. Withers yelled, "Jimmy, don't drop off so far."[2]

But by then it was too late. From about thirty-five feet out, Little Chief literally shot from his right hip. The ball barely cleared the rim, hit the backboard, and slammed through the goal. Game over! Big Sandy had just shattered the dreams of Cougarland in their bid to further extend the 66-game winning streak.[3]

And to make matters worse, Buna's losses after that bombshell continued to pile up. Despite the season's feeble start, there were occasional spurts where Robinson's boys played brilliantly, such as the Sixth Annual December YMBL Tournament in Beaumont. Even though Buna returned as a two-time defending champion—having won in 1955 and 1956—the Lamar Redskins of Houston were highly favored to take this year's title with Big Sandy running a close second.[4]

The Cougars of 1957–58. From left, front row: Jimmy Cobb, Charles Simmons, Jerry Goins, Dan Stancil, William Withers, Paul Swearingen, Robert "Bull" Muckleroy; top row: Kenneth Cobb (student manager), Phillip Rogers, Tom Westbrook, Coy Fletcher, Herman Davis, Raymond Stancil, Wayne Franklin, Dwaine Reese, Donald Vaughn, Charles Chesnutt (student manager)

—Courtesy Kay Cobb Simmons

The Cougars, who'd been belittled too much already, stiffened in their resolve to play above what their current record otherwise indicated. They had been through a rough patch, for sure, but now the time came for them to step up. In the opening round, they beat Port Neches by four, Beaumont High removed Big Sandy in a shocker, Lamar fell in the quarterfinals, and in the championship game, Cotton's team edged the Royal Purples of Beaumont High, 35–32, for their third YMBL title. Dan Stancil, the Cougar center, played so well, scoring twenty-four of Buna's thirty-five points, that he was named to the All-Tournament Team.[5]

Cotton Robinson had not expected his Cougars to outlast the field; in fact, he was absolutely shocked. "The boys played their best games of the year in this tournament," he said. "Somebody told me the record for most championships in this tournament was three [held by Houston's Milby], and I told them, 'Well, we're gonna stop at two.'"[6]

"I was more surprised than anybody that we won. The boys really seem to be coming around."[7]

Still, there were ominous signs that the Cougars had serious problems. Including the four wins at the YMBL, their record so far this season stood at eight losses out of fifteen starts. The Junior Chamber of Commerce Tournament in Houston punctuated the issue, when after suffering two straight defeats, Buna was eliminated.[8]

A degree of normalcy returned in early 1958. The boys have made the turn, the optimists said, and everything will be okay. Cotton will see to it. It seemed they were right, at first. The Cougars waltzed through their district, posting a perfect record of ten wins and no losses, and when the announcement came about whom they would meet in bi-district, even the most ardent cynics heaved a sigh of relief.[9]

Last year, the Cougars had humiliated the Cypress-Fairbanks Bobcats in bi-district by scoring fifty-six points to their twenty-four. Fortunately for the current Buna team, they would meet the same foe, likely to offer little resistance.[10]

On Tuesday, February 25, 1958, Cotton told his boys to be more diligent than usual on the night. Cypress-Fairbanks, he believed, would play aggressively, given the pounding they took the previous season. By the end of the first quarter, the Cougars led 18–5, and it looked like smooth sailing ahead. When the half ended, Buna still held the edge, 29–21. In the stands, the jubilant followers, who'd driven over to see their venerated Cougars play, were already talking about the return trip to the regionals in College Station—and imagining what it would feel like to have their team win there, and then take a fourth straight state title in Austin. If they could carry out this reasonable plan of action, Buna would be right up there with Bowie, who had won four consecutive state championships between 1951 and 1954.[11]

With forty-five seconds left in the game, Buna maintained a six-point lead, but that's when all hell broke loose. Bull Muckleroy, the Cougar guard, recalled the exact point. "They knocked me down at midcourt," he said, "and got the ball. How it happened, I don't know."[12]

From there, Cypress-Fairbanks went on a rampage—bobcat gnashing at cougar—allegedly condoned by some of the most atrocious officiating ever witnessed by those from Buna who attended the game, including Cougar basketball greats, J. C. Smith and Jimmy Burke. As time on the clock was about to expire, Dick Duke of Cypress-Fairbanks hit a free throw that gave the Bobcats a one-point win, 48–47.[13]

Considering the heartbreaking ending, and how the game was played, one can only visualize Coach's mind-set. After Cotton had his say with the referees, Charles Burke, Dick Muckleroy, and Charles Flowers, Cougar superfans, made a beeline for the one they thought most responsible for the fiasco. They cornered him, this referee, a guy named Pontikas, and it's a wonder that he wasn't assaulted and bodily harmed. Luckily for him, he escaped injury by ducking through the door of a dressing room—obviously not Buna's.[14]

Elsewhere, on the same Tuesday, two other defending state champions went down for the full count. Houston Smiley, who'd won the 3-A title, and White Oak of Conference A, both lost their bi-district games. It had been a good night for contenders.[15]

Next day on the Buna campus and around the entire community, the scene was reminiscent of a pall cast by a great national tragedy. This is hard to believe, folks said, that our team will not be represented in the regional and state tournaments. But we'll show 'em next year; we will be back.[16]

Cypress-Fairbanks may have won the battle with Buna in 1958—but they lost the campaign, because the Bobcats never made it to Austin. In an article written for *The Belton Journal* on January 4, 2001, Dr. Billy Wilbanks concluded that the Belton Tigers, who went on to win the State-AA title in 1958, profited most when they won a "Buna-less region."[17]

Did Cotton hold a grudge against Cypress-Fairbanks and the referee involved? Unquestionably, he must have in the short term. Years later, Harold V. Ratliff wrote a book titled *Texas Boys' Basketball: A*

History, and in that connection, he interviewed Robinson and asked how he felt about referees in general. Tongue in cheek, Cotton said, "The officiating was pretty good when we won, but when we lost, it was rotten." Within this humorous response, Coach must have been thinking back to the once-painful memory associated with the Cypress-Fairbanks game of 1958, which by now had been diluted by the passage of time.[18]

Cotton Robinson, circa 1958
—Courtesy Kay Cobb Simmons

The editor and staff of *The Cougar, 1958*, Buna High School's yearbook, tried to present the second-rate season in the most favorable light. "Due to the teams the Cougars played this past year, their record is not as impressive as it has been in the years before," they wrote. "Records only show the won and lost column. Many of the Cougars' contests were crowd thrilling and spine tingling."[19]

In spite of Buna's twenty-two wins and eighteen losses, the Texas Sportswriters Association bestowed upon Cotton Robinson "The Coach of the Year" award, which he shared with Ford King of Big Sandy, ironically the leader of the team that started Buna's current season off so badly. At any rate, Cotton was finally getting the recognition that he so richly deserved.[20]

Two days after Buna High School began classes in 1958, Cotton and Monte Sybil became the proud parents of a second daughter. On September 4, Janice Marie was born at the Baptist Hospital of Orange.[21]

CHAPTER ELEVEN

The 1958–59 Season

"Innovation distinguishes between a leader and a follower."
—STEVE JOBS

When Cotton Robinson first came to Buna in 1948, his responsibilities included coaching both the boys' and girls' basketball teams. However, after a year and a half of juggling his time between the two, he petitioned the school administration to assign someone else to head up the girls' program. After deliberating, all agreed that Coach needed to devote his full attention to the boys' team, so others stepped in to fill the void.[1]

In 1953, Clifton Gary resigned as girls' coach, and the program would have probably been disbanded, except for the entry of Richard Clemit "R. C." Hyden, the high school principal. Hyden volunteered for the job, and in 1954, his team finished the season with a winning record. But as with all sports, players come and go. As described in *Buna Remembered: The Times,* "Graduation left him with an all sophomore offense that featured two tall gangly girls, one [Lewine Germany] a natural left hander and the other [Virginia Shannon] a right. . . ."[2]

All boys' basketball offenses of that day and age were pretty basic. Coaches utilized two guards, two forwards, and a center, commonly called a post. But the girls' setup was different, because they played what is referred to as "six-on-six," with three forwards on one end of the court handling the

R. C. Hyden
—Courtesy *The Cougar, 1958*

ball, and three guards on the other end trying to keep their opponent from scoring.

Hyden thought that by utilizing one of his forwards as the play-maker, he could get better production from Germany and Shannon by rotating them into what he called high post and low post positions. Consequently, defenders had no idea which one to cover, so the other was usually open for an unobstructed shot. This innovation would prove the downfall of many an adversary. The "double post offense" turned the Texas girls' basketball world on its ear.[3]

Hyden's 1954–55 team did extremely well, but at regionals, they were defeated in their first bid to make the state finals. By the following year, though, everything clicked. With the addition of an unusually strong defense in 1955–56, the Cougarettes used the double-post pattern—at times identified as the Hyden Offense—to win Buna's first girls' basketball title. Robinson took notice.[4]

Cotton became convinced that he could use the new tool in his lineup, so he went to Hyden. "Clemit," he said, "I'm going to use the double post, and you're going to help me." Hyden gladly obliged, and Robinson began to experiment.[5]

"In practice we would run it for one quarter, keeping the score,"

The Cougarettes of 1948–49. From left, front row: M. N. "Cotton" Robinson, Shirley Scott, Betty Muckleroy, Ruth Simmons, Jeannette Thomas, Dora Scott; center row: Betty Nicolson, Georgia Nicolson, Bonnie Worsham; top row: Norma Walters, Verna Richardson, Ima Reese, Odean Dickerson, Gracie Williams
                                                              —Courtesy Lynda Robinson Sanford

Coach stated, "then use our old system for a quarter. We soon found we could do better with our new offense." Cotton was describing what came to be labeled as the *Buna Offense*, and he was about to unveil it to the public—and much to their lament, his competition.[6]

Robinson had several great years in which he exhibited extraordinary talents as a coach, but Jimmy Burke, a sophomore backup on the 1958–59 squad, viewed Cotton's eleventh season as the finest. "This was probably his least talented team at the beginning of the year," said Burke. "Our record was terrible up until the Nacogdoches Tournament, right before the holidays and the start of district play. I think we had lost eleven games out of our first fifteen to seventeen, and nearly everyone had written us off."[7]

The Huntington Red Devils also entered the tournament at Nacogdoches, and unknowingly, their coach, Jack Whitton, had a great part in what happened next. After the Cougars' first win, they had to play the Red Devils in the quarterfinals, the same team that had beaten them twice earlier in the season, 57–53 and 55–37. During a brief conversation, Whitton flippantly asked Cotton whether he was going to stay around after their game and watch some more action—or immediately drive his team back home. Robinson took the matter very seriously and as a throwing down of the gauntlet. In fact, he shared the rhetoric with his Cougars who didn't like the offhanded query anymore than their coach. The game ended with a Cougar one-point victory, 42–41, and Huntington, not Buna, made the early exit from the tournament. The Red Devils, however, were still a great team. During the upcoming March, they proved it by capturing the Conference-A state championship.[8]

Prior to the Nacogdoches Tournament, Jimmy Burke is correct in his analysis regarding Buna's prospects for the remainder of the year. The Cougars had begun the season with a win over Big Sandy, but they lost thirteen of the next eighteen games, many to teams they used to beat on a regular basis. Buna was twice defeated by Huntington, Smiley, French, and Beaumont High, while others such as Milby, Jeff Davis, and Port Arthur managed a split in their series.[9]

Admittedly, things looked grim for Cotton. It seemed doubtful that his current team would ever make the cut, and furthermore, it appeared that Coach's perfect district record since 1953–54 would not long stand. In the dead of winter as the fog and mist hung over Buna's Gum Slough Road and the swamps of the area's Big Thicket National Preserve, doubts draped across Cougarland like a black shroud. Buna fans could only cross their fingers and wish for the best.

But as history shows, great leaders rise to the occasion. "Coach literally rebuilt the team at midseason around Jimmy Cobb, the best 'clutch' high school player I've ever seen," said Burke. "Under his direction, Cotton made outstanding players out of those with rather limited talent."[10]

Cobb, a stocky five-foot-eleven forward, had been around basketball his entire life, just like teammates Tom Westbrook and Charles Simmons, the six-foot brother of ninth-grade basketball coach Harold Simmons. Westbrook, on the other hand, was almost lost before Cotton could draw out his true potential.

As a freshman, Tom had played basketball, but he sat out his sophomore season for medical reasons. During a baseball game coached by Cotton, the young man had been hit in the head with a ball, and the resulting blow sent him to the hospital for a week's stay. His discharge orders contained a grave warning from the doctors—any further injury might result in permanent brain damage and perhaps, even death. Naturally, Westbrook was scared when Coach approached him about once more wearing the blue and white uniforms of the Cougars' basketball team.[11]

At first, Tom said no. It's much too dangerous. Cotton presented an alternative. "What if we get other medical opinions to show that you are fine?" he asked.[12]

"My family doesn't have the money to pay for those types of expenses," Westbrook answered.[13]

Cotton would not give up. Since Tom had been hurt during a school-sponsored event, Coach felt that Buna High should be morally bound to do the right thing. At the least, the school could help alleviate the student's concerns for his well-being. Robinson went to Superintendent Bob Cummings, who in a subsequent meeting, assured Westbrook that he would cover all fees associated with the issue about whether it was safe to continue his sports career.[14]

Tom received three separate all-clear physical examinations and resumed basketball as a junior during the 1957–58 season. He rejoined the team, albeit on the Cougars' "B" squad. As Coach suspected he would, Tom lived up to his high standards. Now, a five-foot-eleven senior, Westbrook was ready to exhibit his prowess on the varsity team, and show that he was an integral member of the starting five, including Cobb and Simmons, along with Raymond Stancil, a six-foot-three junior, and Melvin Ellison, a five-foot-eleven sophomore.[15]

The Cougars went on to win the Nacogdoches Tournament that

December, and they emerged as battle hardened veterans, intent on salvaging the season. They then turned their attention to district foes that would once again experience the pain meted out by a superior team. One after the other, worthy competitors fell mangled by the wayside. On January 20, 1959, Buna's Raymond Stancil and Charles Simmons combined for a total of twenty-eight points in the massacre of Kirbyville, 64–32, and during the last district game on February 13, 1959, the win over the Little Cypress Bears, 58–38, assured Robinson his ninth district title. In the latter victory, Tom Westbrook and Wayne Franklin of Buna scored twenty-five and fourteen points, respectively, with Jerry Isbell of the Bears contributing only twelve for the losers.[16]

Considering the impressive comeback of late, folks around Buna were still nervous about their team's chances in the playoffs. However, Cotton and his players had regained their self-confidence, and they were ready to prove their mettle.

In bi-district, the Cougars' romp over Center, 50 to 42, earned for them another trip to the Regional III-AA Tournament in College

The Cougars of 1958–59. From left, front row: Jimmy Cobb, Tom Westbrook, Raymond Stancil, Charles Simmons, Melvin Ellison; center row: Phillip Rogers (student manager); Jimmy Burke, William Martin, Tate Harwell, Billy Kirkpatrick, Charles Chesnutt (student manager, standing); top row: Dwaine Reese, Herman Davis, Wayne Franklin, Glen Stancil, M. N. "Cotton" Robinson (standing)

—Courtesy *The Cougar,* 1959

Station, their fifth in the last six years. The Taylor Ducks were their first-round opponents.[17]

Taylor proved no equal for the Cougars' onslaught. Cotton's team jumped off to a 19–8 lead in the first quarter, and while the second and third frames were more evenly balanced, the fourth favored the Ducks. Nevertheless, the Taylor "Five" never found a way to contain Tom Westbrook of Buna who pumped in nine field goals and eight free throws for a combined twenty-six points, with teammates, Jimmy Cobb and Charles Simmons, adding sixteen and ten, respectively. The Cougars won the game in easy fashion, 58–44, and with it, a spot in the regional finals against the Belton Tigers, the defending Conference-AA champion.[18]

Cotton and his boys were especially pleased to face Belton. They wouldn't have had it any other way. The reason being: they wanted to show Texas basketball fans that if they'd only gotten past Cypress-Fairbanks in last season's bi-district debacle—one they should have taken—it might have been the Cougars, not the Tigers, who were the current AA champion.

Coach counseled everyone to expect a tough game. Belton would not go down as easily as Taylor just did, he said. Besides, the heavily favored Tigers had four starters back from last year's team, and they would be out for a repeat.

The pace of the game proved Cotton's assumption correct. At the end of the first quarter, the score was tied at eleven, it remained tied 29–29 at the half, and by the third, the Tigers led 37–36. As the clock wound down in regulation, Buna had fought back to take the lead, 55–53, but in the last three seconds, a jump shot by Belton's Dennis Watson knotted the score at 55–55. As the two teams lined up to begin the overtime period, Cotton looked toward Cobb and Westbrook to break the stalemate. Up to this point in the game, Jimmy had played like a man possessed—a scoring machine, netting thirty-two points. Tom Westbrook, too, was having a good showing with twelve of his own, supplemented by opportune rebounding.[19]

In overtime, Belton and Buna continued just like two brawling heavyweights settling a feud. Each time the Tigers scored, so did the Cougars. By now, Buna held a two-point lead, 61–59, but a Belton free throw brought the Tigers within one, 61–60. With forty-five seconds to go, Buna's Cobb went high on a jumper. Everyone in the gym gasped, and then followed the ball as if it were in slow motion. When Jimmy's shot fell through the bucket, the Cougar crowd roared.[20]

In any other game, the Tigers' performance might have been good enough to allow them to win. But on this occasion, they were no match for Cotton's shooting ace, Jimmy Cobb, and his thirty-eight points. Against Buna, Belton's best boiled down to nothing more than runners-up. In contrast, the Cougars, as Regional III-AA champions, would advance to the state tournament.[21]

With this miracle win of 63–60, and given the way their season had started with so many losses, every player and Coach must have been astonished at how far they'd come. Despite Buna's current record of 29–15, their team had created magic and enough momentum, most believed, to carry them to a fourth state title in five years.[22]

In sports columns and in radio and television studios, much is said about the word—*momentum*, commonly referred to as "The Big Mo." Winning streaks, they say, prove a psychological advantage in the playoff picture, and if that's so, going into the 39th Annual UIL State Championship Tournament, the Cougars certainly had Big Mo on their side. In their last twenty-one games, they'd lost just once, and to find that one, you'd have to go way back before district competition began. Buna had just taken down the defending AA champion, and they were on a mission.[23]

The State Semifinal Game of 1959

THE TEAMS

Buna Cougars Coached by M. N. "Cotton" Robinson	Seminole Indians Coached by Metz LaFollette
Players	Players
Burke, Jimmy	Billings, Walter
Cobb, Jimmy	Brasfield, L. A.
Davis, Herman	Carter, Noel
Ellison, Melvin	Cobb, Dan
Franklin, Wayne	Davis, Bill "Wig"
Kirkpatrick, Billy	Dow, Dwight
Martin, Willie	Doyle, Harold
Reese, Dwaine	Hugghins, Glen
Simmons, Charles	Jones, Milton
Stancil, Glen	Norton, Ronnie
Stancil, Raymond	Vining, Jim
Westbrook, Tom	Wilson, Lynn "Chig"

Participating Teams, First Round, Conference AA
—Courtesy UIL, Austin

Coaches Cotton Robinson of Buna and Metz LaFollette of Seminole were no strangers. Their teams had met for the Conference-AA championship title in 1957 when Don Stanley established his 51-point record, and the Cougars won by twenty-nine, 74–45. When LaFollette heard that he was meeting Buna in the first round, he must have thought, *Oh, no! Here we go again.*

As Buna and Seminole squared off on Thursday, March 5, 1959, their teams appeared evenly matched in both size and height. But that's about as far as the similarities went. The Indians kept the game close in the early stages, holding the Cougars to a lead of 17–10 late in the first quarter, but when Buna's Jimmy Cobb and Tom Westbrook caught fire, Seminole found themselves behind, 31–25, at the half.[24]

Except for the valiant effort of Harold Doyle, the Seminole guard, Buna's lead might have been more. By the end of the third quarter and ahead, 43–37, the Cougars went on a scoring spree, sinking seventeen points, fifteen of those by free throws in the final period. Seminole's Doyle, Lynn Wilson, and Bill Davis could only muster a total of five points in the fourth, and Buna won the game going away with a score of 60–42. Jimmy Cobb, the Cougar forward, had one of the best head fakes in the business, and he took every advantage of his talent to draw a foul. He finished with twenty-six points, followed by Westbrook's fifteen. Teammates Raymond Stancil had seven, and three others, Melvin Ellison, Herman Davis, and Charles Simmons, accounted for four each. Two of the most telling differences in the game came down to free throws—Buna hit twenty-six of thirty-two, while Seminole only connected on six out of eighteen—and shooting percentages, with the Cougars ending at 53 percent compared to Seminole's 30.[25]

In an earlier game that same evening, the Bowie Jackrabbits defeated the Devine Warhorses, 63–52; consequently, they had won the right to meet Buna in the final AA action, set for Saturday night, March 7. The Jackrabbits, led by six-foot-two senior Jim Thompson, an All-State center, would be gunning for their fifth state title, while Buna aimed for their fourth. Thompson scored twenty-eight points in Bowie's win over Devine, and helped put a stop to the Warhorses' winning streak and undefeated season of thirty-one games. On the other side, Jimmy Cobb of Buna finished with twenty-six in the Cougars' win over Seminole. From all perspectives, the Bowie-Buna matchup appeared to be a good one.[26]

At the state tournament in 1959, the two players that Southwestern Conference coaches viewed as the best prospects were Lewis Qualls, the seven-foot All-State center from Smiley, and Jim Thompson, his counterpart from Bowie. In fact, most of them looked upon Thompson as the better candidate of the two.[27]

Thankfully, in this year's tournament, Buna would meet neither Qualls nor his teammates, because the Smiley Golden Eagles were in a larger conference. The Cougars had already seen all they wanted of this monster center in two early season drubbings. When the Golden Eagles visited Buna and Qualls bent over to clear a doorway to make his way that night onto the playing area of Cougar Gym, no one had ever seen anything like him, purported to be the tallest basketball player in the world.[28]

That left Jim Thompson and the Bowie Jackrabbits on whom Buna had to concentrate. Perry Smith, sportswriter for the *Beaumont Enterprise*, said it best with his March 5, 1959, headline: "Cougars Must Stop Thompson." That's the key, said Smith, stop him, and the Cougars might have a real shot, that is, if Jimmy Cobb and Tom Westbrook play anything like they did in Buna's win over Seminole.[29]

Like Buna, Bowie, too, had a highly decorated basketball history. The Jackrabbits were making their eighth state tournament appearance, extending back to 1946, and they'd brought home titles in four consecutive years: 1951 through 1954, all under Coach R. E. Mattingly. Now, it was Coach Bobby Brashear's turn to try and win the fifth, which would be a record-tying achievement. Coach Brashear liked his chances.[30]

Compared to each of the Cougars, the Jackrabbits were an inch taller per man—and they were fast and well known for being able to drive to the basket. Furthermore, Coaches Robinson and Brashear could not have been more different in their styles and how their teams approached the game. But it would appear that on paper anyway, Bowie's 31–4 record gave them the upper hand. On Saturday, March 7, right before tip-off, most observers were hard-pressed to give Buna the edge; after all, the Cougars had lost fifteen games during the current season. Only South San Antonio (San Antonio) of District 14-AAA had a shoddier record, 14–24, going into the current state championship tournament, but that was simply because twenty-two of their non-district games had been forfeited due to using an ineligible player.[31]

As expected, Bowie got off to a quick start; they scored six points in the first seventy-five seconds. Buna's Cobb, Westbrook, and Ellison finally broke out of their shooting slump, and when the first quarter ended, Buna led 11–10. In the second, the Jackrabbits regained the

The State Final Game of 1959

THE TEAMS

Buna Cougars Coached by M. N. "Cotton" Robinson	Bowie Jackrabbits Coached by Bobby Brashear
Players	**Players**
Burke, Jimmy	Bradfield, Terry
Cobb, Jimmy	Cantwell, Jerry
Davis, Herman	Compton, Ronnie
Ellison, Melvin	Coplin, Keith
Franklin, Wayne	Cordell, Lee
Kirkpatrick, Billy	Cornelison, Bob
Martin, Willie	Cornelison, Roy
Reese, Dwaine	Ford, Charles
Simmons, Charles	Lancaster, Robert
Stancil, Glen	Latham, Pat
Stancil, Raymond	McKinley, Bob
Westbrook, Tom	Powers, Tommy
	Sadler, Mike
	Thompson, James
	Welch, Orville

Participating Teams, Final Round, Conference AA
—Courtesy UIL, Austin

advantage, 22–18. So far, however, the most positive sign for the Cougars lay in the fact that they had held Thompson to a mere six points.[32]

During halftime, Cotton was back in the dressing room delivering instructions to his players on what to do when the game resumed. Jimmy Cobb spoke up. "Don't worry about a thing Coach," he said, "we've got 'em just where we want 'em."[33]

At the end of the third, Bowie still led 37–33, and it seemed they would eventually win. The Cougars bent but refused to break. They began to claw their way back. Cobb, a ball-handling magician, hit a corner jumpshot, and then Simmons made one of his own. Stancil was fouled, and he put the Cougars ahead. For the Jackrabbits, though, the worst was yet to come. Their All-State center, Jim Thompson, fouled out with 5:13 remaining in the game. At that point, the score was tied 41–41, but it wouldn't remain that way for long. Buna took the lead for good at the 3:38 mark and immediately went into slowdown mode that resulted in five fouls from the Bowie players. These costly penalties converted into seven more points for Cotton's team.[34]

When the buzzer sounded, Bowie appeared stunned, in a state of shock. Their players—and coach could not believe it. *How did it happen, they asked themselves? How could we lose to Buna by a score of 53 to 48?*

Cotton Robinson met with reporters, and he commented about how his team pulled off the upset. "It just seemed from the last of December on that these boys improved with every game," he said. "We didn't play as well tonight as we did against Belton in the regional finals—but then Belton and Bowie are so close in ability that one can hardly say which is better."[35]

"Those boys had to work for everything they got," Coach added. "It wasn't like two years ago when we knew we had a great team."[36]

Now, Cotton had to make good on an earlier promise. Charles Simmons, a starter on the 1958–59 championship team, said that Coach had told the Cougars if they won the championship, he'd take them out to eat at Hill's Steak House, and so he did. After everyone enjoyed an excellent meal, they returned to the Oak Motel before departing the next morning for Buna.[37]

Years later, R. C. Hyden, the Buna High School principal at that time and a great basketball coach in his own right, offered the real explanation as to how Buna roughed up Bowie in the finals of 1959. "Our kids wouldn't let them run," he said. "We fought their guards all the way up the court every time they had the ball. You could see the pressure and the frustration building on them as the game wore on, and in the fourth quarter they came apart. They made a bunch of critical mistakes and we won the game."[38]

Statistically speaking during the state final with Bowie, the Cougars shot 54.3 percent, while holding their opponent to 47.8. At four different times, Buna trailed as many as six points, but they never panicked. Buna's Tom Westbrook was high man for his team with twenty-two points, followed by Jimmy Cobb at sixteen, Melvin Ellison at seven, with four each by Charles Simmons and Raymond Stancil. Orville Welch scored eighteen, the most for the Jackrabbits. In his March 7, 1959, column, sportswriter Perry Smith reported that "Jim Thompson, Bowie's big gun, accounted for eleven with Buna's Cobb hawking him like a Siamese twin." When the All-State Tournament Team was announced, it included Jimmy Cobb and Tom Westbrook of Buna, Jim Thompson of Bowie, Carroll Davidson of Devine, and Dan Cobb of Seminole.[39]

Once again, the Cougars ruled the AA Conference with Coach's slow, methodical phalanx that called for ball control and attempting only high percentage shots, combined with a blistering full- and half-court press on defense. After the smoke and dust cleared, Cotton Robinson had just tied the record of R. E. Mattingly, the former Bowie coach, with four state championships each. Despite the many earlier losses in the season and a drab overall record of 31–15, it had been a great year for Cougar basketball, and for the future, Buna fans had no cause to be anything other than optimistic.[40]

H. S. R. No. 280

RESOLUTION

WHEREAS, The mighty Buna Cougars, displaying courage and team spirit, won the State Class AA basketball championship; and

WHEREAS, Jimmy Cobb, Tom Westbrook, Charles Simmons, Raymond Stancil, Melvin Ellison and Herman Davis brought recognition to Buna and all of East Texas with their talent and fine Christian sportsmanship; and

WHEREAS, Cotton Robinson is the efficient coach of this victorious team; now, therefore, be it

RESOLVED, That the Texas House of Representatives of the Fifty-sixth Legislature congratulates the coach and these fine young men of Buna and wishes them all continued success in the game of life.

Collins

Waggoner
Speaker of the House

I hereby certify that H. S. R. No. 280 was adopted by the House on March 10, 1959.

Dorothy Hallman
Chief Clerk of the House

Resolution Number 280, March 10, 1959, honoring 1959 Cougars, originated in the Texas House of Representatives.

—Courtesy Lynda Robinson Sanford

CHAPTER TWELVE

Reversal of Fortune

"Robinson faces a good rebuilding job before constructing another state champ."

—TOM BEARD, *Beaumont Journal,*
Dec. 10, 1959

Cotton Robinson had to confront another rebuilding year, so often discussed amongst high school and college coaches as a pattern all too familiar. Gone were his go-to guys, Jimmy Cobb and Tom Westbrook; and the dependable Charles Simmons, whose play in the 1958–59 season had helped guide the Cougars to their fourth title in the last five state tournaments. Only two starters returned, Raymond Stancil, a six-foot-three senior center, and Melvin Ellison, a six-foot junior who'd started at guard during his sophomore year.

Relatively speaking, Buna fans considered this a nonissue, simply because Cotton seemed to always have a steady supply of good players in the pipeline. This season was basically the same, with one exception. It took Coach more time than usual to decide on a lineup that he'd stick with. About two games into the district race, he settled on Stancil and Wayne Franklin, a six-foot-one senior, at the low and high post positions, respectively, with Ellison and Dwaine Reese, a five-foot-eleven senior, at forward, and James "Jimmy" Burke, a five-foot-six junior, as the single guard. Glen Stancil, a six-foot-two junior who was Raymond's younger brother, became the sixth man in the rotation. That's not to say, however, that Cotton did not change lineups when the need arose; often, he used Ellison as a guard.[1]

The Cougars opened their season on November 3, and by December, they owned a record of 9–2, losing only to the Beaumont High Royal Purples and the Port Arthur Yellow Jackets. As usual, Cotton entered his team in the annual YMBL Tournament in

Beaumont, and in the first game, they met the Milby Buffaloes, whom the Cougars had already beaten earlier in the year. Oddly enough, both Buna and Milby had previously won three championships in the Beaumont tourney, and each hoped to break the tie.[2]

Before the tournament began, Tom Beard of the *Beaumont Journal* asked Robinson to assess his 1959–60 team. In a candid response, Cotton expressed grave reservations. "Our defense so far this season isn't as good as it has been," he said. "We don't have the speed to play a half-court press [as] we like to. I'm having to adapt my defense to the material."[3]

The Lamar Redskins of Houston won the tournament. Buna would have to wait until another day to take home their unprecedented fourth YMBL title.[4]

As had become ordinary at this juncture, the Cougars finished with another spotless record in their district, going 9–0. Red Hebert, a sportswriter for the *Beaumont Enterprise*, hailed the upcoming bi-district bout with the Jasper Bulldogs as "two teams without an individual star." Buna had made it to this level on several occasions, but "this is the first time in Jasper basketball history that the Bulldogs have captured a district crown," Hebert said. The article's undertone was apparent; Jasper didn't stand a snowball's chance in hades.[5]

The Cougars of 1959–60. From left, front row: Melvin Ellison, Glen Stancil, Raymond Stancil, Wayne Franklin, Dwaine Reese, Jimmy Burke; top row: Phillip Rogers (student manager), Jerryl Stanley, Charles Westbrook, Billy Kirkpatrick, Raymond Cleveland, James Simmons, Derryl Stanley, Bobby Simmons, M. N. "Cotton" Robinson
—Courtesy *The Cougar, 1960*

"The Buna Offense" district action in Kountze, 1960. The Cougars, in dark uniforms, left to right, Raymond Stancil, No. 15, low post; Wayne Franklin, No. 13, high post; Glen Stancil, No. 12, right forward; Melvin Ellison, No. 11, guard; Dwaine Reese, No. 10, left forward (not shown)
—Courtesy Melvin Ellison

On Tuesday, February 23, 1960, the Bulldogs under Coach Hubert Boales received quite a defensive lesson from Cotton Robinson. When it was all over, the Cougars had soundly whipped an inexperienced foe with no clue about how to cope with a half-court press. Jasper managed only six field goals in the entire game, and in the absence of fifteen free throws, they would have fallen by more than the ending score of 48–27. Raymond Stancil and Dwaine Reese led Buna with sixteen and twelve points, respectively, while Ray Brown of Jasper accounted for sixteen in the losing effort.[6]

Just like clockwork, the Cougars made the annual pilgrimage to College Station to participate in the Regional III-AA Tournament. Here, they would meet the Belton Tigers in the first round, scheduled for Saturday, February 27. The regulars from Buna were there, along with an unusually large contingent of Buna High School students bused in to cheer for the home team and see their Cougars do what they customarily did during these occasions. The required steps that followed were considered as nothing more than obligatory blips on the radar that would plot Buna's steady course through the regional finals to Austin, where they would most assuredly bring home another state title.[7]

Early, the Belton Tigers proved to be no pushover, and for the Cougars, everything seemed out of sync. Buna used the tried-and-true full-court press, but that didn't work either. Too many fouls provided the Tigers with more points. Belton also held the edge in rebounding with most of those pulled in by six-foot-five Dale West. Although the Cougars jumped out to a 1–0 lead in the first few seconds, they would trail for the rest of the game. By the end of the first half, Belton led 27–24. Each time the Cougars tried to climb back, they failed to find any traction.[8]

This isn't anything new, the Buna crowd told one another. We've been in this same spot many times, and Cotton always worked his magic. Dwaine Reese, one of the Cougar forwards, went high for a rebound on an errant Belton shot, and Buna supporters, including Lionel Reese, Dwaine's older brother, groaned when he accidentally tipped the ball into the Tigers' goal. That can't be helped, they said, Dwaine tried his best. It could have happened to anybody. We'll get those two points back. Nothing to worry about; there's plenty of time left. Just wait and see. But as the game clock wore down, so did their positive attitude.[9]

Even though the Cougars outscored the Tigers in the last half, 17–16, the nineteen charity shots by Belton compared to Buna's five made all the difference. As the game came down to the wire, the score was 43–41. Cotton called a timeout.[10]

He looked toward his guard, Jimmy Burke, who had so far pumped in eleven points. "Jimmy, let's get the ball to the inside," Cotton directed. "If we don't have a shot, maybe we'll draw a foul."[11]

Burke passed the ball to Melvin Ellison. But he had nothing open, so he threw the ball back to Jimmy. Again, Jimmy went to the inside, and for the second time, Ellison passed the ball back to him. With just enough time left to take a desperation shot, Burke let loose. The ball rolled around the rim and bounced out.[12]

Belton had won by only two points, 43–41. At that instant, Buna fans could only fault those hateful Tigers, the ones with the audacity to take away their dream of winning a fifth state title. The long ride home to Cougarland, expected to be joyful, turned somber and comparable to the event described in Ernest Lawrence Thayer's famous poem titled "Mighty Casey at the Bat." With a play on words, Buna's loss to Belton can be characterized as follows:

Oh, somewhere in this favored land the sun is shining bright;
The band is playing somewhere, and somewhere hearts are light,
And somewhere men are laughing, and somewhere children shout;
But there is no joy in Buna—the mighty Cougars have bowed out.[13]

There was some measure of consolation to the torturous ending and this disappointing season of thirty wins and ten losses. Cougars Raymond Stancil and Melvin Ellison were named to the 23-AA All-District Team, while another, Wayne Franklin, made the second squad. Ellison also received a special national honor when the February 1960 edition of *Dell Sports Magazine* listed him as a top high school basketball star in Texas.[14]

1959–60 23-AA All-District Team, Texas A&M Club, Beaumont, TX, March 29, 1960. From left, front row: John Murdock, Little Cypress; Wayne Franklin, Buna; Raymond Stancil, Buna; Melvin Ellison, Buna; Dennis Roberts, Kountze; top row: Jackie Bond, Little Cypress coach; M. N. "Cotton" Robinson; Herbert Muckleroy, Kountze coach
—Courtesy Melvin Ellison

CHAPTER THIRTEEN

The 1960–61 Season

"Winning isn't everything, but the will to win is everything."
—VINCE LOMBARDI

After the previous season's bitter two-point loss to the Belton Tigers in the Regional III-AA semifinals, Cotton Robinson was anxious to begin anew. Obviously, he'd miss Raymond Stancil, Wayne Franklin, and Dwaine Reese, the three seniors who'd graduated, but across the board Coach liked his current team. Guard Jimmy Burke, five-foot-seven, was back for his senior year, as was one of the forwards, Billy Kirkpatrick, five-foot-eleven. Returnees Glen Stancil, six-foot-three, and Melvin Ellison, six-foot-one, both seniors, filled the two post slots, while James "Sambo" Simmons, six-foot, the only junior starter, claimed the other forward position.[1]

By November 26, 1960, the Cougars had already notched five impressive wins without a defeat. But, on that particular night in Buna, the Beaumont High Royal Purples gave them quite a fight. Although behind at the half, Cougars Kirkpatrick and Ellison with fourteen and thirteen points, respectively, brought their team back, and Buna won 49–46. Four nights later, the Port Arthur Yellow Jackets came to town to try their luck, and until midway in the fourth period, they were on top. But Melvin Ellison and Glen Stancil, the same duo that unleashed the defensive charge, also led Buna in scoring with nineteen and thirteen points, respectively. Robinson's boys walked off their home court with a 44–42 victory and their seventh consecutive win.[2]

On December 2, the Cougars thumped Jasper, and then four days later, they turned in a well-balanced effort by beating the French Buffaloes of Beaumont, 39–31. This had been a tune-up game, their ninth win in a row, to get Robinson's team primed for the annual YMBL Tournament, set for the coming weekend.[3]

In a run-up to the YMBL, Coach Donald Longcope of Houston Lamar, the defending tournament champion, met with the media. "We've got height, depth and pretty good shooters," he said. "But if Roemer's [Lamar's six-foot-five center] back isn't all right, we'll have a mighty rough time in that meet."[4]

As it turned out, Dave Roemer's back did not improve, and he didn't play during the tournament. But that mattered little as Lamar got by their opponents, West Orange, South Park, and Milby, on their way to the championship round. Meanwhile on the other side of the bracket, Buna beat Port Neches-Groves, Port Arthur, and Nacogdoches for the right to face the Lamar Redskins for the crown.[5]

Up to this point, both Buna and Houston's Milby had each won three YMBL titles, but by Saturday night's end, the Cougars owned four YMBL championship trophies, making them the tourney's most winningest team. All five of the Cougar starters put up points against Lamar in the 50–46 victory, but Stancil and Kirkpatrick had the most with four-

The Cougars of 1960–61. From left, front row: Johnny Cochran, John Richardson, John McHugh, Pat Stom; center row: John Hatch, Herbert Ross, Pete Hillin, Jimmy Burke, Billy Kirkpatrick; top row: M. N. "Cotton" Robinson, Melvin Ellison, Raymond Cleveland, Glen Stancil, James Simmons, Macarthur Gibson (student manager)

—Courtesy *The Cougar, 1961*

teen and ten, respectively. Lamar's Tommy Nelms was high scorer for
his team with twenty-one. Due to a tie vote, the All-Tournament Squad,
comprised of six players instead of the usual five, included Melvin
Ellison of Buna, Carlos Gutierrez of Milby, Larry Franks of
Nacogdoches, T. Nelson Bruce of Beaumont High, Tommy Nelms of
Lamar, and Bill Gasway of Burkeville.[6]

The following week, Buna entered their second tournament of the
season, the Stephen F. Austin College Invitational at Nacogdoches,
where they swept by Mineola, 57–30, Sam Houston of Houston, 42–39,
and Jeff Davis, 56–50. In the finals, the Cougars tangled with the
Frankston Indians and beat them 55–40 to win the event. The Indians
would go on the following March to become Conference-B state champion.[7]

On December 20, Buna whipped Port Arthur, 47–37, and within
three days, they defeated Milby, 52–45, for their twenty-first consecutive win of the season. While Cotton Robinson prepared to take his undefeated team to the Port Arthur Tournament, Hal Reagan of the
Beaumont Journal printed some favorable comments. "Twelve of Buna's
wins have come over Class 4A and 3A clubs—mostly the former.

YMBL Action, December 1960. *Buna in Dark Uniforms. From left: Jimmy Burke-13,
Billy Kirkpatrick-10, James Simmons-69, Melvin Ellison-jumping, Glen Stancil*
—Courtesy Melvin Ellison

Champion. Stephen F. Austin College Invitational Tournament, December 1960. From left, kneeling, holding trophy: Melvin Ellison, Jimmy Burke; center row: Macarthur Gibson (student manager), James Simmons, Billy Kirkpatrick, John Richardson, Herbert Ross; back row: Pete Hillin, Glen Stancil, Raymond Cleveland, John Hatch; standing extreme right: M. N. "Cotton" Robinson

—Courtesy Bill Kirkpatrick

They've knocked off Port Arthur three times, Beaumont High twice and hold single verdicts over French, South Park, Houston Milby, Port Neches-Groves, Houston Lamar, Nacogdoches and Houston's Sam Houston," he wrote. "It really isn't much of a surprise to Buna's hoop-crazy populace or Robinson. They saw it coming late last year when the 1959–60 Cougars shrugged off a mid-season slump and came on strong with three underclassmen [Glen Stancil, Melvin Ellison, and Jimmy Burke] leading the way."[8]

"Boiled down, it's tough beating a team that hits almost half of its shots, plays picture-perfect defense and takes its basketball dead serious."[9]

In the Second Annual Port Arthur Holiday Basketball Tournament, the Cougars came up against a determined bunch from West Orange in the first round, but finally put them away, 37–30. In the quarterfinals, they beat Lamar Consolidated (Rosenberg), 45–34, and then in the semifinals, they dispensed with Aldine by one of their lowest outputs of the season, 32–19. Buna took the tournament title in a thrilling overtime victory against the Port Arthur Yellow Jackets, 41–39. After losing his fourth game of the season to Cotton Robinson, Port Arthur Coach Pete Pense remarked, "As they used to say in Brooklyn, we'll just have to wait 'til next year, I guess."[10]

On New Year's Eve in Cougar Gym, Buna met the Spring Branch Bears of Houston in what was to become for both teams the tensest game of the year. After thirty-two minutes of nail-biting action, regulation play concluded with a 38–38 deadlock. Six minutes later, at the end of two overtime periods, the score was still tied, 40–40. Just before the Cougars lined up for jump ball at center court to begin "sudden death," Coach called everyone to come in close.[11]

"Okay boys, the first team to score two points wins the game, so here's what we'll do," he said. "On the jump, move into the circle. The referee will call a violation, and Spring Branch will get possession. And then, after the inbound pass, I want you to go after the ball and foul, but don't make it look intentional. Since we have not put them in the bonus yet, they'll only get one free throw. Even if they make it, we'll go down, score a bucket, and win the game."[12]

At this stage, it was incredible that Buna had not picked up five team fouls, which would have given the Bears a bonus shot. And, too, it's a tremendous testimony to Cotton Robinson that his team remained so disciplined on defense in such a hard-fought contest. By and large, the Cougars did not reach and foul; they played smart basketball. Moreover, Coach's grasp of the game in tight situations clearly gave his team an advantage.

Robinson walked over and conferred with the referees, because he didn't want any controversy to arise when or if Spring Branch scored first on a free throw. So, to be on the safe side, he sought to make sure that everyone understood the "first two-points" rule that applied only to sudden death overtimes.[13]

As instructed, a Buna player moved into the circle, and as Cotton expected, the referee blew his whistle. Everything was set up. Spring Branch inbounded, and immediately, Billy Kirkpatrick fouled the ball handler who stepped to his free-throw line and sank a single point. With the Bears now up by one, Cougar Melvin Ellison missed a lay-up. Teammate Glen Stancil recovered the ball, but he also came up short. Ellison never gave up on the rebound which he eventually controlled underneath the basket. He scored, and the game ended on the two-point play. The Cougars had just picked up their twenty-sixth win of the season, 42–41.[14]

True to form, the Buna crowd jumped to their feet and went wild, but Cotton's reaction was out of the ordinary. Normally, he displayed little emotion at the end of a game; this time, however, he bolted from the bench and hollered, "Yea!" Furthermore, his large grin showed his appreciation for a job well done. The dispirited losers shrugged their shoulders in disbelief, but whether they'd won or lost, each team had played a great basketball game. And most assuredly, everyone in attendance had seen Cotton Robinson, the epitome of a coach, perform at his very best.[15]

The Cougars kept up their blistering pace, blasting South Park, 54–26, French, 50–35, Woodville, 67–22, Kirbyville, 74–29, Kountze, 61–28, Little Cypress, 61–34, Newton, 88–31, and Woodville again, 60–43. As they left Kirbyville on February 3, 1961, Buna had a perfect district record of 7–0 and thirty-five consecutive wins behind them.[16]

For the second time this season, Kountze fell to the Cougars, 64–18, and then came Little Cypress's turn to bite the dust yet again, 56–36. George Pharr of *The Orange Leader* put together in words the helpless feeling of the teams that were being dominated at every turn by Robinson's boys. "The death punch, which killed off Little Cypress in the District 24-AA race, came quickly," he wrote. "It was effective and climactic."[17]

In beating Newton on February 14, the Cougars reached another milestone: 100 district wins without a defeat and their thirty-eighth victory of the season. The score was so lopsided, 80–29, that Cotton sent in five members of his B-Team to get all-important playing time.[18]

Buna wrapped up a perfect record in district, their eighth in as many seasons, and then took on the Dayton Broncos in a bi-district tilt held at Lamar Tech's McDonald Gymnasium in Beaumont. Buna's Ellison poured in twenty points, along with Stancil's fifteen. In the rebounding department, the Cougars were masters on the boards, hauling in forty-seven to Dayton's twenty-six, and in the shooting category, they completely outgunned the Broncos, 59 to 38 percent. Red Hebert reported for the *Beaumont Enterprise*. "When the clock reached exactly 4:00 even in the final quarter," he wrote, "a loud round of applause [arose] from the Cougar fans as the entire first unit pulled out and headed toward the showers, leaving the second team at the controls." The final score, 58–35.[19]

The Cougars of 1958–59 had met the Taylor Ducks in the first round of the Regional III-AA Tournament in College Station, and Buna easily won that game, 58–44. And now, these two would again face one another in the same stage of this year's playoffs. Coach Rick Sherley of Taylor was realistic. "We are aiming for the state championship, like all the other teams here," he said. "If we are going to win it, we have to beat the best. So we would just as soon play Buna in the first game."[20]

"I know Buna has a fine ball club, much better than us. But if we have any hopes of going all the way, then we shall have to play some tough teams, and Buna is one of them."[21]

In spite of his team's superlative record of 23–5, Coach Sherley fully agreed with the prevailing opinion of those who regularly followed Texas high school basketball. The road to the Conference-AA state championship ran through Buna.[22]

From the initial tip-off, it was obvious that the Taylor Ducks were in over their heads as they ran headlong into a smoothly functioning machine, hitting on all offensive and defensive cylinders. In the first eleven minutes of the ball game, the Cougars had scored twenty-one points, compared to only one free throw by the Ducks. During the first half, Buna's Melvin Ellison connected with sixteen points, Glen Stancil put in thirteen, and the three other starters, Jimmy Burke, Billy Kirkpatrick, and James Simmons accounted for six each. With his team so far out front, 32–9, at the half, Robinson let his reserves finish out the game. The final score: Buna, 64; Taylor, 23. It had been nothing less than a sacrificial slaughter.[23]

Earlier, Cotton Robinson had called it. He believed that the Madisonville Mustangs, "one of the best teams in the state," would be in the regional finals. And so, they were. The two teams, Buna and Madisonville, slugged it out on Saturday night, February 25, 1961, to determine which one would advance to the state tournament in Austin. Late into the contest, the score was tied at 42–42, but in the last minute and forty-five seconds, Jimmy Burke of Buna went four times to the free-throw line and hit all four. That gave the Cougars all the motivation they needed to carry through to win over the Mustangs, 48–43. Cotton's boys had just qualified for the state tournament with its forty-first straight victory. Johnny Carter, a member of the Madisonville team, offered his version of why the Mustangs lost. "We were quicker, more athletic, had better shooters," he said, "but they had Cotton Robinson and that Buna mystique."[24]

Four teams, Buna, New Boston, Needville, and Dimmitt, had all reached the Conference-AA UIL Boys' State Championship

Tournament in Austin, scheduled for March 2–4, 1961. But the Cougars were established as early favorites to take home the championship trophy in their division, based on their fantastic win streak with many of those victories coming at the expense of much larger 3A and 4A schools.[25]

Long before the first semifinal game against New Boston, sports pundits were comparing Cotton's current team to that of 1957 with their undefeated season of forty wins and a state championship. "This team probably shoots as well as any we've had here," Robinson said, "but it is not as strong physically as the 1957 team and doesn't rebound as well." Coach had learned a long time ago that it was best to downplay his boys' abilities; never give an opponent a leg up. "We've won nine of our ball games by five points or less," he continued, "and we've had two overtime games and one sudden death. About the only thing that's keeping us alive is our shooting."[26]

New Boston and Buna had played previously for consolation honors, back in 1954, in the Cougars' first trip to the state tournament. Although Buna had won that day by a score of 49–37, a lot of water had flowed under the proverbial bridge since then. The New Boston Lions of 1961 were bringing into the tournament an excellent record of 28–3,

Buna Champions of the Future. *Regional B-Team Action, Texas A&M, 1961. Cougars (dark uniforms) vs. Taylor Ducks. From left: Herbert Ross, Pete Hillin-11, Raymond Cleveland-43, John Hatch-31, John Richardson-21*
                                                                    —Courtesy Melvin Ellison

and as Cotton Robinson had so often said, "The teams are all good when they get into the state meet."[27]

The State Semifinal Game of 1961

THE TEAMS

Buna Cougars Coached by M. N. "Cotton" Robinson	New Boston Lions Coached by Richard J. Rittman
Players	**Players**
Burke, Jimmy	Alford, Rea Eddy
Cleveland, Raymond	Chapman, James
Ellison, Melvin	Cox, Frank W.
Hatch, John	Grider, Boyce W.
Hillin, Pete	Grimes, George
Kirkpatrick, Billy	Holt, James L.
Reese, Wade	Jordan, Michael
Richardson, John	Looney, Frank
Ross, Herbert	McCright, David C.
Simmons, James	Pinkham, Chester
Stancil, Glen	Sowell, Thomas
Stom, Pat	Stone, William
	Tuck, Billy W.

Participating Teams, First Round, Conference AA
—Courtesy UIL, Austin

Thirty-five seconds into the game, New Boston scored first with a free throw, but that would be the only lead the Lions would enjoy. Tommy Ayres, a sportswriter for the *Beaumont Enterprise*, was there. "Ellison notched ten of Buna's sixteen points in the initial period," he wrote. "Buna's Glen Stancil and Jimmy Burke combined to send the Cougars to a 22–9 advantage early in the second stanza. A pair of jump shots and two free throws by Ellison extended the gap to 30–14 with two minutes left in the period."[28]

When the second quarter ended, Buna led 32–19, and by then, the Lions had dug the hole so deep, they couldn't climb out. During the third quarter, the Cougars scored another sixteen, and New Boston fell further behind. The trend continued until two minutes and thirty seconds were left in the game. Buna held a 19-point lead, 58–39, at which point Cotton pulled his starters and emptied the bench. The final score read: Buna, 62; New Boston, 45.[29]

Tommy Ayres summed it up. "The famed Buna defense allowed New Boston only eleven field goals, and the Lions managed to get off only thirty shots against the ball hawking Cougars," he stated. "Buna hit twenty-four of forty-eight field goal attempts for an even 50 percent." The Cougars had proved once more that it was most difficult to beat a team with that type of shooting success.[30]

For Buna, Melvin Ellison finished with twenty-four points, Glen Stancil-fourteen, Billy Kirkpatrick-eight, James Simmons and John Hatch each had six, with Jimmy Burke contributing four. Boyce Grider and David McCright had thirteen and ten points, respectively, for New Boston.[31]

While the Cougar players were on the sidelines celebrating with the folks from back home, Robinson stole away to a dimly-lit break room, where he could get a soft drink and relax a little. But Carlos D. Conde, another reporter, caught up with him and asked about his illustrious coaching career.[32]

"It's funny how people always ask me what magic I use," Cotton said. "They want to know if I use any type of psychology to gear the boys into action. It's just hard work. We don't do anything different than other teams. In fact I know our offense is not spectacular or flashy . . ., but it gets the job done."[33]

In closing, Cotton gave credit to Harold Simmons, the long-standing high school freshman coach at Buna. "That's Harold's team out there," he said. "He put them together when they were in the ninth grade."[34]

The second semifinal Conference-AA game of the night involved the Needville Blue Jays with a record of 24–11 going up against the Dimmitt Bobcats at 29–5. The Bobcats had no trouble at all as they took the Blue Jays to the woodshed and soundly whipped them by a score of 60–31.[35]

Overnight, some of those who had foretold that Buna would win the Conference-AA championship changed their minds. The Cougars' odds were now put at 50-50, due to the performance of Dimmitt's Junior Coffey, the six-foot center who scored twenty-three points in the win over Needville. Moreover, Coffey had averaged twenty-four points per game on the season, and he had hit 51 percent from the field.[36]

There was, however, a subtext that could not be dismissed. A single sentence of less than twenty words, which appeared in an article of *The Austin American-Statesman* on March 2, brought to the forefront the major weakness of the Dimmitt squad: "The brilliant Negro athlete

[Coffey] has been the heart of a team which hasn't much experience [or] exceptional height."[37]

On Friday afternoon, Cotton held a team practice, a 30-minute affair, to iron out the kinks and ready the Cougars for the following night's face-off against Dimmitt. Afterward, he sat down with reporter Tommy Ayres. "They will be as good as anyone we've played this year," said Robinson. "They [had] a tough schedule and have beaten a lot of good teams."[38]

Back in the dressing room, Cotton built up the ability and sheer athleticism of Junior Coffey, and he cautioned his team in no uncertain words to completely disregard the fact that he was African-American, the first that any Cougar had played against. In all probability, the big Bobcats' center would guard Melvin Ellison, pitting All-Stater against All-Stater. Just that week, the Texas Sportswriters Association had named both Coffey and Ellison as members of the Conference AA All-State Basketball Team. Kent Hance, a senior, was also on the Dimmitt squad. Hance, a lawyer by training, later became heavily involved in the Texas political scene, and he is the current chancellor of the Texas Tech University System in Lubbock.[39]

Cotton told Melvin to play his usual game. As the meeting broke, Coach got Billy Kirkpatrick's attention. "Billy," he said, "you're guarding [Coffey]."[40]

On Saturday night, two minutes had lapsed before Cougar Jimmy Burke connected on a 15-foot jump shot to give his team a two-point advantage. As the game progressed, the 8,000 fans packed into Gregory Gymnasium expecting to see a shooting clinic had to settle for another brand of basketball. The Cougars ended the first period with fourteen points, and they held the Bobcats to just six. Junior Coffey, closely guarded by Billy Kirkpatrick at times, and James Simmons others, could manage but four, with two of those coming by way of charity shots.[41]

Early in the second quarter, however, it appeared that Coffey had found his way into the game; his four free throws and one jump shot cut Buna's lead to four, 16–12. But that's when the celebrated Robinson defense kicked in, and Dimmitt was as close as they ever got. On the offensive side, Cougars Glen Stancil, John Hatch, and Burke picked up the tempo, and by the end of the first half, Buna maintained a 25–14 margin.[42]

An analysis of Dimmitt's production in the first two quarters reveals a stark certainty. Their fortunes lay with whether Coffey could break loose and score his usual twenty-four points. So far, his eight were far

The State Final Game of 1961

THE TEAMS

Buna Cougars Coached by M. N. "Cotton" Robinson	Dimmitt Bobcats Coached by John Ethridge
Players	**Players**
Burke, Jimmy	Blackwell, Jerry
Cleveland, Raymond	Bradley, Gene
Ellison, Melvin	Calvert, Michael
Hatch, John	Cates, Kelton
Hillin, Pete	Coffey, Junior
Kirkpatrick, Billy	Cowsert, Jim
Reese, Wade	Golden, Harold
Richardson, John	Hance, Kent
Ross, Herbert	Meacham, Wayne
Simmons, James	Neumayer, Lowell
Stancil, Glen	Nichols, Jackie
Stom, Pat	Ratcliff, Jim

Participating Teams, Final Round, Conference AA
—Courtesy UIL, Austin

below average, and his four teammates were held to only six points between them. Things were not looking good for Coach John Ethridge's Bobcats.[43]

There was a combination of reasons as to why the Cougars ran roughshod over Dimmitt. Even though Buna's Melvin Ellison, whom Coffey had so far shut down, was limited to just four points in the first half, he was able to feed the ball to his teammates who scored. That, plus strong rebounding by the Cougars, basically drove a nail in the coffin of Dimmitt's dream and ended the game at halftime.[44]

Coffey eventually scored nineteen points, but he was not able to carry his entire team, either on offense or defense. Normally, he got ten rebounds per game; this time he was held to just two. The other Bobcat starters, Gene Bradley, Michael Calvert, Kelton Cates, and Jim Ratcliff, and the substitutes who came in during the second half, struggled as well on both sides of the ball. In the meantime, Buna's Glen Stancil pulled in eleven rebounds of his teams' forty-one total off the boards.[45]

No one from Dimmitt had come up against a player like Jimmy Burke. "The fourth quarter saw Burke give the Bobcats a lesson in ball handling as he stalled the game with his dribbling," wrote Tommy Ayres, "and caused [the] Dimmitt cagers to continuously foul him."[46]

"Burke led the Cougar attack with nineteen points, fourteen of them coming in the second half," Ayres continued. "The scrappy little guard sank an amazing eleven of eleven from the charity circle and whipped in four of eight field goal attempts."[47]

When the game ended, the score was 60 to 36. With a perfect record of 43–0, Buna had won their fifth state basketball championship, and in so doing, tied Athens who'd taken titles in 1927, 1929, 1931, 1933, and 1934. For the Cougars, Jimmy Burke netted nineteen points, Glen Stancil-thirteen, Melvin Ellison-ten, Billy Kirkpatrick-seven, James Simmons-six; substitutes John Hatch and Pete Hillin put in four and one, respectively.[48]

George Breazeale, veteran sportswriter for *The Austin American-Statesman*, provided a simple, straightforward explanation as to how Robinson and his team beat the Dimmitt Bobcats so convincingly. "There was only one Junior Coffey. There were five Buna Cougars dedicated to the task of winning. . . ."[49]

"On Top of the World." 1961 Conference-AA Champion. Buna's Dressing Room, Gregory Gym. From left, bottom row: Raymond Cleveland, James Simmons, Jimmy Burke, Melvin Ellison; middle row, John Hatch (flashing V sign), Herbert Ross, Glen Stancil; top row: Billy Kirkpatrick, Pete Hillin, John Richardson

—Courtesy Bill Kirkpatrick

After his boys showered and put on their street clothes, Robinson took them back into the gym to see the last game of the state tournament, Clear Creek of League City vs. South San Antonio in the Conference-AAA final. Besides, the Cougars had to wait around to accept their championship trophy which would be presented during half-time ceremonies.[50]

Johnny Carter, a starter on the Madisonville squad that was ousted by Buna in the recent regional tournament in College Station, was also a spectator in the stands. A fellow sitting beside him said of Clear Creek, "Wow, these boys are 36–1. I wonder who beat them?"[51]

Before Carter could respond, this same man looked inside his program and asked aloud, "Where in the heck is Madisonville?"[52]

At that point, Johnny explained that he lived there, and in fact, he played on the team that handed Clear Creek their only loss of the season. "He looked at me in amazement," Carter said, "and asked, 'Why aren't you guys up here?'"[53]

Pointing to the left where the Buna Cougars dressed smartly in their blue jackets were, Johnny answered, "Because of those fellows right over there; they're 43–0!"[54]

With the season concluded, many of the Cougars received additional awards. Melvin Ellison, Jimmy Burke, and Glen Stancil were named to the All-Tournament Conference-AA Team along with Junior Coffey of Dimmitt and David McCright of New Boston. Ellison and Stancil were also members of the Beaumont A&M Honors Team of District 24-AA.[55]

The folks around Buna were walking on cloud nine. Imagine, their Cougars had just gone undefeated for the season, they were the reigning Conference-AA boys' basketball champion, and their coach Cotton Robinson, still a young man, not yet thirty-six years old, had already led his teams to five state championships. How it would end, no one could say. But for the present, they were going to enjoy the ride—for a few days, at least, until talk of next season's expectations began to surface.

By: Dies

SENATE RESOLUTION NO. 162

WHEREAS, The Buna High School Basketball team of
Buna, Jasper County, Texas, won their fifth Class AA
Basketball Championship and their forty-third straight game in
Austin, Texas, on March 4, 1961; and

WHEREAS, By so doing they have brought much credit to their
school, city and the East Texas region; and

WHEREAS, They were ably coached by M. N. (Cotton) Robinson,
an able athletic coach, and a person of high ideals; and

WHEREAS, The victory in Austin, Texas, on March 4, 1961,
represented hard work and determination on the part of each
member of the team and the coach; and in winning the title, the
team did credit to Jasper County and the deep East Texas area;
now, therefore, be it

RESOLVED, That the Senate of the State of Texas
congratulate Buna High School; the members of the basketball team
and coach; the people of the Buna community; that a copy of this
Resolution be sent to Buna High School, and to each member of
the team and to the coach.

Ben Ramsey
President of the Senate

I hereby certify that the
above Resolution was adopted by
the Senate on March 8, 1961.

Charles Schnabel
Secretary of the Senate

Resolution Number 162, March 8, 1961, honoring 1961 Cougars, originated in the Texas Senate.

—Courtesy Lynda Robinson Sanford

CHAPTER FOURTEEN

The 1961–62 Season

"Winning takes talent, to repeat takes character."
—JOHN WOODEN

For the few privileged teams in the world of sports, winning begets tradition, tradition sires dynasty, and dynasty generates a fan base whose ferocious loyalty is never called to question—that is, unless things start falling apart. Yet, there is an indisputable downside to this succession, as in the case of Buna. The Cougars' dynasty produced an enormous weight for Cotton Robinson to bear, a situation that he often discussed candidly with members of the press corps.

For the present, however, Coach had a job to do, and he put aside all personal feelings. What's more, his drive and ambition would tolerate no less.

Even before basketball season began, Cotton had a scare. John Richardson, whom he planned to use at guard, sustained a football injury, severe enough to keep him out for the year and maybe indefinitely. On top of that, Pat Stom, who would have normally filled in for Richardson, had left school at the end of his sophomore year, and he told Cotton that he would not return. Hence, the guard position—the linchpin of the Buna Offense—remained in serious doubt. Fortunately, "[John's father] built an exercise machine which his son utilized extensively to rehab his leg," explained Jimmy Richardson, John's younger brother. "He came back to start at guard that fall. While the injury did impair him, John managed to feed the ball to his teammates and punish his opponents every game."[1]

For reasons that will become abundantly clear, Cotton had an easy time this season picking his starting lineup. He set John Richardson, a five-foot-eight junior, at guard, along with Raymond Cleveland, a six-foot-three senior, and John Hatch, a six-foot-one junior, in the post positions. Pete Hillin, a five-foot-eleven junior, and James Simmons, a five-foot-eleven senior, took the two forward slots. Although only one of them, Simmons, started for the 1960–61 team, the other four were certainly experienced enough. Cleveland, Hatch, Richardson, and Hillin had all seen extra duty during the previous year, because when Buna jumped so far ahead in many of the games, Robinson allowed them to take the wheel of a team that went 43–0.[2]

While other sportswriters were once more bemoaning Cotton's having to butt heads with another of those pesky rebuilding years, Hal Reagan of the *Beaumont Journal* offered a different perspective. "Before swallowing that 'rebuilding' line, here's a look at the Cougars' tracks so far this season," he wrote. "They've shot down three quints in District 11-4A—French [twice], Port Arthur, Beaumont High—and perennial Class B toughie Big Sandy."[3]

The Cougars of 1961–62. From left, front row: *John Richardson, Jimmy Richardson, John McHugh, Derwood Goins; center row: Raymond Cleveland, James Simmons, John Hatch, John "Nickie" Meaux, Barry Turner, Herbert Ross; top row: Wade Reese, Robert Lane (student manager), Jimmy Horn (assistant coach), M. N. "Cotton" Robinson, Pete Hillin*
—Courtesy Lynda Robinson Sanford

"Buna may be experiencing the hard knocks of reconstruction but there could hardly be a nicer fate."[4]

By the time the Cougars rolled into Beaumont in December to de-

Buna and Their Opponents. *10th Annual YMBL Basketball Tournament. Cover by Jack Shofner.*
                                        —Reprint courtesy *Beaumont Journal*

fend their YMBL Tournament crown, they were sitting atop a 48-game winning streak going way back to the beginning of the previous season. In order to win another title, though, they would have to go up against none other than Milby, lurking in the wings to take their fourth. As strange as it may seem, no team from Beaumont had ever won the local event, but this year, French had one of the better opportunities.[5]

None of the conjecture that appeared in the local press fazed Cotton Robinson in the least. He told his boys to play their game, and let the rest take care of itself. In the opening round, the Cougars beat the Orange Tigers 38–28, and in the quarterfinals, Port Arthur became their latest victim, 59–36. Now it was time to see if the French Buffaloes measured up to the hype.[6]

Buna caught the Buffaloes asleep at the wheel and defeated them 40–33. Meanwhile on the other side of the bracket, Milby had been steadily moving up the tournament ladder, and it was no real surprise that they were one of the last two competitors standing. Of course, Buna was the other.[7]

On the night of December 9, the Cougars made it official; they captured their fifth championship in the tournament's ten-year existence. But the game was no cakewalk. Milby had erased a first period deficit, and they were on top, 19–12, at the half. "Buna then caught fire in the third period, while holding Milby to only four," wrote Jack E. Mooney, a *Beaumont Enterprise* reporter. "Both teams tallied ten points in the final quarter." The low scoring affair ended with a Buna victory, 36–33. John Hatch, with twelve points, was high man for the Cougars, and he also scored more combined, fifty-five, than any other player in the tournament.[8]

Following their victory at the YMBL, Buna dropped Jasper, Nacogdoches, Huntington, and Spring Branch before Jeff Davis put an end to the 56-game winning streak at the Nacogdoches Tournament. The Cougars then beat South Park 46–33, but in the very next game with the Port Arthur Yellow Jackets, they went down, 50–42, for their second defeat of the season.[9]

After the loss to the Yellow Jackets, Buna got back up, dusted themselves off, and began to play up to their potential. On December 29, they captured their second consecutive Port Arthur Basketball Tournament championship by destroying South Park, 55–35. The Cougars' John Hatch, Raymond Cleveland, and Pete Hillin scored eighteen, fifteen, and eleven points, respectively, while Robert McNeill only mustered eleven for the losers.[10]

Next, Beaumont High and Sour Lake fell to Buna; both were one-sided games. And even without the services of John Hatch, out of the lineup because of a broken hand, the Cougars whipped South Park once more, 48–28.[11]

In their second district game, the Cougars were scheduled to play the Little Cypress Bears. Beforehand, the Bears' coach had interviewed with *The Orange Leader*, in which he'd issued an ill-advised statement that came back to haunt him. "Buna has lost four starters from the previous year," he said, "so they have the weakest team they've ever had."[12]

"Cotton wasn't one to give rah-rah speeches," said Raymond Cleveland, a senior on the 1962 team, "but in the locker room, before we went out on the court, he pulled out his billfold, removed the article and read it to us. After the half, the game was going so badly for Little Cypress, Coach sent some of us to get dressed." Buna won 55–32.[13]

In the District 24-AA stretch, James Simmons chipped in fifteen points and grabbed eighteen rebounds to lead his Cougars to a 44–31 victory over a stubborn Woodville team. And as expected, Cotton's boys finished district competition with another flawless record.[14]

Thereafter, they met Dayton in bi-district and beat them 46–29. Before the first round of Region III-AA competition in College Station, the Cougars' opposing coach, Joe Leach of Lampasas, talked to the news media. "All I can say is we'll show up. We know all about Buna and what they can do to a team," he said. "Our boys do not have a lot of ability. What they've won this year, they won on desire. They like to win, and we'll be trying our best to do the same against Buna."[15]

Actually, Coach Leach did not think much of his team's prospects; either that or he was trying to lull the Cougars into a false sense of security. Another newspaper article reported him as saying, "I just hope they don't laugh at us when they beat us."[16]

Observers were already predicting that Buna would have little problem going back to the state tournament. "As one [unidentified] coach said last year, 'Give Robinson five timeouts, and he'll beat anybody in the country.'"[17]

Lampasas did show up, but desire alone was no equivalent for the overpowering Cougars, who coasted to an easy conquest, 57–24. However, Buna's meeting with the Rockdale Tigers in the regional championship game left most everyone thunderstruck. Even though Cotton's charges posted leads in the first three periods, the Tigers came back in the fourth to tie the score, 41–41, sending the game into overtime. For a precious few minutes, Rockdale had a remote chance of dethroning the current Conference-AA state champion, but fell short when they were outshot by 8–1. It seemed that Robinson had willed his team to another win. And so, the boys of Cougarland escaped with yet another close call, 49–42, on the heels of strong shooting by Raymond Cleveland, Pete Hillin, John Hatch, and James Simmons, with fourteen, twelve, eleven, and eight points, respectively. John Richardson, the Cougar guard, added another four. Buna had just taken their seventh regional championship title in the last nine seasons.[18]

Back on familiar turf in Austin's Gregory Gym, the Cougars were slated to meet Coach Bennie J. LaPrade and his Donna Redskins in the first round of state competition on March 1, 1962. The Redskins were making their first tournament appearance, while the Cougars—called "the winningest team of them all"—were back for their seventh.[19]

The State Semifinal Game of 1962

THE TEAMS

Buna Cougars Coached by M. N. "Cotton" Robinson	Donna Redskins Coached by Bennie J. LaPrade
Players	**Players**
Cleveland, Raymond	Avila, Alfredo
Goins, Derwood	Avila, Richard
Hatch, John	Badeaux, Johnnie
Hillin, Pete	Chambers, Paul
McHugh, John	Edwards, Fred
Meaux, John	Hulme, Jim
Reese, Wade	Padraza, Luz
Richardson, Jimmy	Roberson, Jackie
Richardson, John	Rodriguez, Alejandro
Ross, Herbert	Villanueva, Frank
Simmons, James	
Turner, Barry	

Participating Teams, First Round, Conference AA
—Courtesy UIL, Austin

The game between Buna and Donna produced a lot of fireworks. While the Cougars led during the first three periods, although by no more than five points, the Redskins rallied and actually went ahead, 40–39, early in the fourth quarter. The Cougars held their ground, though, and retook the lead when James Simmons scored from the outside. His team never trailed again, and Buna won by eleven, 59–48.[20]

Donna shot a remarkable 55 percent from the field, but they only took thirty-four shots. On the other hand, Buna hit 45 percent. The real key to the victory was the Cougar defense that hamstrung their opponents in the fourth period. For the winners, John Hatch, James Simmons, and Raymond Cleveland scored twenty, sixteen, and eight points, respectively, with Pete Hillin, John Richardson, Herbert Ross, and Wade Reese accounting for the remaining fifteen between them. Jim Hulme, who played center for Donna's 1961 state championship football team, the subject of a sports documentary film, "Miracle at Donna," contributed eighteen points to the losing cause.[21]

On Saturday, March 3, the Cougars went up against the Jacksboro Tigers, the comeback winner in their first round game with Fort Stockton in the semifinals. As with the Donna Redskins, Jacksboro had never before been to a state tournament, and Cotton wanted nothing more than to spoil their debut.[22]

The State Final Game of 1962

THE TEAMS

Buna Cougars Coached by M. N. "Cotton" Robinson	Jacksboro Tigers Coached by Dan Owen
Players	**Players**
Cleveland, Raymond	Breding, Ed
Goins, Derwood	Davis, John
Hatch, John	Dickson, Kenneth
Hillin, Pete	Leach, Robert
McHugh, John	Miller, Eddie
Meaux, John	Neely, Jerry
Reese, Wade	Sikes, Marty
Richardson, Jimmy	Simpson, John
Richardson, John	Wheelis, Steve
Ross, Herbert	Winton, Gary
Simmons, James	
Turner, Barry	

Participating Teams, Final Round, Conference AA
—Courtesy UIL, Austin

Jacksboro entered the tournament with a record of 28–3, but they were mindful of Buna's reputation and strength. Moreover, Robinson's Cougars had themselves lost two games during the season, and the Tigers saw no reason why they couldn't hand them a third. Coach Dan Owen and his team were thinking upset.[23]

About 7,800 fans packed into Gregory Gym to see the Conference AA final—and if they were Cougar fans, they were extremely pleased. "Buna led throughout," wrote Orland Sims of the *Beaumont Enterprise*. "[Pete] Hillin started things with a jump shot seventy seconds after the opening whistle and it was 6–1 before Jacksboro scored a field goal."[24]

Buna built up a 20–8 lead in the second quarter, and by halftime, the Tigers had scored only thirteen points, total. At the end of the third quarter, the Cougars were on top 37–17, but finally, when the scoreboard reflected 42–20, Cotton figured that he had punished Jacksboro enough. He put in his reserve players. "Substitute James [Jimmy] Richardson neatly wrapped up the title," said Sims, "dropping in a short jump shot for the final basket of the 1962 season just two seconds before the final horn."[25]

"The Cougars were having none of that upset business," Sims con-

Cougars' Timeout. 1962 State Tournament. From left, front row: John Hatch, Pete Hillin, Raymond Cleveland, James Simmons, John Richardson; kneeling: Herbert Ross, Cotton Robinson; standing: Barry Turner, John McHugh, John "Nickie" Meaux, Jimmy Horn, Jimmy Richardson, Wade Reese

—Courtesy Lynda Robinson Sanford

tinued. "Their constantly tight defense rattled the Tigers, limiting them to single field goals in each of the two middle quarters, and thoroughly defeated the North Texans [49–30]"[26]

In the title game, Buna shot 42 percent from the field versus Jacksboro's 27, and once more, defense had been the key. John Hatch and Pete Hillin were high men for the state champion, with twelve and eleven points, respectively. James Simmons and Raymond Cleveland followed with eight each. John Richardson put in five, Herbert Ross-three, and Jimmy Richardson-two. Jacksboro's leading scorer was Steve Wheelis with eight. The All-Tourney Team consisted of John Hatch and James Simmons of Buna, Eddie Pruitt of Fort Stockton, Steve Wheelis of Jacksboro, and Jim Hulme of Donna. When the 1962 All-State Team was announced, Buna's James Simmons was named to the first team, and John Hatch took a spot on the second roster.[27]

"In Texas high school basketball, there's nothing like the Buna High Cougars," Sims added. "They gave additional proof of that here Saturday night as they set the biggest of all possible records by winning state again. The sixth championship is [one] unmatched by any other school in any other class. Until Saturday night, Athens had held a tie with Buna with five championships [the Athens record had stood for twenty-eight years]."[28]

Some of the luster surrounding a team that finished 39–2 for the year with a record-setting state title became lost when, suddenly, folks around Buna began to hear rumblings. In a small town such as this, it seems that no one can keep a secret, much less when an occasional hint finds its way to the press. One newspaper article even mentioned it during the recent state tournament. "There has been talk that Robinson will give up the coaching post this year at Buna and concentrate on the private business which he has in that town," the article stated. "If that is the decision by Robinson, Texas will lose one of its all-time great basketball coaches."[29]

The notion of Cougar basketball without Cotton Robinson bordered on lunacy. But in fact, Coach had been thinking about stepping down for quite a while now, and before the end of the school year, he presented his decision to a stunned Superintendent Bob Cummings and a board of trustees. Robinson announced the unimaginable—he was handing off next season's team to another. That way, he said, whoever replaced him would start with a strong lineup and therefore, be better equipped to continue the winning tradition. Only two seniors from the current squad, Raymond Cleveland and James Simmons, would be lost to graduation.[30]

Superintendent Cummings, however, could be as persuasive in matters of administration as Robinson was on the basketball court. He argued that Cotton had groomed these boys, and all would be best served by his continuation at the helm. Finally, he convinced Coach to stay for one more year.[31]

CHAPTER FIFTEEN

The 1962–63 Season

"Success is almost totally dependent upon drive and persistence. The extra energy required to make another effort or try another approach is the secret of winning."

—DENIS WAITLEY

For Cotton Robinson, the summer leading up to the 1962–63 basketball season proved to be a real life changer. He honored a pledge made to Bob Cummings that postponed his resignation as head basketball coach but now, it came time to embark on a two-part plan for the future. After stepping down as coach at the end of this season, he would remain on the payroll for one more year as a teacher in Buna High School. And then, he would elevate from part-time to full-time status as a salesman with the Amicable Life Insurance Company. However, no public announcement would be made until later.

The 1962–63 season started with great fanfare, and Cotton readily chose his starting lineup, all seniors. John Hatch, six-foot-one, and Pete Hillin, five-foot-eleven, took the two all-important post positions, with John Richardson, five-foot-eight, returning at guard. Each of these three had played on the previous season's state championship team. To fill out the roster, Cotton tapped Wade Reese, five-foot-ten, and Herbert Ross, five-foot-eleven, as the two forwards. And when Coach needed to go to the bench for early substitutions, he could always depend on another senior, John Meaux, and the lone junior on the squad, Jimmy Richardson.[1]

The Cougars reeled off thirteen wins in a row, twice beating Big Sandy, Port Arthur, South Park, and Milby, before powerful Jeff Davis handed them their first defeat. But Robinson's team rebounded, and they trounced French for a second time and Milby for the third. They also had no trouble getting by Port Arthur once more, 41–27.[2]

The Cougars of 1962–63. From left, front row: Rusty Sowell (student manager), Doug Barclay, Mike Barley, James Norris; center row: Larry Hatch, Jimmy Richardson, Wade Reese, John Richardson; top row: Herbert Ross, John "Nickie" Meaux, John Hatch, Pete Hillin

—Courtesy Rusty Sowell

As the Eleventh Annual YMBL Tournament dates of December 7 and 8, 1962, approached, the *Beaumont Journal* ran a caricature that displayed Buna's potential victims and what might be the outcome.

The Cougars added a sixth YMBL championship to their résumé. But right before the Christmas holidays at the Port Arthur Tournament, Robinson and his team were shocked to the core—the Port Arthur Yellow Jackets, whom they'd earlier blasted on three occasions, took a surprising victory of 43–35. "We were lethargic and had been for a week or two," said Jimmy Richardson, a member of the Buna squad. The Port Arthur loss sent the Cougars into the consolation championship bracket and here, they would face Pasadena, the very team they'd hoped to meet in the finals for overall first-place honors.[3]

Cotton was furious, so completely disappointed by his team's performance that he reacted completely out of character. "He said we were not engaged," Richardson continued, "and that we played nothing but *hully gully*, his term for sloppy and undisciplined."[4]

"He just gave us lunch money and told us to eat whatever we wanted for a pre-game meal, because it did not matter. He also said we were so undisciplined that he was not even going to coach us in the

[Pasadena] game. He did not care how we played, whether we ran fast breaks, or even used the Buna Offense. He was just going to send players in and out."[5]

Buna's Goodies. 11th Annual YMBL Basketball Tournament. *Cover by Jack Shofner.*
—Reprint courtesy *Beaumont Journal*

True to his word, Cotton did exactly that. Given Coach's new attitude and perhaps, low player morale, some might have expected that the Cougars would fold in such adverse conditions. Quite the opposite occurred. Against Pasadena, Richardson said, "We ran fast breaks and literally whipped the dickens out of the team we feared most." The final score: Buna, 70; Pasadena, 52.[6]

Instead of reverting to the slow, ball control methodology, Cotton used the Pasadena experience to his advantage. During the next fourteen games, including the ones in district competition, he let loose his Cougars to maraud at will. With "the run and gun," Buna averaged seventy-eight points to their opponents' thirty-eight, and in that span, they even broke the century barrier when they demolished Port Acres, 116–34. Unlike previous blowouts, this one had special significance. During a football game this past season, Port Acres took on a relatively new Buna team and defeated them 66–0. Cotton was not at all happy that they ran up the score. When his basketball Cougars had the opportunity to reciprocate, he allowed his starters to play extended minutes—and full throttle at that. For the receiver, payback can be hell![7]

Undoubtedly, the new approach worked, but that didn't keep Robinson's players from wondering, *How long will Coach let us keep this up?*

When the Cougars beat Kountze, they closed out their tenth consecutive perfect district race. The *Buna East Texan* reported the feat as "an all-time record for high school basketball in Texas."[8]

Before the playoffs began, Cotton reined in his charges and went back to basics. In this, his last season, he wasn't about to damage his reputation on an offense that he viewed as contrary to everything that had proved for him so successful. "He reminded us that when the playing got tough, discipline would prevail," said Jimmy Richardson.[9]

In the first round bi-district game, the Cougars beat Humble, 52–37, and they strolled into the Region III-AA Tournament in College Station with a glowing record that included just two losses on the season. Next, Rockdale fell, 56–50, and in the regional finals, Buna won the championship by smashing West by thirty-five points, 72–37.[10]

From College Station, the Cougars took a well-traveled route to Austin, where they would play in the 43rd Annual UIL State Championship Tournament, set for March 7–9, 1963. On Thursday, after the Canyon Eagles won the first game in the Conference-AA bracket, Buna and Gladewater met in the second semifinal to determine who would play the Eagles in the finals.[11]

The State Semifinal Game of 1963

THE TEAMS

Buna Cougars Coached by M. N. "Cotton" Robinson	Gladewater Bears Coached by Bill Waters
Players Barclay, Doug Barley, Mike Hatch, John Hatch, Larry Hillin, Anthony "Pete" Meaux, John Norris, James Reese, Wade Richardson, Jimmy Richardson, John Ross, Herbert	**Players** Branum, Jerry Buchanan, Charles Cagel, Paul Cowan, Perry Elliott, Jerry Gibbons, Johnny Jones, Ross Lange, Eddie O'Brien, Joe O'Neil, Butch Phillips, Dickie Ray, Wesley Sawyer, Tommy Sorrels, Larry Strickland, Danny

Participating Teams, First Round, Conference AA
—Courtesy UIL, Austin

Buna's John Richardson scored first with a field goal, then a free throw, and from that point forward, the Cougars never trailed the much-taller Bears. Buna led 20–6 at the end of the first quarter, 40–15 at the half, 61–26 at the third, and when the game ended, they had won 71–39. According to an article in the *Beaumont Enterprise*, "[Pete] Hillin, a second team All-Stater, garnered twenty-six points to pace the Buna attack. First team All-Stater John Hatch chipped in fourteen markers, and Jimmy Richardson added thirteen for the Cougars. The first string sat out the final period after rolling up an insurmountable 61–29 lead."[12]

"But the decisive factor in the lopsided fray was Buna's full court press defense," the article continued. "Gladewater . . . was so rattled, the Bears had trouble just getting the ball across the mid-court line, especially after senior playmaker, Joe O'Brien, fouled out early in the third canto [quarter]. He had ten of Gladewater's seventeen points when he went out."[13]

All but two of the eleven Cougars who got into the game scored at least two points, but for the losers, only six boys tallied. Larry Sorrels, with twelve, finished as high man for Gladewater.[14]

Following the game, Cotton talked to reporters who wanted to know how it was possible for such a small school as Buna to come back year after year to the state tournament. "You must remember I drive these kids hard, and it's because of the support we get back home that I can," he commented. "We work hard and sometimes that helps to win."[15]

"The main thing we teach at Buna is to get our kids to play as well under pressure as they [do] in practice," he said. "They get to believing in themselves and such confidence will pay off in the long run."[16]

As he made his way toward the locker room, someone asked how it felt to be coaching the Cougars in his last state tournament. "I wanted to come this year more than ever, unless maybe that first year," he said. "It's been a privilege."[17]

Meanwhile, the Cougars waited patiently. For sometime, they'd known this would be Cotton's last season, and they wanted to give him a good send-off. When Coach entered the doorway, all of them stood up. Holding his emotions in check, Cotton complimented his boys on the recent win, and with a simple statement, he provided them with all the incentive they needed going into the final. "Men," he said, "we have one more game to a championship."[18]

Robinson stressed the strengths of the Canyon Eagles. However, they were beatable, because seven different teams had already handed to them nine losses during the season. The man to watch and the one who would cause the most damage, Coach warned, was All-Stater Bob Begert, the Eagles' six-foot-five center. But Buna had just seen Begert in the afternoon's early game as his team dismantled John Foster Dulles of Missouri City by a score of 75–39. Additionally, the Cougars were equally familiar with the four other probable starters for the Eagles: Don Breitling, six-foot, Eddie Poole, six-foot-three, Davis Price, six-foot, and Harry Lisle, five-foot-eight.[19]

Cotton closed with the usual summation delivered during post-playoff game meetings. "Wear your caps, and don't kiss any girls," he counseled. "We cannot afford for anyone to get sick."[20]

It seemed that 7:35 P.M., Saturday, March 9, would never arrive. But when it did, finally, the Cougars walked onto the court with all the confidence of a defending champion.[21]

Buna led 15–10 at the end of the first quarter, but by the end of the second, the Eagles had cut their advantage to one, 25–24. Robinson's boys were working the renowned Buna Offense to perfection, a real

The State Final Game of 1963

THE TEAMS

Buna Cougars Coached by M. N. "Cotton" Robinson	Canyon Eagles Coached by Allen Simpson
Players	**Players**
Barclay, Doug	Begert, Bob
Barley, Mike	Breitling, Don
Hatch, John	Burgess, Steve
Hatch, Larry	DeSchweinitz, Alex
Hillin, Anthony "Pete"	Evans, Bobby
Meaux, John	Lisle, Harry
Norris, James	Metcalf, Glen
Reese, Wade	Poole, Eddie
Richardson, Jimmy	Price, Davis
Richardson, John	Whinnery, Jim
Ross, Herbert	

Participating Teams, Final Round, Conference AA
—Courtesy UIL, Austin

tour de force (refer to the diagrams in Chapter Sixteen). When the Cougars' point guard, John Richardson, took the ball toward Wade Reese at right forward, Pete Hillin moved from the left side, low post area to the high post position above the free-throw line. Conversely, whenever Richardson took the ball toward Herbert Ross, the left forward, Hillin would slide down into the low post area. This allowed John Hatch to adjust to the high post position just vacated by Hillin.[22]

If Richardson remained on the right side, Hatch continued at low post and worked across the lane as the ball moved from the right side to the left. But if Richardson initiated the offense on the left side and remained there, Hillin continued at low post, working across the lane, while Hatch stayed high.[23]

By using these well-timed maneuvers, Buna had four boys positioned around the perimeter, and this setup allowed the low post to work one-on-one in the paint. Each Cougar, other than the low post who remained stationary, probed the defense and waited for Canyon to commit. When that occurred, the ball was passed to the low post, who struck either with a power lay-up or a short jump shot.[24]

Last season, John Richardson and Pete Hillin had started every game for the Cougars—John Hatch would have as well, except for the broken hand—and their playoff experience showed. Canyon held on, though, and trailed by just two, 34–32, as the fourth quarter began. With 6:31 left in the game, Buna had extended their lead, 39–32.[25]

The Eagles' Lisle, Metcalf, and Price would not go quietly, and with 1:12 remaining, they rallied and pulled within two, 43–41. That's when the Cougars took over. Between John Richardson and Reese, they scored another two points each and so, the ball game ended with Buna's winning by 47–41.[26]

Oddly enough, the Cougars lagged behind in shooting, 45 percent to Canyon's 48. Even so, Cotton's team made the shots that counted. In the rebounding department, Buna held their own, matching the much-taller Eagles. Another key to the Cougars' success is that Canyon never adjusted to Cotton's full-court press defense, which continually kept them off-kilter. For the victors, Hatch and Hillin scored twenty-two and eleven points, respectively, with Herbert Ross adding five, Wade Reese-four, John Richardson-three, and Jimmy Richardson-two. Bob Begert's seventeen earned for him the Eagles' high point honors.[27]

Buna's Hatch and Hillin were named to the State All-Tournament Team, along with Bob Begert and Harry Lisle of Canyon, and Joe O'Brien of Gladewater. Hatch was also selected to represent the

Buna Crowd Cheering for the Cougars. *Photo taken at Gregory Gym, Austin. Monte Sybil Robinson, front row, seated second from left; Janice Robinson is the little girl seated on floor.*

—Courtesy Charles Breithaupt

Cougars on the All-State First Team, and his teammates Hillin and John Richardson took places on the second and third teams, respectively.[28]

By winning over Canyon, Cotton Robinson was able to take back to Buna the seventh state boys' championship trophy and another overall record of 39–2. In his career, he had fifteen straight state tournament victories. Only Sweeny ever beat one of his teams in Austin, and that was by just two points in the 1954 semifinals. Robinson had long set the bar high, and then raised it time and again to a point, where perhaps no other coach will ever match his record. He had truly become *King Cotton*, the undisputed sovereign of Texas boys' high school basketball.

H. S. R. No. 270

R E S O L U T I O N

WHEREAS, The State of Texas is genuinely proud of the Buna Cougars, whose victory in the Class AA finals of the University Interscholastic League tournament Saturday, March 9, 1963, and their amazing record for the 1962-63 basketball season deserves the applause of the entire populace; and

WHEREAS, Buna, Saturday, won its seventh Class AA championship in State tournament play, thereby setting a new record in Texas schoolboy basketball. The school has sent eight teams to the finals in the last ten years; and

WHEREAS, This year's team was as valiant and talented as any in the past and the school's tradition of victories was a formidable challenge; and

WHEREAS, Their outstanding coach, M. N. (Cotton) Robinson, is ending a fifteen-year basketball career; and

WHEREAS, No team has played with greater determination to win than this one, whose members are: John Hatch, Anthony Hillin, John Richardson, Wade Reese, Herbert Ross, Jimmy Richardson, John Meaux, Doug Barclay, Larry Hatch, Mike Barley and James Norris; now, therefore, be it

RESOLVED, That the House of Representatives of the Fifty-eighth Legislature of the State of Texas heartily congratulates the Buna Cougars on their tremendous victory, and on their ability and their perseverance; and, be it further

RESOLVED, That a copy of this official Resolution be given to each member of the team with the best wishes of this House.

Collins

Byron Tunnell

Speaker of the House

I hereby certify that
H. S. R. No. 270 was adopted by
the House on March 18, 1963.

Dorothy Hallman

Chief Clerk of the House

Resolution Number 270, March 18, 1963, honoring 1963 Cougars, originated in the Texas House of Representatives.
—Courtesy Lynda Robinson Sanford

CHAPTER SIXTEEN

Ahead of the Curve

"The easy way doesn't put any hardware in the trophy case."
—Cotton Robinson

No story about Cotton Robinson would be complete without a discussion of the *Buna System*, which consisted of two key components taken as a whole: an aggressive defense and a two-post offense. From the very beginning, the famed Buna coach ran half- and full-court press defenses in combination with the commonly accepted offense that utilized a single center. Buna won three state championships prior to the 1957–58 season, but after Robinson implemented the two-post pattern, opposing coaches remained baffled about how to defend it. With the new system in place, the Cougars brought home another four state titles in 1959, 1961, 1962, and 1963, and amazingly, during the last three of those seasons, they lost a total of only four games. How did they do it?

The Buna Offense

Numerous teams claimed to have won championships utilizing the Buna Offense, which has become legendary. Larry Dean Jackson, a former coach and author of an e-book titled *The Buna Offense*, states that thirty teams have won state titles mimicking Cotton's strategy. Jackson describes it as "effective versus all half-court defenses."[1]

In fact, Snook High School in Texas won ten state titles from 1965 through 1984 with three different coaches who used the Buna System as an integral part of their program. Coach Jimmy Horn, who started Snook on the road to this tremendous accomplishment, explained his first exposure to it. "I was an assistant coach to Robinson at Buna, and he showed me how to coach," said Horn. "Now you must know why I called Cotton the greatest tutor in the business."[2]

Luke Winn writes a column titled "Inside Basketball" for SI.com. On November 17, 2008, he posted the following on his website.

> An obscure offense that popped up in just two places in our survey—both in the Southland Conference—was the "Buna," a simple, post-focused spread motion that Buna, Texas, high [school] coach M. N. "Cotton" Robinson [used to win several state titles]. Northwestern State—the team of Verne Lundquist's 'Northwestern Wins' fame—used it to post an upset of Iowa in the first round of the 2006 NCAA Tournament. And 2008's Southland Conference tourney champ, UT-Arlington, also used the "Buna" to reach the big dance (The Mavericks didn't fare as well, losing by 24 to Memphis in their opener). Both are up-tempo teams that segue their transition games nicely into the "Buna," by having their post sprint all the way to one block and a wing sprint to each baseline corner—all of which are base positions for the offense.
>
> Why would two coaches who never worked together— Northwestern State's Mike McConathy and UT-Arlington's Scott Cross—be running the same rare offense in the same conference . . . ? It's not by coincidence. Cross' Mavericks got off to an 8–0 start last season running the Triangle Offense, but lost their second-leading scorer, shooting guard Brandon Long, to a season-ending thumb injury in the next game. "After that," said Cross, "we couldn't score with the Triangle, because teams would just sag on us." The solution was to borrow from McConathy, whom Cross calls "the mastermind" of the "Buna." "We had some similar personnel," said Cross, "so I started putting in some of the Buna Offense to change the tempo. Down the stretch when we started winning again [victories in five of their last seven games helped them reach the NCAA], we basically just went all 'Buna.' This year, I like it so much that it's going to be our main offense."[3]

Jimmy Burke, an All-State guard on the 1961 Buna state championship team, discussed the main features of the Buna Offense. "Over the years, there have been so many changes in the game of basketball that it would be almost impossible to identify all of them," he said. "But the core principle of the game remains, and that is for one team to outscore the other. Cotton Robinson's teams accomplished that on a regular basis using his double-post pattern that became widely known as the Buna Offense."[4]

Burke continued:

> Control the ball and set the tempo of the game; this was Robinson's philosophy on offense. He always stressed that any offensive strategy should be based on an opposing team's defense. He repeatedly said,

"Take what the defense gives you." A lot of people thought that Buna played a stalling game, when actually they were patiently trying to get the defense out of position. One of Cotton Robinson's main coaching points was: the closer to the goal when taking a shot, the higher the percentage it would go into the basket. This viewpoint—the main emphasis on inside play—remained constant throughout his coaching career. However, his offense changed accordingly and morphed from a single post pattern with player movement into a double post with more ball movement, especially against a zone. It is amazing that fifty-plus years later, we still find articles and books about it, and some forms of the offense are being used today by high school and college coaches.

When Robinson first came to Buna in 1948, his offense featured a center, two forwards, and two guards. The forwards and guards would sometimes change places or set screens for each other and then shoot from the outside. But Coach wanted the ball to first go to the inside; the outside shot was the last option. At that time, the free-throw lane was only six-feet wide, and that made the basketball court seem much larger than it was. It actually gave the offense more room to operate without getting a three-second violation. Up until the 1940s, the game primarily focused on shorter, quicker, and stronger players, while the center mainly passed off to them. This changed as taller players began to develop and coaches recognized their height as a benefit. Cotton Robinson was always ahead of the curve and so, he designed his offense to take full advantage of inside players.

The double-post offense consists of two inside or post players, two forwards, and a point guard. In today's basketball vernacular, these are labeled as the 1, 2, 3, 4, and 5 positions with the guard as number 1, the forwards as numbers 2 and 3, and the post players as numbers 4 and 5 [refer to the charts below for clarification].

Any secret to the success enjoyed by the Buna Offense lay in the coaching of each position during daily practice sessions and the execution of those skills during offensive work periods and scrimmages. During position-work time, each player worked on different shots, passes, and moves that he would use in games. There are two good examples: have post players work on receiving the ball and practice a minimum of six different moves and shots. Meanwhile, the two forwards worked on passes to the posts, in addition to receiving the ball and practicing their offensive moves and shots.

Coach Robinson taught his players to recognize different offensive options and therefore, be able to carry out each of them. A very large part of his success came directly from the detail he put into having each player understand the intricate details of the game. Other coaches have used the Buna Offense, but they probably did not stress the finer points that he did.

There are five fundamental options of the Buna Offense, all based on the position of the ball. Each one creates at least four or five others depending on the defense. It is a simple set but in reality, it is rather complicated and takes time and repetition to master. Coach started using it in 1958, and by the end of his coaching career in 1963, he had refined it into a smooth functioning offensive scheme that has withstood the test of time.

Robinson expected his teams to shoot 40 to 50 percent from the field and 80 to 85 percent from the foul line. He maintained a chart during every game and afterward, he provided each of his players with a sheet of statistics, plus a critique of their performance. With both positive and negative feedback, he hoped to give each player an incentive to do better.[5]

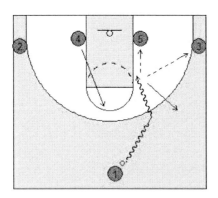

O1 in transition, looks for O5.
O4 comes to high post,
O1 relocates to the guard spot

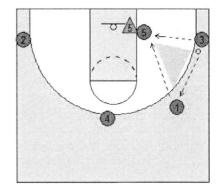

Like the Triangle offense, O1-O3-O5
Look to get the ball into O5 for low-post shot

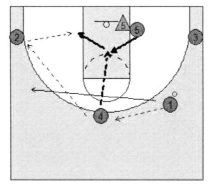

Patterns of the Buna Offense
—Courtesy Bruno Chu,
StormingtheFloor.net

If O5 not open, reverse the ball.
O4 looks for O5 for the high-low.
O1 relocates to form new strong-side

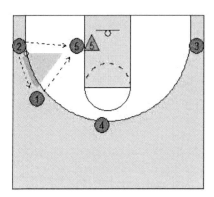
Triangle formed on the other side.

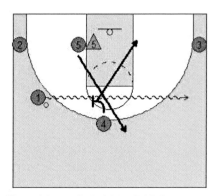
The guard can relocate through dribble. O4 sets the pick for O1, then moves to low post O5 moves up to the high post spot.

The following examples of critiques that Jimmy Burke mentioned above are quoted verbatim from Coach's actual handwritten notes that were directed to individual players on his 1961–62 championship team.

Raymond Cleveland–Post—You pass the ball out too quick before seeing what you can get in the pivot. You must get low when we feed you, react to your defense and see what you can get. Our whole offensive pattern depends on how much of a threat we are on the pivot. Put stretch on feeding #3. You are still not faking and clearing ball on your power shot. No boy in Texas should be able to keep you from power shooting.[6]

James Simmons–Forward—Don't hurry outside shots—make them give us what we want. Do not telegraph passes especially when we are against a press. You lead Harvey [Raymond Cleveland] too much with feed. Don't put too much arch on feed.[7]

Herbert Ross–Forward—Learn to apply what you learn in practice to games. Don't hurry outside shots—make them give us something good. Play your defense on pivot, stay low, keep ball low and let defense decide how and what you do.[8]

John Hatch–Post—Keep tail on man on pivot and be rough and mean as you play. Roll quick and low after screening on free pitch.[9]

Jimmy Richardson–Post—One of the first things you need to do is forget you are a sophomore and take your part of the load. Stay low, keep the ball low, keep tail on man and get under. When you jump shoot, fade away by stepping away from goal.[10]

John Richardson–Guard—First of all you must use your head to take care of your knee [referring to John's earlier injury suffered while playing football]. Know when to fade to open it up after starting drive.[11]

Pete Hillin–Forward/Post—You are still weak on ball handling, especially feeding—you telegraph your passes. Put your stretch on your forward position. See what you can get on drive before passing back to guard.[12]

Wade Reese–Forward/Guard—See your complete picture—try to face everybody as you work ball. Know how to play at the last of the game. Get down low and be real tough handling, protecting and working ball.[13]

Simply put, the double-post offense used by Cotton Robinson involved a patient, probing attack that called for limited player movement. The Cougars "rested" on offense, and based on the positioning of the defense, they made decisions accordingly about which option play they'd run.

Coach Robinson took great pride in teaching his boys the fundamentals of "feeding the post," but he elevated the process to an art form that threw the unexpected at other teams to keep them from sticking to their game plan. At times, Buna players would actually roll the ball into the post. But the overall logic never changed. The idea was to keep the ball away from the defense and allow the post man to score one on one.

In a lengthy interview with George Pharr of *The Orange Leader* in 1961, the reporter questioned Coach Robinson about the reasons for the Cougars' great achievements. Did Buna outthink their opponents?[14]

"No. It isn't that," Robinson said. "Perhaps our boys might do a better job of their individual skills, though."[15]

Pharr asked Cotton to describe his style. "We don't play flashy basketball," Coach responded. "We have even been called unimpressive."[16]

"I figure a boy can learn a few things better than trying to do a bunch of things," he continued. "Like a shortstop in baseball . . . put him in the outfield and he is lost. I like to put a boy in one place and leave him there. You can't be moving them around and changing their natural habits."[17]

"It is all in the philosophy you use. I have gone to the state meet and [have] seen every kind . . . single post, tandem post, the works . . . and all these teams have gotten there by doing the best with what they [had]."[18]

"Basically our offense hasn't changed much in three or four years. In 1958 we set it up [Buna Offense]. I didn't 'invent' this system though. Credit should be given to R. C. Hyden, our girls' basketball coach."[19]

Many quotes by Cotton Robinson are found in other source material. "Our offense is a blend of patterns and quick breaks. We play the offense and let them make the mistakes and then shoot. We try to play percentage basketball."[20]

What about the differences between single and double post offenses? "We felt we could score one-on-one if we had a good post," he said. "We . . . went to the double post in latter years because defenses were getting more sophisticated."[21]

Robinson went on to explain why the center or post was so important, and why the player who would step into that role was determined so early, generally by his sophomore year. "We wanted to make sure he was good and he could develop a lot of confidence in his abilities. In fact, in our 43–0 season of 1961, our post was only 5-11."[22]

"Our teams probably did as well as they did because of hard work, and we conditioned ourselves as a team to carry out the game objectives," Cotton said. "We feel we prepared ourselves as a team so that we were able to control the type of game being played."[23]

"We used a double post with two wingmen [forwards] and one guard or ball handler. We had our inside . . . and outside attack, and the defense always decided the option, regardless of whether we were running the outside . . . or inside pattern. The key was to keep it all simple."[24]

Even in the twenty-first century, the Buna double-post offense has proved to be successful at every level of play. Both professional and college teams have been known to line up with it. But whether coaches of those teams made use of its minute particulars—or engaged it simply for spacing purposes—is unknown. What is evident, however, is that the model, first developed by R. C. Hyden and later adapted by Cotton Robinson, has continued to thrive.

The Buna Defense

Earlier in this chapter, Jimmy Burke, who so effectively described the Cougars' offense, continues with an explanation of the second vital element that led to their amazing record. "A lot of recognition and emphasis has been given to Cotton's offense," he said, "but another key to his success was the man-to-man defense. This was the phase of the game where it should be glaringly visible that in coaching, he was far ahead of the times and his contemporaries."[25]

In an article that he wrote in 1956 for *Coach & Athlete* magazine, Cotton Robinson stated, "At present, the boys . . . in Buna take a great deal of pride in their defense. It is the result of constant yelling, begging, pleading, crying, explaining, and reasoning. I think that they are beginning to realize that a sound defense makes a sound ball club." In his own words, Cotton said it best.[26]

"A player must first learn the basic defensive points. We depend upon the one vs. one drill to help . . . master these points," he commented. "No time is spent trying to teach a boy to have a certain foot forward, etc. We want him to maintain a natural stance from which he can react the quickest."[27]

"Our objective . . . is to keep as much pressure as possible on the ball whether it is in shooting territory or not. We want to keep our opponent from getting off an easy pass as well as an easy shot. We do not want to press to the extent that we foul or let our opponent drive by. We want to apply as much pressure as possible and no more or less. If we over press, we have made the mistake."[28]

"We tell the boys to keep three things in mind: their man, the ball, and plugging the middle. We switch every time our man crosses in front of our teammate. For this type of defense to be successful, we must have all five men working equally hard at all times. It is no stronger than the weakest man."[29]

"The following rules have helped us immeasurably, and I definitely think that they are the most important . . . to keep in mind [while running] the half court pressure defense: Never reach for the ball. Never let a man cut between you and the ball in the direction of the goal. Keep the point of the ball covered. Always concentrate on getting in the dribbler's path. Play tight when the dribbler stops," Coach concluded.[30]

"As Cotton's offensive philosophy evolved, so did his defense," said Jimmy Burke. "He tweaked and refined it continuously. He started his coaching career with more of a sagging man-to-man defense, then moved to a switching man-to-man, and in his last few years, he went to a very tight, full court man-to-man in order to spread pressure over the entire court. This was not to say, however, that he wouldn't adjust the defense if it became necessary. In summary, he wanted his defense to force the other team to do something they did not want to do."[31]

The Buna Pipeline of Talent

When asked to talk about his personal triumphs on the hardwood, Cotton Robinson quickly pointed to the contributions of others. He always said that the community, parents, school administrators, teachers, and especially, Harold Simmons, the ninth-grade coach, had provided him with a nucleus of winning players. But what sort of impact did the lower grades—Buna's Farm Club—really have on Cotton's career? Up until now, very few have ever touched on this intangible, yet relevant aspect.

Jimmy Richardson, a valuable member of the last two Cougar championship teams, weighed in on the subject. "The seventh, eighth, and ninth-grade teams, along with the "B" squads, ran the same offense and defense as the high school [varsity]," he said. "Consistently, for the entire time between the first bounce of the ball in the seventh grade until the final championship game, all of those players were under Cotton's influence. They were saturated with his values, rules, and expectations."[32]

Of course, some may argue that all schools have access to the same type pipeline. But in Buna back then, there is no question that Clarence Riddle and David Stark, who tutored boys' basketball in the lower grades, and Harold Simmons in the ninth, brought along young cubs that would one day indelibly stamp their paw prints onto the cloth of Cougar legend.

CHAPTER SEVENTEEN

Life Outside Coaching

"The pressure I put on myself just wore me out. That's when I decided to retire. I was ready to retire, and I've never really considered going back to coaching."

—COTTON ROBINSON

For Buna, Texas, its boys' high school basketball program, and all of the Cougar resolute, the earth stood still on Saturday, February 9, 1963. At age thirty-seven, Cotton Robinson called it quits; he'd had enough. As part of his retirement announcement, he said, "I think it's our tradition and willingness to work that's made this a good basketball town."[1]

Cotton Robinson was usually correct about everything, and this is one of his most accurate statements. He had built up capital within the community, but he had never sought to cash it in, opting instead to give his best as long as he served as the Cougar head basketball coach. Yes, Cotton was right. Buna had been a good basketball town, and Buna would have followed him to the very end, if only he'd asked.

Back in 1956, right after the Cougars had won their second state championship, and the Cougarettes, their first under R. C. Hyden, the townspeople took up a collection and presented gifts to the two coaches. Cotton got a new 1956 red and white Chevrolet station wagon, and R. C. walked away with a new boat and motor.[2]

Later on, April 1962, the citizens got together again and took up another collection. According to a *Beaumont Enterprise* article dated April 25, 1962, Superintendent Bob Cummings had lured Robinson under false pretenses "to come to the school about 6:30 P.M. [on Monday] for a 'discussion.'" Cotton thought the message so urgent that he never took the time to change clothes. He rushed over to Cummings's office, and for a while, the two talked about the team's recent accomplishments and Coach's plans for the future. The article continued, "At 7 P.M.

Cummings asked him to step out on the football field to 'look something over.'"[3]

When the two reached the exit door, members of the basketball team picked up Cotton and on their shoulders, they carried him to the stadium where about 200 people awaited. D. L. Ross, pastor of Parkwood Baptist Church of Buna, and father of Herbert Ross, one of Cotton's Cougars, completed a short speech and then handed to the surprised recipient the car keys to a new white 1962 Bel Air Chevrolet.[4]

"It has been a wonderful privilege to live here in Buna and to be associated with its fine school system," Cotton responded. "You have already paid me for more than my actual worth by letting me work and live in this community and in giving me such fine boys to work with. My family and I are more grateful than we can ever say."[5]

Players carrying Cotton Robinson to football field for car presentation
—Courtesy Lynda Robinson Sanford

Presentation of 1962 Bel Air Chevrolet. From left, Pastor D. L. Ross, Monte Sybil Robinson, and Cotton Robinson
—Courtesy Lynda Robinson Sanford

Cotton Robinson, Insurance Executive
—Courtesy Lynda Robinson Sanford

The Cougars of 1962–63 won for Buna their seventh boys' state championship, after which Cotton retired as head basketball coach. However, he remained with Buna High School for one more year as a teacher of history and civics [political science].

Then he went full-time into the insurance business as a sales representative with the Amicable Life Insurance Company based in Waco and later, he became district manager. He still lived in the modest frame house by the school, fronted by his Monte's Dairy-D-Lite, where former Buna High students like Roland Cleveland, Mildred Smith, Fred B. McKinley, and Pat Turner learned values in their first-ever real paying jobs outside the home. He kept up with his brothers and sisters, now scattered, but very much in touch. Plus, he continued to be a devoted husband and father to two growing daughters.

The Robinson Family, May 1954. From left, front row: Mathea "Ruth" Robinson, Lucy "Lillian" Robinson, Lyndall Robinson; back row: Robert "Stanley" Robinson, James "J. W." Robinson, William B. "Willie" Robinson (in hat), Lenard "Lindberg" Robinson, Ersell Robinson, Elton Robinson, Marshall N. "Cotton" Robinson
—Courtesy Lynda Robinson Sanford

Family Photo, circa 1967. *From left: Lynda Nell, Janice Marie, Monte Sybil, and Cotton Robinson*
—Courtesy Lynda Robinson Sanford

Throughout his active coaching years, Cotton had received many honors for his outstanding achievements at forums such as the Texas Coaching School. But as time wore on, formal accolades became few and far between, except the occasional newspaper print that emphasized the usual: where one could locate Buna, Cotton's statistics, and the most asked question of all, what was his secret?[6]

Ten years after Robinson had retired, Mike Ramsey of *The Orange Leader* interviewed the legend. "I've never regretted my decision," Cotton said. "The pressure to win kept getting greater and greater."[7]

"The more you win, the more you want to win," he continued. "I saw where the average tenure of a Texas high school coach is twelve years. I was in it fifteen years. I guess I was overdue."[8]

As Robinson quietly went about his new life selling insurance, and continuing to enjoy hunting and fishing, he got word that he was being inducted on April 7, 1983, into the Texas High School Basketball Hall of Fame. As a prelude to the ceremonies, *The East Texas News* of Buna put out a special section honoring Cotton, his teams' records, and the memories created. It also announced Saturday, May 14, 1983, as "Cotton Robinson Day." A luncheon with former players was held at the junior high cafeteria, and later that night, the community gathered at the Buna High School Gymnasium to pay their respects to the great one and enjoy a scrimmage between Cougars of the past.[9]

During the earlier luncheon with the former players, one of them "asked Cotton if his daughter had grown up to become an All-American," said Bobby Ener. "He answered no and responded, 'Why the question?' 'Well,' this person said, 'you told me that you had a five-year-old daughter that could play basketball better than I could, and I was just wondering.'"[10]

At the Hall of Fame induction ceremonies held in Waco, five other worthy candidates were honored that day, including Robinson's All-American, Don Stanley. The four others were Calvin W. Battise, Gilbert "Gib" Ford, Bennie Lenox, and Jim Murphy.[11]

Cotton opened his home during this period and many times before, the Buna Gym as well, to field question upon question from various coaches who sought to learn the secret of the Buna System. There is no secret, he told them. "I really don't know what makes a good coach," Cotton answered. "But I do believe that motivation and discipline are the keys to winning."[12]

That said, he'd go further and unselfishly share the intricacies of the system that he always credited to R. C. Hyden. Just ask the many that he mentored: Charles Breithaupt, Jimmy Burke, Melvin Ellison, Pete Hillin, Jim Horn, Billy Kirkpatrick, John Rich, Bobby Stratton, Lionel

Texas High School Basketball Hall of Fame Induction, April 7, 1983. From left: Don Stanley, Cotton Robinson, and Bill Martin, President, Texas HOF

—Courtesy Lynda Robinson Sanford

Reese, Tom Westbrook, and William Withers, who used it in their own coaching careers.[13]

When Herbert Muckleroy came to Kountze in 1956 as head basketball coach, he called upon Robinson, whom he'd known from Sam Houston days. Since Muckleroy had never coached the sport, he asked Cotton to give him some pointers and especially, help set up a practice schedule. Even though Kountze and Buna were in the same district, Coach gladly obliged. Later, however, when the two met as rivals on the court, the Cougars came out on the winning side. Herbert said, "Cotton, you must have left something out when you told me how to coach basketball." Robinson responded only with a large grin.[14]

Along these lines, Ardie Dixon, current owner of Dixon Industries of Lufkin, acknowledged his gratitude to the veteran Buna coach. Dixon was born in Lufkin, where he attended school. Thereafter, he went off to college, graduated, and then coached basketball at Ennis High School from 1962 through 1965. Early on, he tried running a very complicated offense that he had been part of in college, but his players were having trouble adjusting. So, Ardie called his former high school coach at Lufkin, Robert Wagstaff, and sought some advice. Very quickly, Wagstaff asked whether Ardie had a low post player. He answered no, to which Wagstaff commented, "You ought to run the Buna Offense."[15]

Dixon had no idea what he was talking about. Wagstaff, who said that he knew Cotton Robinson well, offered to set up an introduction, and he did. Cotton instructed Ardie to be in Buna at 7:30 on a Monday morning and be prepared to spend all day—he would be given a free crash course on the Buna System.[16]

Ardie went to his Ennis superintendent, Jim McCoy, a big basketball fan who'd heard about Cotton, and asked for the day off. McCoy told Ardie not to mention to anyone about his appointment with Cotton. "Just go ahead and cover the time off with a sick day," he directed.[17]

As planned, until 4 o'clock in the afternoon, Cotton gave the young coach the ins and outs, and when Ardie returned home to Ennis, he implemented the offense and won quite a few games. From then on, he's been a devotee of Cotton Robinson.[18]

CHAPTER EIGHTEEN

Transformation and Aftermath

"Heroes are remembered but legends never die."
—George Herman "Babe" Ruth

The 1963–64 school year began with the Cougars looking to defend their three consecutive state championships. Hopes and expectations were high; however, several key pieces of the team were missing.

Cotton Robinson, the architect of seven state titles in the past nine seasons, was rightfully viewed as the larger loss. When he retired as coach of the Buna boys' high school basketball team at the end of the 1962–63 season to eventually funnel his talents into a full-time insurance career, he passed the mantle to Harold Simmons, a man he'd known and respected for many years. In fact, Simmons had served as student manager on Coach's first three teams, and there was no question in Cotton's mind that school administrators had made the right choice in their selection to replace him. A new page in Buna basketball history was turned.[1]

Way before the beginning of the new season, many concerns lingered about the departure of Coach Robinson from the Cougar bench. Naysayers claimed the golden era was over, while others hoped that tradition and the inherent strengths of the program would carry their team to yet another title. In any event, the massive pressure was placed squarely on the studious and reserved shoulders of Simmons, the long-time understudy.

Harold Simmons was born on December 1, 1931. He grew up in Buna, where he graduated from high school. Afterward, he attended Lamar State College of Technology in Beaumont, Texas and in 1956, he obtained a Bachelor of Science degree in physical education. During the fall of that same year, he returned to Buna to teach chemistry, biology, and physical science—and to coach ninth-grade basketball. He held that position for five consecutive years, and then for one more during the school term of 1962–63.[2]

Simmons had the know-how, but he faced an uphill battle from the very first practice session that marked his debut as head coach. In all likelihood, even if he'd stayed, Cotton Robinson might have faced an impossible task trying to rebuild a team capable of matching ones of his bygone days. Regardless, it now became Harold's responsibility to do just that, and he was about to find out what it

Coach Harold Simmons
—Courtesy *The Cougar,* 1965

was like to follow in the footsteps of a folk hero who'd reached iconic status.

To begin with, Harold had only one returning player with extensive experience. Several seniors on last year's squad and the lone junior, James "Jimmy" Richardson, had produced the bulk of scoring that accumulated a sparkling record of 39–2, culminated by a Conference-AA state championship. But John Hatch, Pete Hillin, John Richardson, Wade Reese, Herbert Ross, and John Meaux had all graduated, and four of those positions now fell to an untested Doug Barclay, Mike Barley, Larry Hatch, and James Norris. Therefore, it became serious business for Jimmy Richardson, now a senior. For sure, he would have to assume a strong leadership role and do everything possible to fill the void. As the sixth man, Paul Sanford completed the rotation.[3]

When asked about the transition from Robinson to Simmons, Mike Barley expressed his opinion. "We didn't think about it. We were kids. We didn't know any difference," he said. "We were more concerned about the fact that we had lost all those All-State players from the year before."[4]

Barley was right on one count. Filling the shoes of five of the six who played significant minutes on the last two championship teams would prove to be very difficult. This rang true from the outset. While practice, organization, and both offensive and defensive schemes remained consistent, the 1963–64 Cougar squad faced a tough non-district schedule.

Everyone on Coach Simmons's team knew of Buna's record under Cotton Robinson. It was well documented and publicized in newspapers far and wide, this stuff of legend—seven state championships and no district losses since the 1952–53 outfit dropped two to Cedar Bayou. They were well aware of the bulging trophy cases that proudly displayed awards of tournaments past, attesting to victories over some of the largest and most heralded schools in Texas.

And even if the current crop of Cougars didn't consciously reflect on the change in coaching staff, it must have been there, way at the back of their innermost thoughts. How could it not? It was certainly the case with many around town who might construe a single district misstep as an irreversible stumble.

Perhaps the 3A and 4A schools had tired of being dominated for the last decade by one from the lower echelon—if so, they showed their revenge by exacting pain upon the blue and white. The Cougars did not win any tournaments that season, but given Cotton's record in these type outings, all was taken into consideration. Regardless, loss after loss dragged down Buna's psyche as they prepared for the district race.

The team took a less than stellar record into District 24-AA play. To top that off, the competition was much stronger than it had been. West Orange and Forest Park were energized by the possibility of wresting the district crown from Buna, and each one had the talent to do so.

The majority of Buna fans, however, found it inexplicable when their beloved team, in their first district disappointment since 1953, fell to West Orange. The loss, which snapped a 132-consecutive district win streak, came on the Cougars' home floor, making it a double punch to the gut of the Buna faithful. This was almost like desecrating the Holy Grail.[5]

Hope arose, though, when the Chiefs of West Orange dropped a district tilt to the Trojans of Forest Park. The district title would come down to the winner of the final contest of the year between Buna and the West Orange "Five" on their home court.[6]

The fate of the Cougars was sealed in dramatic style as they went down in their second district loss to the Chiefs. Toward the end of the game, Buna's Jimmy Richardson fouled out with about five minutes left on the clock. West Orange won the game, 52–50, but it took a sudden death overtime to do it. For the Cougars, their season came to an abrupt end. Shocked Buna fans could only shake their heads in disbelief and cancel their hotel reservations in Austin. The Chiefs advanced to the next round, and the Cougars stayed home for the first time in a decade.[7]

Mike Barley, a member of the team, summed up the heartbreak. "We struggled against some really good teams early in the year, and we faced the same tough schedule as Cotton's teams. Playing in the YMBL, Nacogdoches, and Port Arthur Tournaments hurt our record, but we never thought we wouldn't win district. It just never entered our minds," said Barley. "Like I said, we were just kids, and we were doing what we always did. We should have beaten West Orange. Jimmy [Richardson] was such a great player, and I was fortunate that he was the post man on my side. When he fouled out in that game, we [were really in trouble]."[8]

The 1964–65 version of Cougar basketball, led by Barley, also met with disappointment. After two key members of the team quit midseason and another moved away with his family, Buna lost a one-game playoff to the Eagles of Port Acres for the district title. The Eagles went on to the state tournament, but were defeated, 60–49, by Lake Worth.[9]

The Cougars, on the other hand, were done. No Buna basketball team since 1963 has won a state championship. No Cougar team has ever made it back to Austin for the state tournament. For the remainder of the twentieth century, only a handful of Buna teams even made the playoffs, and only one got as far as the regional finals. That team, coached by Jamey Harrison in 2000, lost to Kountze on a last second shot in the regional final played in Huntsville.[10]

The *Buna Dynasty* was over! No longer would the Cougars—the once proud behemoth—riddle defenses and decimate offenses. Even so, a 15-year avalanche of victories and championships, led by an incredible coach, left behind a huge mark on the history of Texas high school sports. Coach Robinson's seven state titles remain the record after ninety years of UIL boys' basketball.[11]

Robinson's 15-Year Record at Buna

(Pertains Only to Boys' Cougar Basketball Teams)

★ During his tenure, Cotton Robinson's teams won 538 games and lost only 98, an 85 percent winning ratio.

★ Robinson coached his teams to thirteen district championships, and of the other two, 1948–49, his first, and 1952–53, his fifth, they placed as runners-up.

"A Man and His Hardware": *Cotton Robinson and his Seven State Championship Trophies*
—Courtesy Lynda Robinson Sanford

★ Extending from 1953–54 through 1962–63, his teams never lost a single district game; thus, a win streak of 126. And during his entire coaching career, the Cougars lost only five district games: two (1948–49), one (1949–50), and two (1952–53).

★ Extending from 1953–54 through 1962–63, his teams competed in eight state tournaments, finishing with a record of 15–1. The single loss in the 1954 semifinals came at the hands of Sweeny, who went on to win the Conference-A championship.

★ Robinson's teams won seven state championships, two in Conference A and five in Conference AA. As a coach, Robinson still holds the record for most Texas boys' basketball championships won.

★ Two of Robinson's teams went undefeated: 1957 (40–0) and 1961 (43–0).

★ Robinson's longest winning streak was sixty-six, extending from the final twenty-six games in 1956 through the perfect season of 1957. The second longest was fifty-six, extending from the perfect season of 1960–61 through the first thirteen games of 1961–1962.

★ During Robinson's last three seasons, his teams accumulated a combined record of 121–4. The four losses were to much larger 4-A schools: Jeff Davis of Houston and Port Arthur (1961–62); and the same two in the following year.

★ Robinson was selected in August 1957 to coach the Texas South All-Star team.

★ The Texas Sportswriters Association selected Robinson as the Texas Basketball Coach of the Year three times: 1957, 1961, and 1963.

★ Eighteen players on Robinson's teams were All-State Tournament selections, and one of these, Don Stanley, made All-American. Don currently holds the scoring record of fifty-one points in a state tournament final against Seminole in 1957.

★ Three players on Robinson's teams were inducted into the Texas Basketball Hall of Fame: Don Stanley (1983), John Hatch (1987), and Pat Stanley (2007).

★ Eight members of Robinson's teams played in Texas North-South All-Star games: Clinton "Radar" Johnson (1952), J. C. Smith, Jr. (1954), Delman Rogers (1955), James Mellard (1956), Pat Stanley (1957), Jimmy Cobb (1959), Melvin Ellison (1961), and John Hatch (1963). A ninth, Don Stanley, played in the 1957 East-West All-Star games in Hutchinson, Kansas.

★ More than thirty of Robinson's players received college scholarships.

Coach Harold Simmons bore the brunt of criticism for his inauspicious beginning—and some totally blamed him for the demise of the dynamic boys' basketball program at Buna, created by his predecessor. This allegation is far from the truth, and before passing judgment, the situation he stepped into should be taken in full context.

Cotton Robinson had seen the future, and he wanted to go out while on top of his profession. As a realist, he knew that if he hung around long enough, the odds would catch up, and one of his teams would fail to win a district title. This is a commendable quality, knowing when to step down. For varied personal reasons, too many notable athletes and coaches don't make similar decisions in time to guarantee their legacy in winning circles. That is the saddest testament of all.

When Cotton started out as a coach, life in Buna was far more innocent and much simpler. Plus, he didn't have to share the spotlight with a football program. The high school now had a football team, and boys who might have previously gone out for basketball did not, instead choosing to become involved in the gridiron. Too, values and attitudes had evolved to the point where students began to openly question authority.[12]

Society had changed as a whole. Robinson gave an example. "Kids didn't have cars to run around in back then like they do now," he said in a 1983 interview. "Athletics didn't have as much outside competition as they do nowadays. Back then, one of the few things they had to do was play [basketball]."[13]

Above all things, Cotton concluded that contemporary players would no longer exhibit the dedication and drive that he demanded. R. C. Hyden, the former Buna High School principal and school superintendent, put a different spin on the subject by discussing the lockstep of integration and Buna's relinquishing their unofficial title of Texas High School Basketball King. At that time, the African-American population of the small community was about 4 percent. "Without significant contributions from top black athletes," Hyden said, "we are not going to dominate."[14]

Harold Simmons remained as Buna's head basketball coach until 1972, when he became athletic director. Although he stepped down from that position after two years, he continued to teach until retiring in June 1993.[15]

Epilogue

"I wish I knew an effective approach so that I might reach every junior high boy and in some way instill within his mind a great, burning desire to expand the extent of his capacity."
—COTTON ROBINSON, 1983

Every interviewer that approached Coach after his retirement announcement wanted to know why. Besides the usual explanations, he mentioned numerous times that the job was eating him up, tearing at his insides, and he no longer wanted to deal with the pressure involved. Lynda Robinson Sanford, Cotton's daughter, said she remembered that her dad often stayed up after a game until about 2:00 A.M., because he couldn't sleep.[1]

Most understand what stress caused by outside factors can do to a person, but for Robinson, it was more intense, more personal in nature. Though Buna expected a great deal from him, he demanded more of himself than anyone. As such, he became a victim of nerve-racking conditions that he'd placed on himself—and in truth, his keen desire to win and fierce competitive nature caused more problems than an adoring public who never wanted to let go.

From the time that Coach first set foot on the Buna campus, team members and all those who knew him joked about his habits, one in particular. Rusty Sowell, the student manager on Robinson's last championship team, said, "Maalox and Beech Nut Chewing Tobacco, these were the two things Coach always warned me to never run without and always have stocked in the bag we carried on trips."[2]

John Rich, one of Robinson's Cougars, expanded on the Beech Nut issue. "Cotton was known to chew a little tobacco. When we would ride with him in his white Mercury, we would try to get in the front seat before everyone else," John said. "The reason, as you might imagine, he

Cotton Robinson, circa 1985
—Courtesy Lynda Robinson Sanford

would roll down his window every once in a while to spit. Those in the back seat would start to laugh, because we would always lean at the same time to prevent the residue from coming back on us. I don't know if Cotton was aware of this or not, but we certainly didn't complain about it [to him directly]." And there were the many reports from various other players who chuckled about making sure that everyone steered clear of kicking over the "tennis ball can," both during practices and games.[3]

Lynda Sanford also stated that her dad "had stomach problems and many ulcers through the years. In the spring of 1985, things really worsened, and he was diagnosed with non-Hodgkin's lymphoma in his stomach." Cotton checked into MD Anderson in Houston, and for a while, treatments appeared successful at the primary location. "But in late fall, things took a turn for the worse," Lynda added, "and it was found in his liver. At that point nothing could be done, and he spent the last seven weeks of his life at St. Elizabeth Hospital in Beaumont."[4]

"It was quite a shock that he only lived seven months after his diagnosis when he had been given a 95 percent chance for a full recovery."[5]

Suddenly, all those who once joked about the tobacco use, wondered just how much it contributed to his terminal illness. Clinton "Radar" Johnson went to see Cotton two days before he passed away. "As sick as he was," Clinton said, "he told me that if he had two players just like me, he would go back into coaching right away. I was there trying to comfort him, yet he was the one who made me feel good and accomplished. But that's just like Coach, all the way to the very end."[6]

"I visited Cotton in the hospital shortly before his death," said John Hatch. "He pulled me down to his bed and gave me a bear hug. I felt as if he was hugging all of his players."[7]

Cotton Robinson's amazing run ended at 9:30 P.M. on Sunday, March 16, 1986, shortly after his sixty-first birthday. Two days later, funeral services were held at the First Baptist Church of Buna. Brother B. A. Carlin officiated, and two of Cotton's all-time greats—Delman Rogers and John Hatch, now ministers—assisted. Marshall Neil "Cotton" Robinson was interred at Antioch Cemetery in Buna.[8]

Some of those who played for Cotton tell of the many times that he could have gone elsewhere to ply his trade. Newspaper reporters, too, usually asked whether he had received tempting propositions to leave the town he loved. Normally, Cotton gave a stock reply. "I've had some, but I have my family, a business, and many friends in Buna," he said. "Naw, it would have to be a pretty good offer before I would leave."[9]

Back in 1963 and during Robinson's last state championship tournament, James Mellard went by his old coach's motel room in Austin. The two talked about many things, James said, but eventually, the subject turned to something strange: Cotton's "disappointment of not having had an opportunity to get a coaching job in college. He seemed genuinely puzzled about that. He knew he was a great coach, so why didn't some college or university come calling? Coach asked me why?" James added. "I could not say, and it broke my heart. Still does."[10]

Historians do not have the luxury of adding opinions as to how things would have evolved, if only this and that had occurred. But in

The Robinson Marker, Antioch Cemetery
—Photo by Fred B. McKinley

this case, wouldn't it have been nice if someone had, at the very least, given him a chance? Might Cotton Robinson have eclipsed Bobby Knight, Dean Smith, and Rick Pitino? It's a shame that we'll never know.

Monument Honoring R. C. Hyden and Cotton Robinson, Buna, Texas
—Photo by Fred B. McKinley

The M. N. "Cotton" Robinson and R. C. Hyden Activity Center, Buna Public Schools
—Photo by Fred B. McKinley

Appendix 1

According to the University Interscholastic League of Texas, four conferences were in effect from the 1947–48 school year through that of 1950–51. Conference B was comprised of high schools with enrollments below 200 students; A ranged from 200 to 500; AA from 500 and up; and a city conference that included schools with 500 students and above.

In 1951–52, the UIL expanded to five conferences. Conference B schools had less than 114 secondary students; Conference A ranged from 115 to 200, AA from 200 to 450, AAA from 450 to 850, and AAAA from 850 and up.

The following table provides the same type data beginning with 1952–53 and ending with 1962–63, the year in which the Buna Cougars won their last state basketball championship under Coach Cotton Robinson.

Note: In 1980–81, Conference B became Conference A, and 4A became 5A. Buna's records at the University Interscholastic League in Austin are currently listed in the 3A category.

1952–55		1955–56		1956–58	
4A	1000 and up	4A	1200 and up	4A	845 and up
3A	500 to 1000	3A	550 to 1200	3A	370 to 845
2A	225 to 500	2A	225 to 550	2A	200 to 370
1A	125 to 225	1A	125 to 225	1A	120 to 200
B	124 and under	B	124 and under	B	119 and under

1958–60		1960–62		1962–64	
4A	900 and up	4A	905 and up	4A	950 and up
3A	390-900	3A	400 to 905	3A	400 to 950
2A	200-390	2A	205 to 400	2A	200 to 400
1A	120-200	1A	120 to 205	1A	115 to 200
B	119 and under	B	119 and under	B	114 and under

Appendix 2

The Close Ones that Slipped Away

During his 15-year coaching career, Cotton Robinson was involved in numerous close games, some he won, and others he lost. But none parallel the magnitude of those that are detailed below, the six that if he had won could have well added even more to the aura of the Buna Cougars, not only in the won-loss column but where those wins might have possibly taken them.

★ 1952—Advanced to the Regional III-A Tournament, where they lost, 27–23, in the semifinals against the Troup Tigers.

★ 1953—Lost two critical games to their district rival, the Cedar Bayou Bears. After winning both by three points each, 46–43 and 40–37, the Bears claimed the district championship. Consequently, Buna had to wait until the following season to make their first trip to the state tournament.

★ 1954—In the first overtime game in state tournament history (set up by a controversial call at the end of regulation play), they lost by two points their semifinal round to the Sweeny Bulldogs, 74–72. The Bulldogs went on to clinch the Conference-A championship by beating Sundown, 92–67. Buna, however, had to wait until the following season to win their first state crown in Conference A.

★ 1958—Advanced to the bi-district round (the first step on the playoff ladder leading to the state tournament). Here, they met the Cypress-Fairbanks Bobcats. With forty-five seconds remaining on the game clock, the Cougars led by six points. Under questionable officiating, the Bobcats mounted an aggressive comeback and won the game by one point, 48–47, on a last second free throw. Buna would go on the following season to win the Conference-AA state title.

★ 1960—Advanced to the regional tournament and played their first round game against the Belton Tigers, who won the Conference-AA title in 1958 and whom the Cougars had beaten, 63–60, in the 1959 regional championship game. This time, though, the Tigers turned the tables by beating Buna two points, 43–41. After Belton defeated Buna, they went on to beat Humble, 56–42, in the Regional III-AA Tournament final, but lost in the state semifinals and in the consolation game as well. During the next three seasons, the Cougars would go on to win the Conference-AA championship three times.

Note: The Cougars lost their last three playoff games (1954, 1958, and 1960) by a combined total of just five points.

Appendix 3

After Buna Basketball

This section contains biographical data on former Cougar basketball players and team managers whom we were able to contact or verify through independent sources. Also, we have attempted to provide as much information as possible about those now deceased. For simplification purposes, Lamar State College of Technology in Beaumont (now Lamar University) is abbreviated as Lamar. All locations are assumed to be in Texas, except for clarification.

It is our sincere desire that after reviewing the following sketches, readers will come away with what we've tried to convey throughout the text of this work. Cotton Robinson's teachings had a great impact on those he coached and guided in his 15-year career at Buna High School. Of course, others, such as parents and teachers, also deserve proper credit, but for the Buna Cougars and team managers who were able to continue their education only because of athletic scholarships, Robinson served as the primary instrument that put them on the road to success. Some, however, chose not to attend college for various reasons—and others dropped out before graduating—but most have expressed that their life rewards depended on large part from the lessons learned from Coach Robinson.

Barclay, Doug. Attended Stephen F. Austin but later transferred to Sam Houston, where he graduated with a degree in criminal justice. In the interim, he worked for the Texas penal system and also announced games for the Sam Houston Bearkats. After graduating, he went into the clothing business with two professors. When these stores were sold, he founded a screen print business that catered to product lines designed for fraternities, sororities, and the Houston Oilers football team. Then he evolved into the music business, licensing and supplying merchandise for musicians. He is now involved in specialty real estate in the Texas Hill Country. The Three Whispers Development is one of his projects. Doug and his wife, Kelly, currently reside in Wimberley.

Barley, Mike. Attended Stephen F. Austin, from which he graduated with a degree in economics. Thereafter, he worked in Houston for Southland Paper and later for J. C. Penney, before returning to Buna as vice president of the East Texas State Bank. After several other jobs, he began teaching and coaching in Detroit, Texas, where he has been the head baseball coach for the past twenty years. Mike and his wife, Cathy, currently reside in Detroit, Texas.

Brown, Adrian. Deceased. No other information available.

Buckner, Jerry Lynn. Received an athletic scholarship as a student manager to Kilgore Junior College. After two years, he went to work for Houston Chemical in Beaumont and then a woods product company in Silsbee. In the interim, he also attended Lamar. Thereafter, he was employed for twenty-two years as a supervisor and then a vice president of manufacturing with RoyOMartin, a large lumber company in Louisiana. He retired in 2001, but later consulted with companies involved in the woods product industry. Jerry and his wife, Karla, currently reside on the Louisiana side of Toledo Bend Lake near Mansfield.

Burke, James "Jimmy." Received an athletic scholarship to Stephen F. Austin, from which he graduated. Thereafter, he earned a master's in health and physical education, along with a certification in all levels of educational administration. He held basketball coaching jobs in Mauriceville, Buna, and Hardin-Jefferson for a total of fifteen years. He served as an elementary principal for another nineteen, and then at Hardin-Jefferson in Sour Lake, he became the technology director and later, Director of Operations. After thirty-eight years in the education field, he retired in 2003. Jimmy and his wife, Sharon, currently reside in Sour Lake.

Chesnutt, Charles. (Student manager 1957–59) Attended Lamar, and then became associated with the banking industry. Thereafter, he went into the real estate business in which he is still involved as owner/broker of Chesnutt Real Estate, LLC. He is a graduate of the Realtors Institute, and through the years, has served as president of the Lone Star State Chapter of Certified Residential Specialists, which has over 1,600 members; on the Education and TREPAC Committee–Texas Association of Realtors; and on several committees of the Houston Association of Realtors. Furthermore, he is certified by the Texas Real Estate Commission to teach mandatory continuing education courses. Charles and his wife, Mary, currently reside in Houston.

Clark, Tommy D. After graduating from high school, Tommy went on to become an officer in the Texas Highway Patrol. He is deceased.

Clark, Tommy G. Graduated from Lamar with degrees in general business and economics. Thereafter, he did graduate work in economic and industrial development at Texas A&M and then graduated from the Institute of Economic and Industrial Development at the University of Oklahoma, where he completed a thesis titled "The John Gray Institute and its Impact on the Business Climate of the Golden Triangle of Texas." He also served in the military, assigned to NORAD in the states and later the Pacific Command in Okinawa. His wife, Jill Slavik Clark, now deceased, enjoyed many retirement years with Tommy in Wildwood Resort City, where he currently resides.

Cleveland, Raymond. Received an athletic scholarship to Stephen F. Austin. After marriage and leaving school, he worked for American Bridge in Orange and then Texaco for thirty years, advancing to the position of Operations Supervisor. When part of Texaco was sold to Ethyl Additives, he continued with them for another seven years before retiring. He now teaches an adult Sunday school class and works with the Texas Baptist Men on Disaster Relief Program. Raymond and his wife, Dian, currently reside in Buna.

Cobb, Jimmy. (Brother of Kenneth Cobb) Received an athletic scholarship to Texas A&M. Although he enjoyed playing basketball, he left the university which he referred to as the "Alcatraz on the Brazos." The reasoning, he said, "Because there were no girls there." Later on, he transferred to Sam Houston State, where he made All-Lone Star Conference. After graduation, he worked for DuPont in Orange until retirement. Jimmy passed away in December 1999. His widow, Britta, currently resides in Sugar Land.

Cobb, Kenneth. (Brother of Jimmy Cobb) No other information available.

Cochran, Johnny. In spite of all efforts, no information has been discovered.

Coyle, Milton. Deceased. No other information available.

Crocker, Dalton. Deceased. No other information available.

Cummings, Robert Dale. (Son of Robert Cummings, former Superintendent of Buna ISD) Graduated from the University of Texas with a pharmacy degree, and after serving two years in the U.S. Army, he returned to UT and enrolled in the pre-med program. He earned an MD degree from University of Texas Medical School in Galveston and completed an internship at Memorial Hospital in Corpus Christi. For the next thirty-two years, he practiced medicine and surgery in Taylor, where he also served on the school board. Thereafter, he was a faculty member for family medicine residency at St. Elizabeth Hospital in Beaumont. Since 2004, he's been affiliated with Sabine-Neches Private Clinic in Evadale that treats family members and employees of MeadWestvaco (formerly East Texas Pulp and Paper Company). Dr. Cummings and his wife, Joan, currently reside in Buna.

Davis, Herman. Deceased. No other information available.

DeVore, Richard. Before he graduated from Buna High School, his family moved to Denver, where he became a state singles tennis champion while attending West High School. Thereafter, he relocated to Texas and worked at Fritz Chemical Corporation of Mesquite for twenty-six years. Richard currently resides in Princeton, near McKinney.

Ellison, Melvin. Received an athletic scholarship to Baylor University, where he majored in English and business administration. After graduation, he pursued a coaching career and then went into school administration. Melvin and his wife, Lori, currently reside in Orange.

Ener, Bobby Guy. After high school, he served two years in the U.S. Army. Upon discharge, he went to work for Magnolia Petroleum Company (Mobil) in Beaumont, and in 1963, transferred to Mobil Chemical. He retired in November 1993. In the interim, he attended Lamar, from which he obtained an accounting degree. Bobby and his wife, Margaret, currently reside in Hemphill.

Fletcher, Coy. After graduating from Buna High School, he worked for fourteen years at B. V. Holmes Chevrolet and then for another four years at Chevyland in Beaumont as service manager. Thereafter, he owned a repair shop and operated a wrecker service. Coy, semiretired, currently resides in Camper's Cove near Woodville.

Franklin, Wayne. Received an athletic scholarship to Allen Academy and later, transferred to Lamar. Thereafter, he worked for the Chemical Division of Mobil Corporation, and in 1998, retired with thirty-five years of service. He passed away on January 29, 2006. Wayne's widow, Syble, currently resides in Buna.

Gibson, Macarthur. (Student manager 1960–61) After graduating from Buna High School, he worked for five years at Britton-Cravens Lumber Company in Silsbee, and was then drafted by the U.S. Army, wherein he served in a top secret atomic program, the Davy Crockett Weapon System. Thereafter, he worked thirteen years for the Beaumont Fire Department, advancing to the position of District Chief. In the interim, he attended Lamar, from which he obtained an associate degree in personnel management. From there, he worked for Marathon Oil as a safetyman on an offshore oil production platform. After three years, he formed his own companies, M&K Gibson Construction, a home builder, and M&K Gibson Properties, which oversees rental properties. Macarthur and his wife, Kay, currently reside in Lafayette, Louisiana.

Goins, Derwood. (Brother of Jerry and Robert Goins) Deceased. No other information available.

Goins, Jerry. (Brother of Derwood and Robert Goins) After graduating from Buna High School, he worked for Kirby, and then for four years with the Buna ISD in the maintenance department. Thereafter, he was employed by East Texas Pulp and Paper Company in Evadale (Eastex), from which he retired after thirty-eight years. Jerry and his wife, Sarah, currently reside in Buna.

Goins, Robert. (Brother of Derwood and Jerry Goins) After graduating from Buna High School, he worked in construction until he was drafted by the U.S. Army. After his discharge, he worked for several companies including Brown & Root. Robert is retired and currently resides in Spurger.

Guillory, Charles "Buddy." After graduating from Buna High School, he served two years in the U.S. Army. Thereafter, he went to work for Schulman, Inc., a plastics manufacturer located in Orange, from which he retired after thirty-eight years. Charles and his wife, Geraldine, currently reside in Buna.

Hargroves, John Ed. Did not play basketball in his senior year at Buna due to an eligibility issue. After graduating from high school, he went on to become a professional rodeo clown. He is deceased.

Harwell, Tate. Moved from Buna before graduating. No other information available.

Hatch, John Allen. (Brother of Larry Hatch) Received an athletic scholarship to East Texas Baptist College, from which he graduated in 1967 with a degree in sociology. He was selected All-Conference for two years. Thereafter, he earned both a Master of Divinity and Doctor of Ministry from Southwestern Baptist Theological Seminary in Fort Worth. Through the years, John has served as pastor in several churches, his last at First Baptist of Lake Jackson for twenty-seven years. In 1987, he was inducted into the Texas Basketball Hall of Fame. At the present, he is Executive Director of the Gregg Baptist Association. John and his wife, Alice, currently reside in Longview.

Hatch, Larry. (Brother of John Hatch) Attended Lamar, from which he graduated with a B.S. in geology. Thereafter, he taught math and physics at Buna High School for eight years, and during that time, he also worked at Kaine's Supermarket. For about ten years, he partnered with Herbert Ross in a construction company that built and remodeled homes in the Buna area. Larry passed away in January 2008. His widow, Cheryl, has remarried and currently resides in Buna.

Hillin, Anthony "Pete." (Brother of Donald Hillin) Received an athletic scholarship to East Texas Baptist College, from which he received a degree in education. Thereafter, he coached in Texarkana and Ore City. He left coaching for a while and went into the private business sector within the oil industry. But once again, he restarted his teaching and coaching career. After earning an M.Ed. and educational certificate at Stephen F. Austin, he has been involved in school administration ever since. He now serves as assistant principal in the

From left, Bill Martin, president, Texas HOF, John Hatch. Photo taken at John Hatch's Hall of Fame induction ceremony.
—Courtesy John Hatch

Kilgore Independent School District with whom he has been employed for eighteen years. Pete and his wife, Lisa, currently reside in Longview.

Hillin, Donald. (Brother of Anthony "Pete" Hillin) After graduating from Buna High School, Donald joined the U.S. Army, and after twenty years of service, he retired. Thereafter, he attended Lamar and earned a B.A. and an M.A., both in history. He worked for the Baptist Hospital of Beaumont, where he served as Director of Personnel. Donald passed away on December 17, 1993. His widow, Helene, currently resides in Buna.

Holland, Billy. Deceased. No other information available.

Johnson, Benny. After graduating from Buna High School, he briefly attended Lamar. Thereafter, he moved to Orange and went to work for American Bridge Shipyard, from which he retired in 1983 after thirty years of service. Benny and his wife, Betty, currently reside in Orange.

Johnson, Clinton "Radar." Received an athletic scholarship to Allen Academy, and thereafter, he enlisted in the U.S. Army. After his discharge, he worked for Gulf (Chevron) in Orange for thirty-eight years. Clinton passed away on November 1, 2011.

Jones, George. Left Buna High School after his junior year and joined the U.S. Marine Corps, in which he served fourteen and one-half years. In what would have been his senior year in high school, George won the singles tennis championship at Camp Pendleton, and he was on the doubles team that also won. In the Corps, he ran track and played on the basketball team at several installations, winning numerous citations and trophies. In 1975, he started his own business, a flight school, that evolved into the largest in Alaska, near Anchorage. He sold out in 1984 and returned to Texas, where as a sideline, he continues to teach aviation classes. George and his wife, Charlotte, currently reside in Lumberton.

Kirkpatrick, Bill. Received an athletic scholarship to Wharton County Junior College. He obtained a bachelor's degree from the University of North Texas and earned an M.Ed. from McNeese State University in Lake Charles, Louisiana. For six years, he served as head basketball coach at Stephen F. Austin High School in Port Arthur, and for another two in Boling, as head basketball, junior varsity football, and golf coach. In June of 1975, he left teaching and coaching to open a life insurance office. In 1981, he became a stockbroker and financial advisor. Bill, now semiretired, and his wife, Paulette, currently reside in Wharton.

Knight, Norman. Received an athletic scholarship to Lon Morris, but due to personal reasons, he had to drop out. He worked as a surveyor and in a machine shop before joining the U.S. Army, in which he served for three years. After discharge, he returned to Texas and enrolled at Lamar, from which he graduated with a degree in mechanical engineering. Thereafter, he worked for twenty-four years at the Baptist Hospital of Beaumont, first as director of maintenance and then as construction manager. He retired in 1995 and afterward pursued a hobby of restoring vintage vehicles. Moreover, he designed activity centers for churches in Buna and Bridge City, and held various offices of leadership in the Buna Methodist Church. He was president of South Jasper County Water Supply Corporation from 1999 until his death in 2005. His widow, Jo Nell, currently resides in Buna.

Lamb, James. Lived near the boundary of Buna and Kirbyville School Districts. He eventually ended up in the latter and played basketball there. No other information available.

Lane, Robert. (Student manager 1961–62) Deceased. No other information available.

Lavender, Lonnie. After graduating from Buna High School, he enlisted in the U.S. Air Force and served for three years. After discharge, he worked for more than thirty years in Irving and Tyler with Texas Power and Light, now Oncor, from which he retired in 1984. He passed away in October 2010. Lonnie's widow, Odean, currently resides in Mesquite.

Lindsey, Charles. Attended Lamar and then served for five years in the U.S. Navy. After discharge, he once again enrolled at Lamar, from which he graduated with a B.S. in geology. Thereafter, he worked for Sperry-Sun, a subsidiary of Sun Petroleum, and then he became involved in the government's underground nuclear testing program in Nevada and Alaska. In 1970, he returned to Houston and went to work as a seismologist for Western Geophysical. Ten years later, he retired. Charles and his wife, Gwen, currently reside in Sugar Land.

McFarland, R. C. Did not play basketball his senior year at Buna due to a back injury, and as a result, had to refuse several athletic scholarships that were offered. After graduating from high school, he worked for a while at Livingston Ship Builders in Orange, and thereafter, for Bethlehem Steel in Beaumont, from which he retired after thirty years of service. At Bethlehem, he began his career as a shipfitter and worked his way up to senior structural planner. R. C. and his wife, Joanne, currently reside in Lumberton.

McGaughey, Robert. Moved from Buna before graduating. No other information available.

McHugh, John. Attended Jacksonville Junior College, where he played basketball for one year. Then he joined the U.S. Marine Corps and served six years. Thereafter, he was employed for more than twenty years as a manager with American General Insurance Company. He is now associated with B&E Resources, Ltd. in Buna, which manufactures and markets field equipment for the oil industry. John currently resides in Vidor.

Martin, William. Moved from Buna before graduating. No other information available.

Meaux, John "Nickie." Received an athletic scholarship to Lon Morris. Thereafter, he graduated from the College of Pharmacy, University of Houston. John retired in 1998, and he currently resides at Lake Conroe.

Mellard, James. Received an athletic scholarship to Lamar and after completing a four-year career as a starter, he emerged as the leading scorer in Cardinal basketball history. As a senior in 1959–60, he won several awards for academic achievement, including the John E. Gray Award, presented to the letterman-athlete graduating with the highest scholastic average, and the Bingman Award for Outstanding Achievement. He was also honored in *Who's Who in American Colleges and Universities*. James graduated from Lamar in 1960 with a B.A. in English. Thereafter, he earned an M.A. in English (1961) from the University of Oklahoma, and a Ph.D. in English (1964) from the University of Texas. He then taught at the University of Southern California and Northern Illinois University, retiring from the latter in 2000 after thirty-three years of service. He has published seven books, produced more than 200 essays, reviews, and scholarly papers, served on advisory boards of leading scholarly journals, and has himself edited a journal called *Style*. James and his wife, Sue, currently reside in Boerne.

Mosley, Andy. (Brother of Mark Kimbrough Mosley) During the summer of 1949, the Mosley family moved to Buna from Marshall, where Andy had made quite a name for himself, playing basketball, football, and baseball. In Buna, he was a sophomore member of the Cougars' team that went 29–8. But soon after his sixteenth birthday in March 1950, he died tragically of an accidental gunshot wound received while on an overnight camping trip with friends. Coach Cotton Robinson took several of the Cougars to Fordyce, Arkansas, where they served as pallbearers at Andy's funeral.

Mosley, Mark Kimbrough. (Brother of Andy Mosley) Received an athletic scholarship to Allen Academy. Later, he attended the University of Texas, from which he graduated with an engineering degree. Thereafter, he entered the oil industry on his way to a 35-year career in the field, retiring as Division Manager of Exploration and Production with Conoco, Inc. Mark and his wife, Sharon, currently reside in Austin.

Muckleroy, Robert "Bull." Received an athletic scholarship to the University of Texas, and later transferred to Lamar, from which he graduated with a business degree. He owns and operates a cattle auction company, a business that his family established in Kirbyville, where Robert currently resides.

Norris, James. In spite of all efforts, no information has been discovered.

Reese, Dwaine. (Brother of Lionel and Wade Reese) Received an athletic scholarship to Allen Academy, and later transferred to Lamar, from which he graduated with a B.S. in chemistry. He taught at Buna and Rusk, and also earned a master's in chemistry from Highlands University New Mexico. Thereafter, he worked for Nalco and retired in 2000. Through the years, he has obtained several patents. He is the CEO of EnerTeck Corp., which specializes in a product developed for combustion enhancement and emission reduction technology in diesel engines. Dwaine and his wife, Ann, currently reside in Richmond, Texas.

Reese, Lionel. (Brother of Dwaine and Wade Reese) Received an athletic scholarship to Sam Houston State, from which he graduated with a degree in business administration and a minor in physical education. Thereafter, he went on to coach basketball for seven years in Warren, and then, three more in nearby Woodville, where he continued to teach in the business department. In 1991, he retired after a 33-year career in education. Lionel and his wife, Beverly, currently reside in Warren.

Reese, Wade. (Brother of Dwaine and Lionel Reese) Attended East Texas Baptist University, where he played freshman basketball. He later transferred to Texas A&M, from which he graduated with a B.S. in animal husbandry. Thereafter, he coached basketball for ten years in Buna, where he also taught biology. Eventually, he left there to go into the construction business, but had just signed a contract to return to Buna as head basketball coach when he was tragically killed in a boating accident.

Rich, John. Received an athletic scholarship to Kilgore Junior College, and then East Texas Baptist College, from which he graduated with a degree in social studies. Thereafter, he earned an M.Ed. from East Texas State University and a certificate in educational administration from Tarleton State University.

Before going into school administration, John coached for years in various places, including Buna and Cedar Hill, where he and his wife, Marty, currently reside.

Richardson, James "Jimmy." (Brother of John Richardson) Received an athletic scholarship to Lamar, from which he graduated with a bachelor's of business administration. From 1968 to 1989, he served in the U.S. Air Force, in both active and guardsman status. During the last two of these years, he was promoted to 147th Fighter Interceptor Group Deputy Commander for Operations with the rank of Lieutenant Colonel. Jimmy's education also includes an M.S. in health administration, an administrative residency at Pasadena Bayshore Hospital in Pasadena, Texas, and a Fellow in American College of Healthcare Executives. He's been associated with the healthcare field for thirty years, serving as chief executive officer to more than twenty hospitals. At the present, he is Vice President of Operations at Quorum Health Resources, the largest contract manager of hospitals and the seventh largest healthcare consulting firm in the country. Jimmy, and his wife, JoAnn, currently reside in McKinney.

Richardson, John. (Brother of James "Jimmy" Richardson) Received several athletic scholarship offers, but he opted instead to enroll in Lamar's pre-med program. However, John still found time to win a walk-on scholarship and thereafter, played freshman basketball for Coach Billy Tubbs's Lamar Cardinals. At the beginning of his sophomore year, he was accepted into the University of Texas School of Pharmacy. He completed the five-year program and then moved to Center, where he began working for Rogers Drug Store. Two years later, he was in the process of purchasing the business when he was tragically killed in a motorcycle accident.

Richardson, Lynn. Deceased. No other information available.

Rogers, Delman. (Brother of Victor and Phillip Rogers) Received an athletic scholarship to East Texas Baptist, from which he graduated. Thereafter, he earned a Master of Divinity at Southwestern Seminary. He has been affiliated with many churches over the years and still pastors at Beulah Baptist Church in Mansfield, Louisiana, where he and his wife, Helen, currently reside.

Rogers, Phillip. (Brother of Delman and Victor Rogers) Received an athletic scholarship as a student trainer to Lon Morris, but later transferred to Lamar. For the next twenty-one years, he was involved in retail. In 1981, he became a landman, acquiring right-of-ways, easements, and leases for various oil companies. His career in that field has now spanned thirty years. After retiring from Mustang Engineering in 2008, he opened an independent operation, Rogers

Land Services, located in Schulenburg, where he and his wife, Vivian, currently reside.

Rogers, Victor. (Brother of Delman and Phillip Rogers) While still a student in Buna High School, he submitted an application for employment with the FBI. By fall, he had not received a response, so he enrolled at Lamar. In December, an agent showed up at Victor's English class and offered him a position. He accepted, and forty-five years later, he retired from the bureau as a supervisor/trainer. In the interim, he also attended the University of Houston. Vic and his wife, Gail, currently reside in Pearland.

Ross, Herbert. Received an athletic scholarship to Jacksonville Baptist College, and thereafter, he joined the U.S. Army and served for six years. After receiving a discharge, he has been self-employed in the construction business, building and remodeling homes. Herbert and his wife, Cecelia, currently reside in Buna.

Simmons, Bobby. After graduating from Buna High School, he worked for Kinsel Ford in Beaumont and then East Texas Pulp and Paper Company in Evadale (Eastex). After serving four years in the U.S. Air Force, he returned to Eastex, but left again to attend a trade school in Houston, after which he became a licensed electrician. Thereafter, he joined Boise Cascade, Ltd., a manufacturer of paper, corrugated containers, and wood products building materials, located in DeRidder, Louisiana, where for twenty-one years, he applied his training as an industrial electrician. After he retired, he went full time into the ministry. He serves as pastor of Carson Baptist Church in Zwolle, near Many, Louisiana. Bobby and his wife, Judy, currently reside in Leesville, Louisiana.

Simmons, Charles. (Brother of Harold and James "Sambo" Simmons) After graduating from Buna High School, Charles worked with his father in the timber and sawmill business. In 1966, he went to work for the East Texas Pulp and Paper Company in Evadale (Eastex), and in 2001, he retired after 35 years of service. Charles and his wife, Nancy, currently reside in Buna.

Simmons, Harold. (Brother of Charles and James "Sambo" Simmons) Served as student manager on Cotton Robinson's first three basketball teams, 1948–49, 1950–51, and 1951–52. A complete biography, including his coaching career at Buna, is detailed in Chapter Eighteen, Transformation and Aftermath. Harold and his wife, Kay, currently reside in Buna.

Simmons, James "Sambo." (Brother of Harold and Charles Simmons) Received an athletic scholarship to Kilgore Junior College; however, he suffered a broken arm before the first season. He then joined the U.S. Navy, and his career spanned twenty-seven years, the last three of which he served as a recruiter in Victoria. After retiring in 1991, he was associated with the oil field industry until 1998, when he went to work for the U.S. Postal Service. James and his wife, Linda, currently reside in Victoria.

Simmons, Richard Charles. Before he graduated from Buna High School, his family moved to Louisiana, where he completed his senior year at Quitman High School. Thereafter, he obtained a degree in physical education at Lamar, and then earned an M.Ed. at Sam Houston. He was with the Port Acres ISD for thirteen years, serving the last one and a half as principal before he moved on to coach at Kirbyville and Hemphill. His basketball and football coaching career spanned thirty-two years. Charles and his wife, Lavella, currently reside in Hemphill.

Smith, Jasper C. "J. C.," Jr. (Brother of Jerry and Joan Smith) Received an athletic scholarship to Texas A&M. In his sophomore year, he transferred to Lamar, from which he graduated with a degree in mechanical engineering. He worked for Boeing in Seattle, and in Garland for LTV on the Corvus missile project. Thereafter, he moved to Deer Park, where for nearly thirty years, he worked for NASA. J. C. and his wife, Dot, currently reside in Buna.

Smith, Jerry. (Brother of Joan and Jasper C. "J. C." Smith, Jr.) Received an athletic scholarship to Kilgore Junior College. Later, he transferred to Lamar and then to Stephen F. Austin, from which he graduated with a degree in mathematics, a minor in physics, and a teaching certificate. He earned an M.Ed. (also from SFA), and then for ten years, he served with the Buna Independent School District, four as assistant superintendent and six as superintendent. Thereafter, he was employed by the Nederland ISD as assistant superintendent and personnel director. After twelve years there, he retired in 2001. Jerry and his wife, Sue, currently reside in San Benito.

Sowell, Rusty. (Student manager 1962–63) Attended Lamar and then joined the National Guard in which he served for six years. Thereafter, he went into the construction industry, and then the restaurant business for about eighteen years. He has also been involved in mission work inside China, Mexico, Brazil, and the states. He is very active in Gideons International, an evangelical Christian organization dedicated to distributing free bibles all over the world. Although Rusty is semiretired, he still works around the family farm near San Augustine, where he currently resides.

Stancil, Dan. (Brother of Glen and Raymond) In spite of all efforts, no contact has been made.

Stancil, Glen. (Brother of Dan and Raymond Stancil) Received an athletic scholarship to Stephen F. Austin, where he was All-Conference and honorable mention All-American. After graduating with a degree in math, he also earned at SFA an M.Ed. Thereafter, he worked for Tennessee Gas Transmission Company (Tenneco) and Gulf Computer Sciences, both in Houston, before he opened his own company, TOSC International, Inc., a software company. Glen and his wife, Joanna, currently reside in Cypress.

Stancil, Raymond. (Brother of Glen and Dan Stancil) Graduated from Texas A&M with a degree in chemical engineering. Thereafter, he worked for Signal Oil and Gas, then Purvin & Gertz, Inc., before forming Muse, Stancil & Company, and then breaking off to become Stancil & Company. In the middle 1980s, he represented Southland Corporation with their many mergers and acquisitions. Raymond passed away on September 15, 2000. His widow, Sharon, currently resides in Coppell.

Stanley, Derryl. (Twin brother of Jerryl Stanley) Left Buna High School after his junior year and joined the U.S. Air Force, in which he served four years. After discharge, he worked construction through Pipe Fitters Local 195 in Nederland. He retired from there and went to work for a while with Hardin County Precinct 4. Derryl and his wife, Mary, currently reside in Lumberton.

Stanley, Don. (Twin brother of Pat Stanley) Received an athletic scholarship to Kilgore Junior College, and while there, he was named All State, All Regional, National Junior College Athletic Association All Tournament, and Junior College First Team All American in 1958. His team won the Junior College National Championship in 1958. He repeated as All State, All Regional, All American and played in the first Junior College World Series game in 1959. Thereafter, he went on to attend Texas A&M from 1959–61. He served as co-captain of the team and won All-Southwest Conference honors. After graduation, he became associated with the oil tools business, working as an executive with Lufkin Industries until he retired. He was inducted into the Texas Basketball Hall of Fame in 1983, and the Kilgore College Hall of Fame in 2005. Don and his wife, Roanne, currently reside in Buna.

Stanley, Jerryl. (Twin brother of Derryl Stanley) Left Buna High School after his junior year and joined the U.S. Air Force, in which he served four years. After discharge, he worked construction through Pipe Fitters Local 195 in Nederland. He retired in 2001. Thereafter, he went to work for Hardin County Precinct 1, where he has been for the last eight years. Jerryl and his wife, Amanda, currently reside in Buna.

Stanley, Pat. (Twin brother of Don Stanley) Received an athletic scholarship to Kilgore Junior College, and while there, he was named All-Regional, All-State, and Junior College First Team All-American in 1958. His team won the Junior College National Championship in 1958, and in 1959, he played in the first Junior College World Series Game. Thereafter, he went on to attend Texas A&M from 1959–61. He served as co-captain of the team and won All-Southwest Conference honors. After graduation, he became associated with the oil tools business, working as an executive with Lufkin Industries International Division, from which he retired in 1999. He was in-

From left: Don Stanley, Pat Stanley. Photo taken at Pat Stanley's Hall of Fame induction ceremony.
—Courtesy Pat Stanley

ducted into the Kilgore College Hall of Fame in 2005, and the Texas Basketball Hall of Fame in 2007. Pat and his wife, Mary, currently reside in Buna.

Stom, Pat. Left Buna High School after his sophomore year and joined the U.S. Navy, in which he served four years as an aviation electronics technician. Thereafter, he went into construction and through the years, he has continued in that profession. He now works for Jacobs Engineering as an industrial construction site manager. Pat and his wife, Alice, currently reside in Beaumont.

Stratton, Bobby. Attended Lamar, from which he graduated in 1956 with a degree in physical education. He coached basketball and football at High Island before moving to East Chambers in Winnie, where he served as head coach of both the basketball and football teams. He left coaching at the end of the 1973 season and went into the insurance and securities business. Before retiring, he owned a chain of ten check cashing outlets located in Louisiana and Texas. Bobby and his wife, Judy, currently reside in Sulphur, Louisiana.

Swearingen, Jackie. (Brother of Paul Swearingen) Received an athletic scholarship to Allen Academy, but opted to join the U.S. Navy. He served for four years as an accountant in the Naval Aviation Unit. Thereafter, he was employed with PPG Industries in Beaumont, from which he retired in 1980. Jackie and his wife, Judy, currently reside in Village Mills.

Swearingen, Paul. (Brother of Jackie Swearingen) After graduating from Buna High School, he joined the U.S. Army for a three-year hitch. Thereafter, he worked for forty years at East Texas Pulp and Paper Company in Evadale (Eastex), from which he retired. In the interim, however, he also served for twenty-six years as associate pastor for Central Baptist Church, and for the last two years, he's been the pastor of Friendship Baptist Church. Both churches are located in Buna, where Paul currently resides.

Turner, Barry. In spite of all efforts, no information has been discovered.

Vaughn, Donald. In spite of all efforts, no contact has been made.

Walters, Raymond Doyle. After graduating from Buna High School, he attended Sam Houston, from which he received an associate degree in industrial arts. Thereafter, he worked for Bethlehem Steel in Beaumont and then Texas U.S. Chemical in Port Neches, which later became Ameripol-Synpol. He retired from the latter in 2001. Raymond also owned and operated Buna Machine and Welding. In the interim, however, he freely gave of his time and service to his community. He spent fifty-three years in the Buna Volunteer Fire Department, for which he received numerous awards; and he was an 18-year member of Buna ISD's school board. He passed away on February 13, 2010. Raymond's widow, Peggy, currently resides in Buna.

Walters, Thomas Richard. After graduating from Buna High School, he joined the U.S. Air Force, in which he served for three and one-half years. Thereafter, he went to work in the Street Lighting Department of Pasadena (Texas), and two years later, he became the city's electrical inspector. In the interim, he earned an associate degree and a master electrician's license from San Jacinto Junior College. In 2000, he retired after a combined thirty-six years with Pasadena, where he and his wife, Jan, currently reside.

Westbrook, Charles. (Brother of Tom Westbrook) Left Buna High School after his junior year and joined the U.S. Navy for four years. After discharge, he returned to Southeast Texas and went to work for various companies including Texas Gulf Sulphur for nine years. Thereafter, he became involved in offshore drilling, working his way up to first engineer of a drill ship. About ten years later, he went back into the construction business, from which he is now retired. Charles and his wife, Donna, currently reside in Beaumont.

Westbrook, Kenneth. In spite of all efforts, no information has been discovered.

Westbrook, Tom. (Brother of Charles Westbrook) Received an athletic scholarship to Allen Academy but later transferred to the University of Corpus Christi. After a hitch in the U.S. Air Force, he worked for a time at Neches Butane in Port Neches while attending Lamar. He earned a degree and coached at Beaumont High for six years. Then for twenty-six years, he was associated with the Evadale Independent School District, serving as a coach and an elementary school principal. He left that job to become business manager for the school district. Tom is now retired and currently resides in Buna.

Whitehead, Ed. After graduating from Buna High School, he joined the U.S. Army, and upon discharge, he returned to Buna. Thereafter, he worked as a welder at various companies and installations. He is retired. Ed and his wife, Pansy, currently reside in Buna.

Whitmire, Revis. After graduating from Buna High School, he went to work for DuPont in Orange. Thereafter, he enlisted in the military, and then returned to DuPont. Ten years later, he went out on his own, operating automobile franchises, from which he is now retired. Revis and his wife, Frances, currently reside in Broaddus.

Withers, James C. "Blackie." (Brother of William Withers) Received an athletic scholarship to Lamar. About a year later, he passed a special examination which established him as the number two candidate to win one of Texas's five appointments-at-large to the U.S. Naval Academy Thereafter, he attended American University in Washington, D.C., from which he obtained a B.S. in chemistry. James was then accepted into a prestigious external program, connected also with American University and under the supervision of Professor Linus Pauling, the only person ever to receive two unshared Nobel Prizes. Upon completion, James earned two doctorates, one in physics and the other in physical chemistry. Since then, he has received a total of nine distinguished "R&D 100 Awards," honoring the 100 most significant, newly introduced research and development advances. He has also been awarded fifty U.S. patents and has published more than 200 technical articles in his field of expertise. He now serves as CEO of the MER Corporation, a materials and electrochemical research corporation. James and his wife, Tiffany, currently reside in Tucson, Arizona.

Withers, William. (Brother of James C. "Blackie" Withers) Received an athletic scholarship to Allen Academy and then transferred to Stephen F. Austin, from which he graduated with degrees in health, physical education, and English. Thereafter, he held coaching jobs at Tomball, Evadale, and Kirbyville, before going into banking at Kirbyville State Bank, where he was first a loan officer, then cashier. In 1976, he returned to teach in Buna, and for a while coached the girls' basketball team. He left teaching in 1982 and became a full-time agent with Farmers Insurance. He has also been associated with the International Mission Board, an entity of the Southern Baptist Convention and as such, has served as a missionary. William, now semiretired, and his wife, Wynna, currently reside in Buna.

Worsham, Velton. Deceased. No other information available.

Endnotes

Abbreviations

CPQ   Completed Player Questionnaire
UIL   University Interscholastic League of Texas, based in Austin
YMBL Young Men's Business League Annual High School Basketball
      Tournament, Beaumont, TX

Introduction

1. Aaron Smith, "Top Five Basketball Dynasties of All Time," (http://www. associat-edcontent.com/article/1387540/top_five_basketball_dynasties_of_all.html), accessed Mar. 2, 2011.

2. Several sources, including "Real 'Hoosiers' Better Story than the Movie's?" Apr. 3, 2010, CBS News.com (http://www.cbsnews.com/stories/2010/04/03/earlyshow/saturday/main6360209.shtml), accessed Mar. 13, 2011, point out that the movie *Hoosiers* was based on the 1954 boys' state high school championship game in Indiana between Milan and Muncie Central. Milan won the game by the final score of 32–30.

3. Betty Barker and Carolyn Rauwerda, eds., *Buna Remembered: The Times* (Nederland [TX]: Cate Media, 2002), 18 (quotations).

Chapter One

1. Buna Area Historical Writers, *Buna Remembered: The Places* (Jasper [TX]: Jasper Printing Company, 1997), 68; Robert Wooster, "BUNA, TX," *Handbook of Texas Online* (http://www.tshaonline.org/handbook/online/articles/hjb22), accessed Mar. 4, 2011.

2. CPQ, John Rich (quotation).

3. It is not the authors' intention to dwell too much on the history of Buna, Texas. The *Buna Remembered*, three-volume series included in the Bibliography, is a great source for that information. We have, therefore, provided a very generalized summary.

4. Wooster, "BUNA, TX," accessed Mar. 4, 2011 (quotation); Brent Snyder, "Buna," BeaumontEnterprise.com (http://www.beaumontenterprise.com/default/article/Buna-748121.php), accessed Mar. 1, 2011. On page 7 of *Buna Remembered: The Places*, there is

mention of Dr. William Walters, who while conducting research for his doctoral thesis, determined how the town got its name. The account is as follows: "Joseph [Carroll] renamed the logging camp, Bunah, in honor of one of his nieces who visited the small community and charmed the residents. Maggie and Emily Richardson, in interviews, recalled her visit and departure and the suggestion that the town be named Bunah. When the post office sent the information to Washington, all the papers came back with the name spelled 'Buna.' The name endured as did the town. Bunah Corley, whose married name was Bass, was last known to live in El Campti, Louisiana, and never was known to have returned to Buna."

5. *Texas Almanac and State Industrial Guide, 1943–1944* (Dallas: *Dallas Morning News*, 1944), 72; *Texas Almanac and State Industrial Guide, 1947–1948* (Dallas: *Dallas Morning News*, 1948), 136; Wooster, "BUNA, TX," accessed Mar. 4, 2011; Buna Independent School District's website (http://www.bunaisd.net/campuses), accessed Mar. 7, 2011.

6. Buna Independent School District's website; Buna Area Historical Writers, *Buna Remembered: The Places*, 119.

7. These statements are based on the personal knowledge of co-author Fred B. McKinley, who lived in Buna and attended school there from 1955 through 1960.

8. Ibid.

9. Ibid.

10. Ibid.

11. Ibid.

12. Ibid.

13. Ibid.

14. Betty Barker and Carolyn Rauwerda, eds., *Buna Remembered: The Times* (Nederland [TX]: Cate Media, 2002), 3–10; Robert Hargrove, telephone interview with Fred B. McKinley, Feb. 9, 2011 (quotation); Phil Rogers (progersland@aol.com), e-mail to Fred B. McKinley, Burleson, Texas, Mar. 9, 2011. According to the Buna yearbook, *The Cougar, 1960*, football returned to the school in 1959 with the hiring of Coach Fred Godwin. Buna's first boys' basketball team, coached by Ernest Davis, consisted of Corbett Whitmire, Norman Woods, Richard Woods, Richard Jones, and Victor Rogers, Sr.

15. Barker and Rauwerda, *Buna Remembered: The Times*, 9-10.

16. *Chalk Talk, 2006*, Texas Association of Basketball Coaches (no publication data available), 1; Hargrove telephone interview with McKinley; Basketball, 1947–1948, Conference B (Tentative List), UIL, n.d., 3; Basketball District Winners–1948, UIL, n.d.; Basketball Official List, 1948, UIL, n.d.; Permanent Record of Marshall N. Robinson [student transcript], Sam Houston State Teachers College [now Sam Houston State University], Huntsville, Texas; Lynda Robinson Sanford, interview with Fred B. McKinley and Larry Gerald, Mar. 26, 2011, Buna, Texas.

Chapter Two

1. Marshall Neil Robinson's Birth Certificate Number 456147, filed May 25, 1942, Texas Department of Health, Bureau of Vital Statistics, County of Travis, State of Texas; Lynda Robinson Sanford (dulcilynda1@hotmail.com), e-mails to Fred B. McKinley, Burleson, Texas, Feb. 11, 13, 2011. According to family records, Mrs. Sanford indicated the birth dates of Marshall Neil "Cotton" Robinson's siblings as: James William "Jack," Oct. 28, 1917; Ersell Powell, Aug. 19, 1919; Elton Erasterus, Nov. 8, 1921; Lyndall

Louise, Oct. 21, 1923; Lenard Lindberg, Aug. 23, 1927; Lucy Lillian, Feb. 5, 1929; Mathea Ruth, Mar. 25, 1931; and Robert Stanley, May 25, 1935.

2. Lyndall Robinson Hale, letter to Lynda and Butch Sanford, Buna, Texas, Feb. 19, 2010 (quotation); Lillian Robinson Pierce, telephone interview with Fred B. McKinley, June 1, 2011. In the first source, Mrs. Hale referred several times to Pleasant Ridge as the "ridge." And in the latter, Mrs. Pierce said, "Before the locals adopted the name of Pleasant Ridge, they called the community Nubbin Ridge, due to the fact that the land was not productive in the growing of corn. Thus, cotton became the mainstay." Most sources, including Cotton Robinson's birth certificate, erroneously reflect his place of birth as Centerville, most probably to identify with a better known location other than Pleasant Ridge. According to another e-mail dated Apr. 5, 2011, Mrs. Sanford advised McKinley that her father, Marshall Neil Robinson, was delivered at home by a Dr. Powell.

3. Hale letter to Sanford; Sanford, e-mail to McKinley, Apr. 4, 2011.

4. Hale letter to Sanford (quotations).

5. Ibid.; Sanford, e-mail to McKinley, Apr. 4, 2011.

6. Hale letter to Sanford; Sanford, e-mail to McKinley, Apr. 11, 2011. Mrs. Sanford said, "I'm not aware of Papa having any problems from the malaria while I was growing up."

7. Hale letter to Sanford; J. D. O'Keefe, telephone interview with Fred B. McKinley, Aug. 13, 2011. In the latter communication, Mr. O'Keefe, Robinson's teammate on the Leona basketball team, said that at times, Cotton would ride his horse to school.

8. Hale letter to Sanford; Sanford, e-mail to McKinley, Apr. 4, 2011. In the latter communication, Mrs. Sanford said that her father's maternal grandmother, Lucy Ward, kept Stanley [Cotton Robinson's youngest brother] during the day because he was not old enough to go to school."

9. Hale letter to Sanford; Sanford, e-mail to McKinley, Feb. 15, 2011. In later years, Bill Bitner served as superintendent of the Centerville Public Schools. He recommended Johnny Carter for a head basketball coaching position with Kennard High School. Carter interviewed with C. L. Bitner, Bill's brother and the superintendent at Kennard, and got the job. During his first season, 1966–67, Carter led his Kennard team to their first state championship in Conference B by defeating Krum, 51–47, in the final. The story of this team's amazing achievement is detailed in Carter's book, *The First Season: The True Story of How a Rookie Coach Took a Newly Integrated Team to a Texas State Championship* (Dallas: Brown Books, 2011). Carter also led the Kennard Tigers to state championships in 1968 and 1970. Carl Owens continued the program, and his team won the state B crown in 1973.

10. Sanford, e-mail to McKinley, Feb. 15, 2011; "Leona Lions Win Regional Basketball Championship," *Leon County News*, Mar. 4, 1943.

11. "District Basketball Tournament To Be Held Here Saturday," *Leon County News*, Jan. 14, 1943; "Leona Wins First District Tourney," *Leon County News*, Jan. 28, 1943; Basketball, 1949–1950, Conference B (Tentative List), UIL, n.d. The first source lists twelve schools in District 43: A&M Consolidated, North Zulch, Leona, Normangee, Flynn, Centerville, Buffalo, Oakwood, Lone Star, Concord, Jewett, and Marquez. The second source, however, shows only nine of those actually competed: Leona, Centerville, Lone Star, Buffalo, Flynn, Concord, Jewett, Oakwood, and A&M Consolidated. The latter source indicates that A&M Consolidated is in College Station.

12. "Second District Basketball Meet Here Saturday," *Leon County News*, Feb. 4,

1943; "Leona Lions Will Play In Regional Tourney Saturday," *Leon County News*, Feb. 25, 1943; "Leona Lions Win Regional Basketball Championship," Mar. 4, 1943; "Regional Basketball Champions," *Leon County News*, Mar. 11, 1943. Other members of the Lions team are listed as Jimmy Mize, Jack Thompson, and Roy Pugh, manager.

13. Dylan Wood, "LEONA, TX," *Handbook of Texas Online* (http://www.tshaonline.org/handbook/online/articles/hll38), accessed Mar. 15, 2011; "Leona Lions Win Regional Basketball Championship," Mar. 4, 1943.

14. 1943 Boys' State Basketball Tourney Records, Conference B, First Round, UIL, n.d.; Tournament Schedule for Texas High School State Championships, Mar. 4–6, 1943 (UIL, n.d.), n.p.; *Chalk Talk, 2006*, Texas Association of Basketball Coaches (no publication data available), 1; Charles Breithaupt (cbreithaupt@uiltexas.org), e-mail to Fred B. McKinley, Burleson, Texas, Feb. 14, 2011.

15. "Leona Basketball Star Enlists in U.S. Navy," *Leon County News*, Mar. 18, 1943; Marshall Neil Robinson's Notice of Separation from U.S. Naval Service, Number 2277, May 6, 1946; Marshall Neil Robinson's Leona High School Class Material; Marshall Neil Robinson's Leona High School Diploma, May 26, 1943.

16. Lynda Robinson Sanford, interview with Fred B. McKinley and Larry Gerald, Mar. 26, 2011, Buna, Texas; Sanford, e-mail to McKinley, Apr. 4, 2011 (quotation).

Chapter Three

1. Marshall Neil Robinson's Notice of Separation from U.S. Naval Service, Number 2277, May 6, 1946; James G Schneider, *The Navy V-12 Program: Leadership for a Lifetime* [second edition] (Champaign: Marlow, 1993), 68; I. Bruce Turner (bturner@louisiana.edu), e-mail to Fred B. McKinley, Burleson, Texas, Feb. 22, 2011.

2. Schneider, *The Navy V-12 Program*, 7 (quotation).

3. Ibid., 236; Cindy D. Menard (cdm2796@louisiana.edu), e-mail to Fred B. McKinley, Burleson, Texas, Feb. 17, 2011.

4. Turner, e-mail to McKinley, Mar. 3, 2011; Cade Sirmans (ctsirmans1126@louisiana.edu), e-mail to Fred B. McKinley, Burleson, Texas, Feb. 15, 2011.

5. Turner, e-mail to McKinley, Mar. 2, 2011; Robinson's Notice of Separation from U.S. Naval Service. In his book titled *Texas Boys' Basketball: A History*, page 45, Harold Ratliff writes that Cotton Robinson "dropped out [of Southwestern Louisiana Institute] because of a broken knee."

6. Permanent Record of Marshall N. Robinson [student transcript], Sam Houston State Teachers College [now Sam Houston State University], Huntsville, Texas.

7. Barbara Kievit-Mason (lib_bak@shsu.edu), e-mail to Fred B. McKinley, Burleson, Texas, Feb. 18, 2011; "SHS Cagers Edge SFA Jacks, 62–57," *The Houstonian*, Sam Houston State Teachers College, Feb. 7, 1947 (quotation).

8. Kievit-Mason, e-mail to McKinley, Mar. 30, 2011 (quotation).

9. Robinson's student transcript, Sam Houston State Teachers College.

10. William Withers, telephone interview with Fred B. McKinley, Apr. 4, 2011. According to Mr. Withers, Cotton boarded in the Withers's household for over two years, before he moved in with Bubba Kaine's family.

11. Ibid.

12. Ibid. (quotation).

13. Buna Area Historical Writers, *Buna Remembered: The Places* (Jasper [TX]: Jasper Printing Company, 1997), 113.

14. "Just a Memory," *The Buna Beacon*, Jan. 10, 1973; Buna Area Historical Writers, *Buna Remembered: The Places*, 115-117. According to the latter source, p. 117, "Bob Wegener was in charge of the W.P.A. for this area and Fate Johnson was foreman for the Buna Gym Project." During the writing of *King Cotton*, the authors focused their attention on developing the story of the winning tradition established by Robinson's boys' basketball teams. Therefore, the coverage of the girls' teams is very limited in scope.

15. CPQ, J. C. Smith, Jr.

16. Ibid.

17. Ibid. (quotation).

18. Betty Barker and Carolyn Rauwerda, eds., *Buna Remembered: The Times* (Nederland [TX]: Cate Media, 2002), 18 (quotation).

19. Geraldine Hyden, interview with Fred B. McKinley and Larry Gerald, Mar. 24, 2011, Buna, Texas (quotation).

20. Barker and Rauwerda, *Buna Remembered: The Times*, 18 (quotation).

21. Buna Area Historical Writers, *Buna Remembered: The Places*, 117; Robert Hargrove, telephone interview with Fred B. McKinley, Feb. 9, 2011; "Just a Memory," Jan. 10, 1973; Joan Smith, telephone interview with Fred B. McKinley, July 27, 2011. In the latter source, Ms. Smith said that she graduated from Buna High School in May 1957, and she was on the girls' team that played in the new Bob Cummings Gymnasium.

Chapter Four

1. Charles Breithaupt (cbreithaupt@uiltexas.org), e-mail to Fred B. McKinley, Burleson, Texas, Apr. 18, 2011; Bill McMurray, "Fabulous Cotton Robinson Career Nearing End at Buna High," *The Buna East Texan*, Feb. 14, 1963. For a full description of Conference B and other conference sizes, consult Appendix 1—Conference Designations, 1947–1964.

2. "Champion Cagers Advertise Two Winners: Hargrove Station and Humble Products," *Humble Sales Lubricator* (Jan. 27, 1949), 2.

3. The Cougar, 1950, Buna School's Yearbook (no publication data available).

4. Ibid.; Boys Basketball, 1949–1950, Conference B (Tentative List), UIL, n.d. The latter source indicates that Bleakwood High School is near Kirbyville.

5. J. C. Smith (jakesmith2836@sbcglobal.net), e-mail to Fred B. McKinley, Burleson, Texas, Apr. 14, 2011 (quotation); *The Cougar, 1950* (second quotation). The University Interscholastic League's records reflect limited documentation for Buna during 1949–1950, other than they were slated to play Yantis in bi-district. Perhaps they played Pickton, but unfortunately, there is no data. At any rate, the Cougars never advanced to regional competition. Robert Cummings's son, Dale (front row, jersey number 4), is identified in the group photo for that year. The overall record of the 1949–50 Cougars is usually set at 30–8, a one game difference from that of the 1950 Cougars Yearbook, which shows 29–8.

6. Permanent Record of Marshall N. Robinson [student transcript], Sam Houston State Teachers College [now Sam Houston State University], Huntsville, Texas. During the period extending from June 6 to August 25, 1950, Robinson took four courses, the grades of which follow the title: P.E. 378, Administration of P.E. and Athletics-A; P.E. 367, Driver Education and Training-B; P.E. 322, Coaching of Basketball-B; and P.E. 263, Boys Club Work and Camp Leadership-A. According to this transcript, Robinson at-

tended several summer sessions, uninterrupted from 1951 through 1953. He took a hiatus until returning on June 6, 1958, and he enrolled again on June 8, 1959, after which, he earned an M.Ed. on July 17, 1959.

7. Lynda Robinson Sanford (dulcilynda1@hotmail.com), e-mail to Fred B. McKinley, Burleson, Texas, Feb. 4, 2011; Marshall Neil Robinson and Monte Sybil Smith, Marriage License, issued June 26, 1950, and recorded in vol. 5, p. 442 of the Marriage Records of Walker County, Texas.

8. Sanford, e-mail to McKinley, May 2, 2011; Johnny and Nelda Sheppard (brother-in-law and sister of Monte Sybil Robinson, respectively), telephone interviews with Fred B. McKinley, May 5, 2011; "Baby Galvez Resort Brought Visitors From All Over Texas," *The Silsbee Bee Sesquicentennial, 2008* (http://issuu.com/gdickert/docs/silsbee_bee_sesquicentennial), accessed May 5, 2011. For more about the rich history of the Honey Island, Texas area, the authors suggest an article titled, "Honey Island, Texas," which can be accessed at (http://www.tshaonline.org/handbook/online/articles/hlh53).

9. *The Cougar, 1951*, Buna School's Yearbook (no publication data available). The scores for the French, Rosenberg, and Nederland games were taken from records prepared at the time by J. C. Smith, Sr., of Buna. These fragile documents, henceforth referred to as the "J. C. Smith, Sr., records," are in the possession of his son, J. C. Smith, Jr., who currently resides in Buna.

10. *The Cougar, 1951*; J. C. Smith, Sr. records; "District 62-B Champions," *Beaumont Enterprise*, n.d.

11. Smith, e-mail to McKinley, Apr. 14, 2011 (Johnson quotation).

12. "District 62-B Champions," n.d.; *The Cougar, 1951*; Harold Ratliff, *Texas Boys' Basketball: A History* (Austin: UIL, 1976), 96; Breithaupt, e-mail to McKinley, Apr. 18, 2011; "Fabulous Cotton Robinson Career Nearing End at Buna High," Feb. 14, 1963; Thomas Foster, telephone interview with Fred B. McKinley, Apr. 29, 2011; Smith, e-mail to McKinley, Apr. 28, 2011; Bobby Ener, telephone interview with Fred B. McKinley, Apr. 27, 2011; Fred Cervelli, "Fabulous Records of Robinson, Hyden Make Buna Basketball Paradise," *The Orange Leader*, Feb. 19, 1961. After the Big Sandy Wildcats ousted Buna from regional competition, they advanced to the state tournament, where they lost the title game to Conference-B champion Cayuga by a score of 44–38.

13. Texas Birth Index, 1903–1997, record for Lynda Nell Robinson, Ancestry.com, Texas Birth Index, 1903–1997 [database on-line], Provo, UT, USA: Ancestry.com Operations Inc, 2005 (Original data: Texas Birth Index, 1903–1997, Texas: Texas Department of State Health Services, microfiche); Sanford, e-mail to McKinley, May 2, 2011.

14. *The Cougar, 1952*, Buna School's Yearbook (no publication data available); Boys Basketball, 1951–1952, Conference A (Official List), UIL, n.d.; Smith, e-mail to McKinley, Apr. 14, 2011; "Cedar Bayou Nips Buna 40–37 To Win 20-A Title," n.p., n.d. According to the latter source, the win over Buna "was the second time in the past three years that the Watkins-coached Bruins [Bears] grabbed off the conference cage title. They won the crown in 1950–51, and finished second last season [Buna won district in 1951-52]." *The Cougar, 1952* reflects the final record of the 1950–1951 Cougars as 41 wins and 3 losses.

15. *The Cougar, 1952*; "Winners Enter State Cage Meet," *Beaumont Enterprise*, Feb. 25, 1952; "Basketball Scores," *Beaumont Enterprise*, Feb. 27, 1952; "Cage Scores," *Beaumont Enterprise*, Mar. 1, 1952; J. C. Smith, Sr. records. The latter source indicates that on Jan.

4, 1952, Buna lost their first game in the Junior Chamber of Commerce Tournament to John H. Reagan of Houston, 53–37. On the same day, the Cougars went on to beat Van, 58–37. The following day, they beat Beaumont High, 43–34, but lost to Port Arthur in the consolation final, 41–33. Also according to J. C. Smith, Sr. records, Buna and Cedar Bayou met twice in district competition, and Buna won both times: Jan. 24, 1952, 36–29; and Feb. 19, 1952, 53–35.

16. "Cage Scores," *Beaumont Enterprise*, Mar. 1, 1952; "Basketball Scores," *Beaumont Enterprise*, Mar. 2, 1952. UIL records show that Lovelady, who had beaten Troup in the Region III-A Tournament final, advanced to the state tournament in Austin, where they fell to Plano, 40–38.

17. Bobby Guy Ener, telephone interview with Fred B. McKinley, Apr. 27, 2011; Smith, e-mail to McKinley, Apr. 14, 2011 (quotation); Bobby Stratton, telephone interview with Fred B. McKinley, July 28, 2011.

18. Smith, e-mail to McKinley, Apr. 28, 2011 (quotation). Smith went on to say, "[Buna] could not afford glass backboards, so Cotton built some out of wood that must have been 3-4 inches thick, trying to make them hard as glass."

19. *The Cougar, 1952*; Breithaupt, e-mails to McKinley, Apr. 17, 18, 2011; Smith, e-mail to McKinley, Apr. 14, 2011. In the latter communication, J. C. Smith said that in the Huntsville Tournament that same year, the Big Sandy Wildcats beat Buna, and that "started a rivalry with them over the years in which Cotton finally got the upper hand." According to Dr. Billy Wilbanks, *Texas Basketball Champions*, Dimmitt beat Plano, 62–40 in the Conference-A final.

20. Smith, e-mail to McKinley, Apr. 14, 2011.

21. First Annual Beaumont YMBL High School Basketball Tournament-1952, listing of teams; Lionel Reese, telephone interview with Fred B. McKinley, May 12, 2011 (quotation).

22. Reese, telephone interview with McKinley (quotation).

23. Ibid.; Blackie Arendale, "Buna, Royal Purples Score Wins," *Beaumont Enterprise*, Dec. 4, 1952; *The Cougar, 1953*, Buna School's Yearbook (no publication data available); J. C. Smith, Sr. records. According to Dr. Billy Wilbanks, *Texas Basketball Champions*, "Jerry Mallett scored 38 points (a 3-A record) in the final . . . and 34 points in the semi-final for a 3-A record 72 points in two games [the 1953 state tournament]." The records of J. C. Smith, Sr. show that on Dec. 5, 1952, South Park defeated Buna, 57–43, in the YMBL finals. Jerry Mallett went on to star in baseball and basketball at Baylor and later played baseball for the Boston Red Sox. Kenneth A. Shouler et al., *Total Basketball: The Ultimate Basketball Encyclopedia* (Wilmington, Del: Sports Media, 2003) expresses the height of a basketball player in terms of the following example: six-foot-seven. The authors have, therefore, chosen to follow this format throughout.

24. Ray Lee, "Buna Tops Buffs 61–49," *Beaumont Enterprise*, Dec. 14, 1952; "Buna Cagers Win 2 From Orangefield," *Beaumont Enterprise*, Dec. 22, 1952; "Buna Topples Nederland," *Beaumont Enterprise*, Dec. 23, 1952; *The Cougar, 1953*, Buna School's Yearbook (no publication data available); "Buna Quintet Wins 71–33," *Beaumont Enterprise*, Jan. 14, 1953; "Buna Victor Over Dayton by 52–39," *Beaumont Enterprise*, Jan. 28, 1953.

25. *The Cougar, 1953*; J. C. Smith, Sr. records; Robbie Muckleroy (robjoy87 @ktc.com), e-mail to Fred B. McKinley, Burleson, Texas, July 16, 2011.

26. Smith, e-mails to McKinley, Feb. 21; Apr. 14, 2011; *The Cougar, 1953*; Boys Basketball, 1952–1953, Conference A (Tentative List), UIL, n.d.

27. "Bears Nose Out Buna To Take League Lead," n.p., n.d.; Smith, e-mails to McKinley, Feb. 21; Apr. 14, 2011.

28. Smith, e-mails to McKinley, Feb. 21; Apr. 14, 2011.

29. Ibid.; "Cedar Bayou Nips Buna 40–37 To Win 20-A Title," n.p., n.d.

30. "Cedar Bayou Nips Buna 40–37 To Win 20-A Title," n.d.; J. C. Smith, Sr. records; Smith, e-mail to McKinley, Apr. 14, 2011; Bobby Ener, telephone interview with Fred B. McKinley, Apr. 27, 2011. In the latter communication, Mr. Ener said that in the second game with Cedar Bayou, some of the Buna players still suffered with side effects of influenza.

31. Smith, e-mail to McKinley, Apr. 14, 2011 (quotation); Breithaupt, e-mails to McKinley, Feb. 20, 21; Apr. 30, 2011; "Cedar Bayou Places Pair on 20-A Stars," *Beaumont Enterprise*, n.d. According to the latter source, Herbert Bishop and Aiden Forsythe of Cedar Bayou, Emery Louvier of Sour Lake, J. C. Smith of Buna, and Rudy Zaruba of Dayton made the *Beaumont Enterprise* 1952–53 All-District 20-A Team. Kimbrough Mosley and Tommy Clark were named to the second team. After Cedar Bayou won their district, they were scheduled to play in the regional tournament in College Station which began on Feb. 27, 1953. During this time, only 32 teams advanced in Conference A. In order to win the state championship, a team had to first win its district, and then follow by winning an additional five games. Due to a revision of the playoff system, the current numbers are much larger. Ninety-six teams now advance, and in order to win the state championship trophy, a team has to win six additional games. The district champions, however, receive a bye, and are required to win five games to take home the state title.

32. The Jimmy Cobb quote is from a personal conversation held with co-author, Fred B. McKinley.

Chapter Five

1. J. C. Smith (jakesmith2836@sbcglobal.net), e-mail to Fred B. McKinley, Burleson, Texas, Apr. 14, 2011 (quotation). Buna twice beat Little Cypress, Sour Lake, and Hull-Daisetta to take the Eastern Zone of District 20.

2. Ibid. (quotation).

3. CPQ, John Rich (quotation).

4. "Buna Cougars-3rd Place State Winners," *The Kirbyville Banner*, Mar. 19, 1954; *The Cougar, 1954*, Buna School's Yearbook (no publication data available); Boys Basketball, 1953–1954, Conference A (Tentative List), UIL, n.d.; "Buna, Orange Win Meet Openers," *Beaumont Enterprise*, n.d.; "Milby Bumps Lamar 54–42 For YMBL Crown," *Beaumont Enterprise*, Dec. 6, 1953; "20 East Texas Quintets Register For 2nd Annual Jasper Cage Tournament," *Beaumont Enterprise*, Jan. 17, 1954; "Buna Grabs Jasper Cage Meet Crown," *Beaumont Enterprise*, Jan. 24, 1954; "Jasper Meet Fetes Teams and Players," *Beaumont Enterprise*, Jan. 25, 1954.

5. "Buna Quint Gains Crown on 82–43 Win," *Beaumont Enterprise*, Feb. 6, 1954; "Buna Raps Bears to Win 20-A Title," *Beaumont Enterprise*, Feb. 17, 1954; Records of J. C. Smith, Sr.; "East Texas Teams Set For [Bi-District] Games," *Beaumont Enterprise*, n.d.; *The Cougar, 1954*; Charles Breithaupt (cbreithaupt@uiltexas.org), e-mail to Fred B. McKinley, Burleson, Texas, Apr. 24, 2011. The latter source provides much-needed background information as to why districts were split into zones. "The purpose was to eliminate as much travel as possible," Dr. Breithaupt said. "In many cases, Buna was

placed in a district with seven other teams. It would appear that they would play each opponent twice, thus a 14-game schedule. However, many years they were divided into two, four team zones. This means that each team played six district games with the winners playing either a two out of three format or a single game for the district title."

6. *The Cougar, 1954*; Records of J. C. Smith, Sr.; "Buna Sweeps Into Regional on 63–41 Win," *Beaumont Enterprise*, Feb. 24, 1954; "East Texas Quints Play In Regionals Saturday," *Beaumont Enterprise*, n.d.; "Buna Edges Troup 46–44 For Regional Title," *Beaumont Enterprise*, Feb. 28, 1954. Other information relative to Buna's opponents and associated scores in both bi-district and regional finals was provided by Dr. Charles Breithaupt, Executive Director, University Interscholastic League, Austin, Texas.

7. *The Cougar, 1954*; "Buna Leaves For Austin Meet Today," *Beaumont Enterprise*, Mar. 3, 1954; "Buna-Sweeny Clash Set Today As State Cage Tourney Opens," *Beaumont Enterprise*, Mar. 4, 1954; Tournament Schedule for Texas High School State Championships, Mar. 4–6, 1954 (UIL, n.d.), n.p.; "Champs from the Past," *The Buna Beacon*, Aug. 14, 2002.

8. Tournament Schedule for Texas High School State Championships, Mar. 4–6, 1954, n.p.; J. C. Smith, telephone interview with Fred B. McKinley, Mar. 15, 2011 (quotation).

9. Dr. Billy Wilbanks, *Texas Basketball Champions* (http://www.texasbasketball champs.com), accessed Mar. 9, 2011.

10. CPQ, Delman Rogers (quotation).

11. Orland Sims, "Sweeny, Sundown 'A' Victors," n.p., n.d.; Bo Byers, "Sweeny Ousts Buna from Tourney 74–72," *Beaumont Enterprise*, Mar. 5, 1954; Smith, e-mail to McKinley, July 25, 2011. According to the latter source, J. C. Smith said, "We [Smith, Ener, Rogers, and Reese] were all about the same height, five-foot-eleven. Tommy [Clark] may have been a couple of inches shorter. Cotton never wanted to exaggerate on the [UIL] program about anything. We were all good jumpers, so we could rebound with those much taller. Cotton also taught us how to block out so that would give us an advantage."

12. Ibid.

13. Verne Boatner, "Sundown to Battle Sweeny for A Crown," n.p., n.d.

14. Smith, e-mail to McKinley, Feb. 19, 2011; Geraldine Hyden, interview with Fred B. McKinley and Larry Gerald, Mar. 24, 2011, Buna, Texas (quotation).

15. Smith, e-mail to McKinley, Feb. 19, 2011; CPQ, Rogers; Sims, "Sweeny, Sundown 'A' Victors," n.p., n.d.; Lionel Reese, telephone interview with Fred B. McKinley, Feb. 20, 2011. In a Feb. 25, 2011, telephone conversation with Fred B. McKinley, Lionel Reese, a senior on Buna's 1953–54 squad, said that much later when he was coaching his second year at Warren, Texas, he had a pretty good team that played a district game against Anahuac, Texas, coached by Russell Boone. When Warren came out on top, Lionel said that he enjoyed the victory ever so much, all the while remembering Buna's two-point loss to Sweeny in the 1954 state semifinals.

16. CPQ, Rogers; Sims, "Sweeny, Sundown 'A' Victors," n.p., n.d.

17. Byers, "Sweeny Ousts Buna from Tourney 74–72," Mar. 5, 1954 (quotation); Dr. Billy Wilbanks, Texas Basketball Champs–Team Narratives (http://www.drbilly-wilbanks.com/basketball/teams.htm), accessed Feb. 10, 2011. According to the latter source, "Carrington scored 66 points in 3 games in 1947 which broke the state record of 61 set in 1935. His 33 points in the first round was a state record for one game and also broke the Gregory Gym record of 32 held by Jack Gray of TX since 1933."

18. Wilbanks, *Texas Basketball Champions*.

19. Ibid. (quotation); "Buna Cougars-3rd Place State Winners," Mar. 19, 1954; Breithaupt, e-mail to McKinley, Mar. 18, 2011; "Buna Takes Third Place in Class A," *Beaumont Enterprise*, n.d.; "Buna Places Two Players on All-State," *Beaumont Enterprise*, Mar. 11, 1954. Buna's J. C. Smith, Jr. played on the South squad of the Texas North vs. South All Star Basketball Game, held at the Dal-Hi Field House, Dallas, TX, on Friday, Aug. 13, 1954. According to a newspaper article (n.p., n.d.), "J. C. Smith, Jr., star basketball player for the Buna Cougars, was a member of the All Star team for the South Zone in a playoff at Dallas Friday. J. C. played four minutes of the game and scored two points. The South Zone won by a score of 62–61. Coach Cotton Robinson accompanied him. Also attending the game were Mr. and Mrs. J. C. Smith and Mrs. Cotton Robinson and daughter [Lynda]."

20. Breithaupt, e-mail to McKinley, Feb. 20, 2011. J. C. Smith, a four-year starter on Cotton Robinson's 1953–54 team, maintains that at one time, film did exist of the game between Buna and Sweeny. Robinson told Smith that when he reviewed Smith's controversial shot, everything was so dark that nothing was visible except the shot itself. Smith said also that "he saw the film several times" and agreed. The film "did show that a Sweeny player guarding me at the free-throw line did hit me," Smith added, "and caused a slight hesitation before I shot." A search of the UIL archives and the library at Buna High School, along with a query of Deon Cummings Thornton [the late Buna Superintendent Bob Cummings's daughter], has not turned up any such film, but of course, this does not dismiss its existence.

21. Julian Galiano, "Robinson Reflects on Top Cage Mark at Buna," n.p., n.d. (quotation).

22. Smith, e-mail to McKinley, Apr. 24, 2011; Records of J. C. Smith, Sr.; *The Cougar, 1954*; Wilbanks, *Texas Basketball Champions*.

23. Boatner, "Sundown to Battle Sweeny for A Crown," n.p., n.d.

Chapter Six

1. During a Mar. 26, 2011, interview with Lynda Robinson Sanford in Buna, Texas, Fred B. McKinley noted these were the only two books in Cotton Robinson's collection.

2. Pat Stanley, interview with Fred B. McKinley and Larry Gerald, Mar. 24, 2011, Buna, Texas (quotation).

3. CPQ, Kimbrough Mosley.

4. Ibid.; CPQ, Delman Rogers.

5. James E. Richardson (jim_richardson@qhr.com), e-mail to Fred B. McKinley, Burleson, Texas, Apr. 18, 2011 (quotation).

6. CPQ, James Burke (quotations).

7. CPQs, Delman Rogers, Pat Stanley, Bill Kirkpatrick, Don Stanley, Melvin Ellison, and Jerry Smith; CPQ, John Rich (quotation). Victor Rogers, Sr. also holds the distinction of playing on the first-ever Texas A&M basketball team of 1913 (source: *Longhorn Yearbook, 1913*, p. 229). The reference to the A&M yearbook name, *Longhorn*, is not a misprint.

8. CPQ, Raymond Cleveland (quotation).

9. CPQ, James Richardson (quotation).

10. Ibid.; CPQs, Cleveland, Kirkpatrick, James Mellard, and J. C. Smith; CPQ, Rogers (quotations).

11. CPQ, Kirkpatrick (quotations).

12. CPQ, Burke (quotation).

13. CPQ, Mellard (quotation).

14. Ibid. (quotation).

15. CPQs, Kirkpatrick, J. C. Smith, and Burke.

16. CPQs, Herbert Ross and Pat Stanley; Delman Rogers, telephone interview with Fred B. McKinley, Mar. 7, 2011 (quotation).

17. CPQ, Richardson (quotation).

18. CPQ, Mellard (quotation).

19. Ibid. (quotation).

20. J. C. Smith (jakesmith2836@sbcglobal.net), e-mail to Fred B. McKinley, Burleson, Texas, Apr. 14, 2011; John Rich, telephone interview with Fred B. McKinley, July 15, 2011 (first quotation); Jerry Lynn Buckner, telephone interview with Fred B. McKinley, Aug. 13, 2011 (another source for first quotation); Robert Hargrove, telephone interview with Fred B. McKinley, Feb. 9, 2011 (second quotation).

21. CPQ, J. C. Smith (quotations).

22. CPQ, Rich (quotation).

23. CPQ, J. C. Smith (first two quotations); CPQ, Mosley (third quotation); Don Stanley, interview with Fred B. McKinley and Larry Gerald, Mar. 24, 2011, Buna, Texas.

24. CPQ, Rich (quotation).

25. CPQ, Mellard.

26. Victor Rogers, telephone interview with Fred B. McKinley, Aug. 5, 2011.

27. Ibid.

28. Ibid. (quotations).

29. CPQ, Charles Simmons (quotation).

30. Ibid. (quotation).

31. Ibid.

32. CPQ, Rogers.

33. Ibid. (quotation).

34. Ibid. (quotation).

35. CPQ, Bob Ener (quotation).

36. Ibid. (quotation).

37. Anthony "Pete" Hillin, telephone interview with Fred B. McKinley, July 29, 2011 (quotation).

38. During a June 30, 2011, telephone interview, Janice Robinson Black, the youngest daughter of Cotton and Monte Sybil Robinson, provided the three attributes that were discussed in this passage.

39. CPQ, Rich (quotation).

40. Ibid. (quotation).

41. Ibid. (quotation); CPQ, Richardson.

42. CPQ, J. C. Smith (quotation).

43. CPQ, Richardson (quotation).

44. Ibid. (quotation).

45. CPQ, Rich (quotation).

46. CPQ, Kirkpatrick (quotation).

47. CPQ, Rogers; CPQ, J. C. Smith (quotation).

48. CPQ, Don Stanley (quotation); Pat Stanley, interview with Fred B. McKinley and Larry Gerald, Mar. 24, 2011, Buna, Texas (quotation).

49. CPQs, J. C. Smith and Tom Clark; CPQ, Mellard (quotation).

Chapter Seven

1. Orland Sims, "Sweeny, Sundown 'A' Victors," n.p., n.d.
2. CPQ, James Mellard.
3. CPQ, James Burke (quotation).
4. CPQ, Mellard.
5. Ibid.; Jerry Lynn Buckner, telephone interview with Fred B. McKinley, Aug. 13, 2011; James Mellard (jsmellard@aol.com), e-mail to Fred B. McKinley, Burleson, Texas, Aug. 13, 2011. Within the latter communication, Mellard said, "Cotton Robinson did understand the principle [of vertical leap], and actually recorded, like growing marks, the vertical jumping abilities of his players in pencil markings on the back wall of Buna's old [log] gym. He also knew that arm length and reach were important to basketball players, and measured that as well." Mellard never played varsity ball in Kirbyville, because he was recovering from an injury received when a cow pony fell on top of him.
6. CPQ, Mellard.
7. Ibid.
8. Ibid. (quotation); Mellard, e-mail to McKinley. Within the latter source, Mellard said, "At first, Robinson . . . was not happy with the maneuver's [fadeaway jump shot] movement away from the basket and thus [the] ability to rebound missed shots. The offset had to be something. It turned out to be accuracy. Soon Robinson conceded that the shot could be extremely effective, for, with the six-foot lane in effect those years, it could be extraordinarily accurate because a post player could commence his posting up not more than three or four feet from the basket. Thus any move away from the basket still left the post player quite close in. It was not long before Mellard, in one-on-one drills, could hit eight and ten or more fadeaway shots in a row. While Robinson was tough and demanding, he did not become Texas's most successful coach because he was inflexible." For more information on James Mellard, his basketball career after Buna High School, and his fadeaway jump shot, the authors recommend Rush Wood's article, which can be accessed at: http://www.beaumontenterprise.com/sports/article/RUSH-WOOD-James-Mellard-has-more-claims-to-fame-701116.php.
9. CPQ, Mellard.
10. Ibid. (quotation).
11. Ibid. (quotation).
12. Ibid.
13. Ibid. James Mellard said, "It was not 'till the summer before my senior year that I bought a car of my own (a 1941 Ford) [for which] I paid $95 with summer money earned bailing hay and cutting silage with one of my uncles."
14. Ibid.
15. Ibid. (quotation).
16. Ibid. (quotation).
17. *The Cougar, 1955*, Buna School's Yearbook (no publication data available).
18. Ibid.
19. "Buna Dumps Smiley Quint Score 74–31," *Beaumont Enterprise*, Jan. 14, 1955.
20. "Buna Bumps Woodville's Eagles 67–37," *Beaumont Enterprise*, Feb. 23, 1955. *The Cougar, 1955*, reflects the score as 69–37, and the *Basketball Pressbook, Tournament Schedule for Texas High School State Championships, Mar. 3–5, 1955* (UIL, n.d.), 20, shows the final score as 60–37. The authors, however, have elected to go with the Feb. 23, *Beaumont Enterprise* article, considered to be the primary source. According to *The Cougar, 1955*,

James Mellard, Jackie Swearingen, and Delman Rogers "were selected on the All District 20-A Team. Donald Hillin received honorable mention."

21. *The Cougar, 1955*; "Buna Wins Regional," *Beaumont Enterprise*, Feb. 27, 1955.

22. Ibid.

23. Ibid.

24. Ibid.

25. "East Texas Quintets Sight Titles," *Beaumont Enterprise*, n.d.

26. Ibid. (quotation); "Buna-Sweeny Clash Set Today As State Cage Tourney Opens," *Beaumont Enterprise*, Mar. 4, 1954. The latter source reflects the fact that Buna was favored to win the Conference-A title in the 1954 state tournament.

27. "East Texas Quintets Sight Titles," *Beaumont Enterprise*, n.d.

28. Dr. Billy Wilbanks, *Texas Basketball Champions* (http://www.texasbasketball champs.com), accessed Mar. 9, 2011; Bob Osius, "Mellard Leads Buna Past Plano," *Beaumont Enterprise*, Mar. 4, 1955; 1955 State Basketball Tournament Bracket, teams and results, UIL records, n.d.; Traxel Stevens, *Basketball Pressbook of the 35th Annual University Interscholastic League Boys' Basketball State Championship Tournament, Austin, Mar. 3, 4, and 5, 1955* (UIL, n.d.), 20-22. In the first source above, Dr. Wilbanks stated that Leon "Pod" Hill and Charlie Lynch, "were both 1st team all-state and later starred at Texas Tech."

29. Stevens, *Basketball Pressbook of the 35th Annual University Interscholastic League Boys' Basketball State Championship Tournament*, 23.

30. "Scoring sheets, quarter by quarter results, Buna vs. Plano, UIL, Mar. 3, 1955; Osius, "Mellard Leads Buna Past Plano," Mar. 4, 1955.

31. Ibid.

32. Ibid.; 1955 State Basketball Tournament Bracket; Stevens, *Basketball Pressbook of the 35th Annual University Interscholastic League Boys' Basketball State Championship Tournament*, 21; Scoring sheets, Buna vs. Plano; Boys Basketball, 1953–1954, Conference A (Tentative List), UIL, n.d. According to the latter source, both Dickinson and Sweeny were in District 26-A.

33. James Mellard (jsmellard@aol.com), e-mail to Fred B. McKinley, Burleson, Texas, May 10, 2011 (quotation).

34. Ibid. (quotation).

35. Ibid. (quotation); CPQ, Delman Rogers.

36. Mellard, e-mail to McKinley (quotation).

37. Scoring sheets, quarter by quarter results, Buna vs. Dickinson, UIL, Mar. 5, 1955; "Buna Nudges Dickinson to Win Class A Crown," *Beaumont Enterprise*, Mar. 6, 1955; Stevens, *Basketball Pressbook of the 35th Annual University Interscholastic League Boys' Basketball State Championship Tournament*, 21.

38. Robert Lynn "Bull" Muckleroy (tee4bull8214@sbcglobal.net), e-mail to Fred B. McKinley, Burleson, Texas, May 1, 2011 (quotation).

39. Scoring sheets, Buna vs. Dickinson; CPQ, James Mellard.

40. Scoring sheets, Buna vs. Dickinson.

41. "Buna Nudges Dickinson to Win Class A Crown," Mar. 6, 1955; CPQ, Delman Rogers.

42. "Buna Nudges Dickinson to Win Class A Crown," Mar. 6, 1955.

43. Ibid.; 1955 Boys Class 1A Final, Buna vs. Dickinson, UIL Basketball Film.

44. "Buna Nudges Dickinson to Win Class A Crown," Mar. 6, 1955; Muckleroy, e-mail to McKinley.

45. "Buna Nudges Dickinson to Win Class A Crown," Mar. 6, 1955; Buna vs.

Dickinson, UIL Basketball Film. According to statistics provided by the UIL, the shooting percentages of both teams were subpar. Buna shot 33.8 percent, and Dickinson 29.3.

46. CPQ, Rogers (quotation).

47. Wilbanks, *Texas Basketball Champions* (quotation). The Cougars' overall record for that year is usually set at 43–4.

48. CPQ, Rogers; CPQ, Mellard; All-Tournament Teams, 35th Annual State Boys Basketball Tourney, 1955. According to the latter source, John Ed Hargroves did not make the All-Tournament Team, but teammates Delman Rogers, James Mellard, and Jackie Swearingen did. Charles Lynch and Leon Hill, both of Sudan; and Wayne Williams of Dickinson completed the roster of six.

Chapter Eight

1. Traxel Stevens, *Basketball Pressbook of the 35th Annual University Interscholastic League Boys' Basketball State Championship Tournament, Austin, Mar. 3, 4, and 5, 1955* (UIL, n.d.), 20; CPQ, James Mellard (quotation). In basketball, the large, weighted medicine ball is used in rehabilitation and strength training. Ranging between 2-25 pounds, its diameter is approximately 14 inches. By comparison, a men's regulation basketball measures 9.39 inches in diameter.

2. CPQ, Mellard (quotation); Don Stanley, interview with Fred B. McKinley and Larry Gerald, Mar. 24, 2011, Buna, Texas. During the latter, Don Stanley said that at the beginning of practice in the tenth grade, Paul Stanley, Pat and Don's father, told them that they were going to have to quit playing basketball. There were too many chores on the farm, he reasoned, and they needed to get home early enough to take care of the cows and horses. Both boys pleaded with their dad and asked him to "just let us try." Fortunately, for all parties, including Buna basketball history, everything worked out, and they remained on the team.

3. Geraldine Hyden, interview with Fred B. McKinley and Larry Gerald, Mar. 24, 2011, Buna, Texas.

4. Dot Smith (dotsmith419@sbcglobal.net), e-mail to Fred B. McKinley, Burleson, Texas, Mar. 21, 2011 (quotation).

5. Traxel Stevens, *Basketball Pressbook of the 36th Annual University Interscholastic League Boys' Basketball State Championship Tournament, Austin, Mar. 1, 2, and 3, 1956* (UIL, n.d.), 20.

6. Ibid.; *The Cougar, 1956*, Buna School's Yearbook (no publication data available); Victor Rogers, telephone interview with Fred B. McKinley, Aug. 5, 2011. The first source shows that Buna lost to Jacksonville by a score of 60–58, while the second source shows 59–57. Relative to the third source, Victor Rogers, the Cougars' student manager who attended the game, said that Buna lost to Jacksonville in overtime.

7. Stevens, *Basketball Pressbook of the 36th Annual University Interscholastic League Boys' Basketball State Championship Tournament*, 20.

8. Ibid.; *The Cougar, 1956*. After reviewing the scores of these individual playoffs, the Joaquin game is the only one that is reported differently. *The Cougar, 1956*, reflects the final as 59–34, while the *Basketball Pressbook of 1956* (p. 20) shows 58–34.

9. Rhea H. Williams, State Athletic Director, letters to Mr. O. E. Greathouse of the Oak Motel, Jan. 24; Feb. 27, 1956; Tournament Schedule for Texas High School State Championships, Austin, Mar. 1–3, 1956 (UIL, n.d.), n.p. Dr. Williams's letter of Feb. 27, 1956, indicated, "They [Buna Cougars] are to pay all bills before leaving, and we in turn will reimburse them on their receipted bills."

10. Stevens, *Basketball Pressbook of the 36th Annual University Interscholastic League Boys' Basketball State Championship Tournament*, 21; Bob Price, "Buna Outlasts Deer Park by 55–39," *Beaumont Enterprise*, Mar. 2, 1956. In an e-mail dated Apr. 22, 2011, Matt Lucas, Director of Communications with the Deer Park (Texas) Independent School District, said, "D. H. 'Cotton' Watkins came to Deer Park in the mid-1950s and was an assistant football coach when the high school team won the state 1-A championship in 1954 and 1955. He was also head basketball coach. He served longest as high school principal and, at the end of his career, spent a short time as superintendent. Cotton [Watkins] was inducted into Sam Houston University's Bearkat Hall of Honor on Nov. 22, 1980." All research points to May 1954, as the date of Cedar Bayou High School's closing.

11. Stevens, *Basketball Pressbook of the 36th Annual University Interscholastic League Boys' Basketball State Championship Tournament*, 21.

12. Ibid.

13. Price, "Buna Outlasts Deer Park by 55–39," Mar. 2, 1956 (quotation); Scoring sheets, quarter by quarter results, Buna vs. Deer Park, UIL, Mar. 1, 1956.

14. Price, "Buna Outlasts Deer Park by 55–39," Mar. 2, 1956 (quotation).

15. Ibid.; Scoring sheets, Buna vs. Deer Park.

16. Price, "Buna Outlasts Deer Park by 55–39," Mar. 2, 1956 (quotation).

17. Scoring sheets, Buna vs. Deer Park; Harold Ratliff, *Texas Boys' Basketball: A History* (Austin: UIL, 1976), 99.

18. Price, "Buna Outlasts Deer Park by 55–39," Mar. 2, 1956 (quotation). It appears that Price miscalculated Buna's average. It should be 42.9, not the 41.9 expressed.

19. Ibid. (quotation); Dr. Billy Wilbanks, *Texas Basketball Champions* (http://www. (texasbasketballchamps.com), accessed Mar. 9, 2011. The latter source indicates that "Buna outshot (42% to 36%) Deer Park . . . and closed the game with a 19–4 run in the 4th quarter."

20. Tournament Schedule for Texas High School State Championships, Mar. 1–3, 1956, n.p.

21. Bob Price, "Buna Wins State A Title," *Beaumont Enterprise*, Mar. 4, 1956; Scoring sheets, quarter by quarter results, Buna vs. Troup, UIL, Mar. 3, 1956.

22. Price, "Buna Wins State A Title," Mar. 4, 1956.

23. Ibid. (quotations); Ratliff, *Texas Boys' Basketball: A History*, 99.

24. Price, "Buna Wins State A Title," Mar. 4, 1956; Wilbanks, *Texas Basketball Champions*. The latter source says, "The Cougars shot 41% (20–49) in the final to 21% (16–52) [should be 31 percent] for Troup and out rebounded the Tigers 32–24."

25. This quote is based on the personal recollections of co-author, Fred B. McKinley.

26. Ibid.

27. Hyden, interview with McKinley and Gerald; Price, "Buna Wins State A Title," Mar. 4, 1956.

28. Stevens, *Basketball Pressbook of the 36th Annual University Interscholastic League Boys' Basketball State Championship Tournament*, 20; *The Cougar, 1956*; Press Release, Mar. 5, 1956, University of Texas, Sports News Service; Price, "Buna Wins State A Title," Mar. 4, 1956. The overall record of the 1955–56 Cougars is usually established at 38–4.

Chapter Nine

1. Boys' Basketball, 1956–57, Conference Designations and Number of Schools, UIL, n.d.

2. George Pharr, "How Does Buna Win? Robinson Gives Philosophy," *The Orange Leader*, Feb. 19, 1961 (quotation).

3. Pat Stanley, interview with Fred B. McKinley and Larry Gerald, Mar. 24, 2011, Buna, Texas.

4. Odis Booker, interview with Fred B. McKinley and Larry Gerald, Mar. 25, 2011, Buna, Texas. The Buna Public Schools were not integrated until the 1965–66 school year.

5. Class (Conference) Champions, 1940–70, Prairie View Interscholastic League Basketball Records (http://www2.uiltexas.org/athletics/archives/basketball/pvil_records.html), accessed Sept. 1, 2011. For more information on the history of and the valuable contributions of the PVIL, the reader may also refer to the University Interscholastic League's website (http://www.uiltexas.org/history/pvil).

6. Roy Moses, *Pressbook of the 37th Annual University Interscholastic League Boys' Basketball State Championship Tournament, Austin, Mar. 7, 8, and 9, 1957* (UIL, n.d.), 26; *The Cougar, 1957*, Buna School's Yearbook (no publication data available).

7. "Buna Massacres Dayton 85–28," *Beaumont Enterprise*, Feb. 6, 1957.

8. "Buna Slips Past Marlin to Take Regional Crown," *Beaumont Enterprise*, Mar. 3, 1957; *The Cougar, 1957*. These two sources have different scores for the Rockdale game. The Mar. 3 *Beaumont Enterprise* article indicates the score as 72–39, while the 1957 Buna Yearbook shows it as 72–31. The authors have elected to go with the primary newspaper source which reflects it as 72–39.

9. Photo of Cotton Robinson, flanked by Pat and Don Stanley, with accompanying article that discusses the 64-game winning streak, n.p., n.d.; "Buna Massacres Dayton 85–28," Feb. 6, 1957. The first source also indicates that over the past four seasons, Buna's record was 158–12.

10. Hunter Schmidt, "Buna Blasts Clear Creek 64–40 to Enter Finals," *Beaumont Enterprise*, Mar. 8, 1957; Scoring sheets, quarter by quarter results, Buna vs. Clear Creek of Webster, UIL, Mar. 7, 1957; George Breazeale, "Seminole, Buna Win," n.p., n.d. George Carlisle created quite a legacy with Clear Creek basketball. He later became the basketball coach at Rice University and finished his career in school administration. He passed away recently after a long bout with Alzheimer's (source: personal knowledge of Dr. Charles Breithaupt).

11. Ibid. According to a Mar. 7, 1957, press release issued by state tournament officials, Carl Mitchell's old record of 35 points, which was set the previous year, had also been in a semifinal game against Clear Creek of Webster.

12. Ibid.

13. Breazeale, "Seminole, Buna Win," n.d.; Moses, *Basketball Pressbook of the 37th Annual University Interscholastic League Boys' Basketball State Championship Tournament*, 28.

14. Hunter Schmidt, "Don Stanley Sets New Record as Buna Hits Seminole for Flag," *Beaumont Enterprise*, Mar. 10, 1957.

15. Breazeale, "Seminole, Buna Win," n.d.

16. Schmidt, "Don Stanley Sets New Record as Buna Hits Seminole for Flag," Mar. 10, 1957.

17. Ibid.; Scoring sheets, quarter by quarter results, Buna vs. Seminole, UIL, Mar. 9, 1957.

18. Don Stanley, interview with Fred B. McKinley and Larry Gerald, Mar. 24, 2011, Buna, Texas (quotation).

19. Ibid.; Scoring sheets, quarter by quarter results, Buna vs. Seminole.

20. Jerry Lynn Buckner, telephone interview with Fred B. McKinley, Aug. 13, 2011 (quotation).

21. Don Stanley interview with McKinley and Gerald; Charles Breithaupt (cbreithaupt@uiltexas.org), e-mail to Fred B. McKinley, Burleson, Texas, Feb. 20, 2011.

22. George Breazeale, "Don Stanley Hits 51 Points as Buna Wins AA Crown," *The American Statesman* [Austin], Mar. 10, 1957 (quotation); Press Release, Mar. 9, UIL Tournament, 1957; Press Release, Mar. 11, 1957, University of Texas, Sports News Service.

23. Ibid.; Breithaupt, e-mail to McKinley, May 23, 2011. According to the latter source, Don Stanley's record of 51 points in a Texas high school basketball championship game still stands; however, on Mar. 6, 1969, Tommy Jones of Crane scored 51 in a semifinal loss to Fort Worth Kirkpatrick. The score was 78–77. In the 1957 title game against Buna, Seminole's Donnie Wilson was held to nine points. His teammates, Leland Caffey and Archie English, scored ten each.

24. "Buna Salutes State Champions," *The Kirbyville Banner*, Mar. 31, 1961; Dr. Billy Wilbanks, *Texas Basketball Champions* (http://www.texasbasketballchamps.com), accessed Mar. 9, 2011; "Buna's All-American," n.p., n.d. In the latter source, the article states: "Don Stanley of Buna, a member of the state Class AA championship Buna Cougars last season, recently was made high school All-American after his East All-Stars defeated the West two games out of three in Hutchinson, Kan. Don, 6'3" and weighing 185 pounds, was a guard on the East five."

25. Schmidt, "Don Stanley Sets New Record as Buna Hits Seminole for Flag," Mar. 10, 1957; Breazeale, "Don Stanley Hits 51 Points as Buna Wins AA Crown," Mar. 10, 1957; Moses, *Basketball Pressbook of the 37th Annual University Interscholastic League Boys' Basketball State Championship Tournament*, 26, 32.

26. Ibid.

Chapter Ten

1. William Withers, telephone interview with Fred B. McKinley, July 24, 2011; Dr. Billy Wilbanks's website (http://www.drbillywilbanks.com/basketball/teams.htm), accessed July 25, 2011. According to the latter source, "Coach Ford King led the Big Sandy Wildcats to the state finals 8 times (1949, 1951, 1952, 1953, 1954, 1955, 1957, 1958) in his 10 years, winning championships in 1952 & 1957. Big Sandy lost finals to Cayuga (3 times), Martin's Mill, Avoca & Blossom. The Wildcats also lost in the finals in 1988 & 2008. The Big Sandy team was made up of Indians from the Alabama and Coushatta Indian reservation plus his son, Ford King, Jr., in 1956–58. The entire reservation supported the team and their road supporters included Indians in traditional attire with their 'papooses on their backs.'" The same season (1957–58) that Big Sandy broke Buna's 66-game winning streak, they went all the way to the state tournament, where they were defeated by Blossom, 67–61, in the Conference-B final.

2. Withers, telephone interview with McKinley (quotation). Mr. Withers went on to explain that the length of the basketball court in those days was eighty-four feet.

3. Ibid.

4. Bill McMurray, "Fabulous Cotton Robinson Career Nearing End at Buna High," *The Buna East Texan*, Feb. 14, 1963; "Tourney Picks Play Openers," n.p., n.d.

5. "Two Favorites Ousted Quickly," n.p., n.d.; "Wide-Open YMBL Meet Rushes Toward Saturday Night Title Tilts," *Beaumont Journal*, Dec. 14, 1957; "Buna Wins YMBL Tourney, *Beaumont Enterprise*, Dec. 15, 1957.

6. "Buna Wins YMBL Tourney," Dec. 15, 1957 (quotation).

7. Ibid. (quotation).

8. *The Cougar, 1958*, Buna School's Yearbook (no publication data available).

9. Ibid.

10. *The Cougar, 1957*, Buna School's Yearbook (no publication data available). This source incorrectly identified the Cypress-Fairbanks's mascot as the Wildcats; however, Rita Willis, Librarian of Cy-Fair High School in Houston pulled their 1958 school yearbook and noted that it should be the Bobcats.

11. "Buna Quint Suffers Last-Second Loss," *Beaumont Enterprise*, Feb. 26, 1958; Roy Moses, *Basketball Pressbook of the 39th Annual University Interscholastic League Boys' Basketball State Championship Tournament, Austin, Mar. 5, 6, and 7, 1959* (UIL, n.d.), 6, 8. Through the 1959 boys' state tournament, Buna still held the record in Conference A for the most state championships (two, 1955–56).

12. Ibid.; Robert Lynn "Bull" Muckleroy (tee4bull8214@sbcglobal.net), e-mail to Fred B. McKinley, Burleson, Texas, May 2, 2011 (quotation).

13. J. C. Smith (jakesmith2836@sbcglobal.net), e-mail to Fred B. McKinley, Burleson, Texas, May 2, 2011; "Prep Survivors Eye Regional Play," *Port Arthur News*, Feb. 26, 1958; "Buna Quint Suffers Last-Second Loss," Feb. 26, 1958; "Rusk, Pineland Advance, Buna Takes Upset," *The Jasper Newsboy*, Feb. 27, 1958.

14. Muckleroy, e-mail to McKinley, May 10, 2011.

15. "3 Champions Are Ousted in Playoffs," *Beaumont Enterprise*, Feb. 26, 1958.

16. These observations are from personal memories of co-author, Fred B. McKinley, who was a student in Buna High School at the time.

17. "Schoolboy Action Opens Thursday," *Port Arthur News*, Mar. 4, 1958; Dr. Billy Wilbanks, "The Unforgettable Tiger Basketball Team of 1960," *The Belton Journal*, Jan. 4, 2001 (quotation).

18. Harold Ratliff, *Texas Boys' Basketball: A History* (Austin: UIL, 1976), 45 (quotation).

19. *The Cougar, 1958* (quotation).

20. "Coach-of-the-Year, 1957–1958," n.p., n.d.

21. Lynda Robinson Sanford (dulcilynda1@hotmail.com), e-mail to Fred B. McKinley, Burleson, Texas, May 2, 2011; Texas Birth Index, 1903–1997, record for Janice Marie Robinson, Ancestry.com, Texas Birth Index, 1903–1997 [database on-line], Provo, UT, USA: Ancestry.com Operations Inc, 2005 (Original data: Texas Birth Index, 1903–1997, Texas: Texas Department of State Health Services, microfiche).

Chapter Eleven

1. Betty Barker and Carolyn Rauwerda, eds., *Buna Remembered: The Times* (Nederland [TX]: Cate Media, 2002), 10. Later on, Cotton Robinson also coached the boys' baseball teams.

2. Ibid., 13, 14 (quotation); Lewine Foster (lewinefoster@sbcglobal.net), e-mail to Fred B. McKinley, Burleson, Texas, Apr. 2, 2011.

3. Barker and Rauwerda, *Buna Remembered: The Times*, 14; Geraldine Hyden, interview with Fred B. McKinley and Larry Gerald, Mar. 24, 2011, Buna, Texas.

4. Ibid. By using the "Double Post System," R. C. Hyden led his girls' teams to four state titles, 1956, 1957, 1960, and 1961. His overall record is 347–38. Cotton Robinson's teams won championships in three of those years, 1956, 1957, and 1961; thus, Buna still holds the record of three, with both the boys' and girls' teams winning basketball championships in the same year.

5. Hyden, interview with McKinley and Gerald (quotation).

6. George Pharr, "How Does Buna Win? Robinson Gives Philosophy," *The Orange Leader*, Feb. 19, 1961 (quotation).

7. CPQ, James Burke (quotation).

8. Roy Moses, *Basketball Pressbook of the 39th Annual University Interscholastic League Boys' Basketball State Championship Tournament, Austin, Mar. 5, 6, and 7, 1959* (UIL, n.d.), 21, 26; James Burke (jburke@cmaaccess.com), e-mail to Fred B. McKinley, Burleson, Texas, July 8, 2011; Dr. Billy Wilbanks, Texas Basketball Champs–Team Narratives (http://www.drbillywilbanks.com/basketball/teams.htm), accessed Feb. 10, 2011. According to the latter source, Huntington repeated as Conference-A state basketball champion in 1960 under Coach Jack Whitton. Led by other coaches, they also won the Conference-B and Conference-A titles in 1962 and 1974, respectively.

9. Moses, *Basketball Pressbook of the 39th Annual University Interscholastic League Boys' Basketball State Championship Tournament*, 26.

10. CPQ, Burke (quotation).

11. Thomas E. Westbrook, telephone interview with Fred B. McKinley, Mar. 5, 2011.

12. Ibid. (quotation).

13. Ibid. (quotation).

14. Ibid.

15. Ibid.

16. CPQ, Burke; "Buna Defeats Kirbyville," *Beaumont Enterprise*, Jan. 21, 1959; "Buna Captures District Title," *Beaumont Enterprise*, Feb. 14, 1959.

17. Moses, *Basketball Pressbook of the 39th Annual University Interscholastic League Boys' Basketball State Championship Tournament*, 26.

18. "Buna, Belton in Region Finals; Bobcats Beaten," *Beaumont Enterprise*, Mar. 1, 1959.

19. Ibid.; Paul Brookshire, "Buna, Huntington Capture Regional Tourney Titles," *The Bryan-College Station Eagle*, Mar. 1, 1959; Perry Smith, "State Cage Meet Starts Today," *Beaumont Enterprise*, Mar. 5, 1959.

20. Brookshire, "Buna, Huntington Capture Regional Tourney Titles," Mar. 1, 1959.

21. Ibid.

22. Moses, *Basketball Pressbook of the 39th Annual University Interscholastic League Boys' Basketball State Championship Tournament*, 26.

23. Ibid.

24. Ibid., 28; Perry Smith, "Buna Slashes Seminole 60–42," *Beaumont Enterprise*, Mar. 6, 1959; Scoring sheets, quarter by quarter results, Buna vs. Seminole, UIL, Mar. 5, 1959.

25. Scoring sheets, Buna vs. Seminole; Dr. Billy Wilbanks, *Texas Basketball Champions* (http://www.texasbasketballchamps.com), accessed Mar. 9, 2011; Press Release, Game No. 8, Mar. 5, UIL Tournament, 1959; Smith, "Buna Slashes Seminole 60–42," Mar. 6, 1959.

26. "Buna Breezes as Pampa, Milby Clash in Feature," *Port Arthur News*, Mar. 6, 1959; Press Release, Game No. 7, Mar. 5, UIL Tournament, 1959; Smith, "Buna Slashes Seminole 60–42," Mar. 6, 1959.

27. Perry Smith, "Cougars Must Stop Thompson," *Beaumont Enterprise*, Mar. 6, 1959.

28. Moses, *Basketball Pressbook of the 39th Annual University Interscholastic League Boys' Basketball State Championship Tournament*, 30. Fred B. McKinley, co-author, was in the stands of Cougar Gym the night that Lewis Qualls made his appearance and he, like the rest in attendance, was awestruck.

29. Smith, "Cougars Must Stop Thompson," Mar. 6, 1959.

30. Moses, *Basketball Pressbook of the 39th Annual University Interscholastic League Boys' Basketball State Championship Tournament*, 25. According to Dr. Billy Wilbanks's website, Coaches with Most State Championships (Boys), Cotton Robinson has seven, followed by Donnie Victorick of Snook with five; and with four each by R. E. Mattingly of Bowie, Clifton McNeely of Pampa, Jack Whitton of Huntington/West Sabine, Bill Ingram of Jacksonville/LaPoynor, Jim Reid of Kerrville/Dumas/Ingram, and James Gamble of Port Arthur Lincoln. This website can be accessed at: http://www.drbilly wilbanks.com/basketball/misc.html#coaches.

31. Perry Smith, "Buna Captures State AA Title," *Beaumont Enterprise*, Mar. 8, 1959; Moses, *Basketball Pressbook of the 39th Annual University Interscholastic League Boys' Basketball State Championship Tournament*, 32.

32. Scoring sheets, quarter by quarter results, Buna vs. Bowie, UIL, Mar. 7, 1959; Scoring sheets, minute by minute, quarter by quarter results, Buna vs. Bowie, UIL, Mar. 7, 1959.

33. Kay Cobb Simmons, telephone interview with Fred B. McKinley, June 14, 2011 (quotation).

34. Scoring sheets, quarter by quarter results, Buna vs. Bowie; Scoring sheets, minute by minute, quarter by quarter results, Buna vs. Bowie; Smith, "Buna Captures State AA Title," Mar. 8, 1959.

35. George Breazeale, "Buna Beats Bowie, Takes Fourth Title," *The American Statesman* [Austin], Mar. 8, 1959 (quotation).

36. Ibid. (quotation).

37. CPQ, Charles Simmons.

38. "Buna High No Longer Best in State, but Memories," *Fort Worth Star-Telegram*, Mar. 10, 1987 (quotation); "'The System' Moves to Snook … and to Dallas," *Texas High School Hoops*, vol. 1, no. 2 (Apr. 1987 Honors Edition), 12 (second source for same quotation).

39. Smith, "Buna Captures State AA Title," Mar. 8, 1959 (quotation); "Westbrook Cobb Named to All-State," *Beaumont Enterprise*, n.d.; Scoring sheets, quarter by quarter results, Buna vs. Bowie; Scoring sheets, minute by minute, quarter by quarter results, Buna vs. Bowie; Press Release, Mar. 9, 1959, University of Texas, Sports News Service.

40. Wilbanks's website, Coaches with Most State Championships (Boys). On Mar. 24, 1959, Buna citizens held a banquet honoring both Cotton Robinson and R. C. Hyden, the girls' coach. Perry Smith, sportswriter for the *Beaumont Enterprise*, spoke during the event. Smiley won the Class AAA championship, and Pampa won the title in Conference AAAA. Clifton McNeely, who coached Pampa, edged Cotton Robinson as 1959 Texas High School Basketball Coach of the Year. Buna finished the 1958–59 season with a 31–15 record (source: *The Cougar, 1959*).

Chapter Twelve

1. James Burke, telephone interview with Fred B. McKinley, Burleson, Texas, May 12, 2011.

2. Tom Beard, "Dusting Em Off," *Beaumont Journal*, Dec. 10, 1959.

3. Ibid. (quotation).

4. "Buna Beats Lamar Redskins for YMBL Title," *Beaumont Enterprise*, Dec. 11, 1960.

5. Beard, "Dusting Em Off," Dec. 10, 1959 (quotations).

6. "Buna Beats Jasper," *Beaumont Enterprise*, Feb. 24, 1960; "Basketball Scores,"*Beaumont Enterprise*, Feb. 24, 1960.

7. "Belton Upsets Cougars," *Beaumont Enterprise*, Feb. 28, 1960; co-author, Fred B. McKinley's personal recollections of the lead-up to the game.

8. "Belton Upsets Cougars," Feb. 28, 1960.

9. Lionel Reese, telephone interview with Fred B. McKinley, May 12, 2011; co-author, Fred B. McKinley was a senior in Buna High School at the time, and he made the bus trip to College Station to see the game. Some of this material is based on his personal recollections.

10. Burke, telephone interview with McKinley; "Belton Upsets Cougars," Feb. 28, 1960.

11. Burke, telephone interview with McKinley (quotation).

12. Ibid.

13. "Casey at the Bat by Ernest Thayer," *Baseball Almanac* (http://www.baseball-almanac.com/poetry/po_case.shtml), accessed May 14, 2011 (quotation); "Belton Upsets Cougars," Feb. 28, 1960.

14. *The Cougar, 1960*, Buna School's Yearbook (no publication data available); Bob Weekley, "Buna Lands Stancil and Ellison on All-District," n.p., n.d.; "Top High School Stars, Texas," *Dell Sports Magazine*, Feb. 1960: 9; Charles Breithaupt (cbreithaupt@uiltexas.org), e-mail to Fred B. McKinley, Burleson, Texas, Apr. 19, 2011. According to the latter source, after Belton defeated Buna, they went on to beat Humble, 56–42, in the Regional III-AA Tournament final, but lost in the state semifinals, and in the consolation game as well.

Chapter Thirteen

1. Roy Moses, *Basketball Pressbook of the 41st Annual University Interscholastic League Boys' Basketball State Championship Tournament, Austin, Mar. 2, 3, and 4, 1961* (UIL, n.d.), 26.

2. "Cougars Nip Purples in 49–46 Contest," *Beaumont Enterprise*, Nov. 27, 1960; "Buna Cougars Squeeze By Yellow Jackets, 44–42," *Beaumont Enterprise*, Dec. 1, 1960.

3. "Buna Drubs French Buff Five 39–31," *Beaumont Enterprise*, Dec. 7, 1960.

4. Hal Reagan, "Lamar, Buna Expected to Collide for YMBL Championship Tonight," *Beaumont Journal*, Dec. 10, 1960.

5. Ibid.

6. "Buna Beats Lamar Redskins for YMBL Title," *Beaumont Enterprise*, Dec. 11, 1960.

7. "Dragons Down Purples, Buna Wins in Tourney," *Beaumont Enterprise*, Dec. 17, 1960; "Buna Wins Division 2, BHS Cops Consolation, *Beaumont Enterprise*, Dec. 18, 1960; Dr. Billy Wilbanks, Texas Basketball Champs–Team Narratives (http://www.dr billywilbanks.com/basketball/teams.htm), accessed Feb. 10, 2011. According to the latter source, the Frankston Indians claimed the Conference-B state championship by beating Hutto, 60–44, in the final.

8. "Buna Downs Port Arthur in 47–37 Go," *Beaumont Enterprise*, Dec. 21, 1960; "Buna Collars Milby 52 to 45," *Beaumont Enterprise*, Dec. 24, 1960; Hal Reagan, "Gift Shots 'Killing' Buna-Saw it Coming," *Beaumont Journal*, n.d. (quotation).

9. Reagan, "Gift Shots 'Killing' Buna-Saw it Coming," n.d. (quotation).

10. Corlis Holt, "Buna Gains 23rd Win," *Port Arthur News*, n.d.; Corlis Holt, "Buna Sinks Jackets, 41–39, in Overtime for News Title," *Port Arthur News*, n.d. (quotation).

11. "Buna Chalks Up No. 26," *Beaumont Enterprise*, Jan. 1, 1961.

12. Robert Hargrove, telephone interview with Fred B. McKinley, Feb. 9, 2011; Charles Breithaupt (cbreithaupt@uiltexas.org), e-mail to Fred B. McKinley, Burleson, Texas, June 27, 2011 (quotation); James Burke (jburke@cmaaccess.com), e-mail to Fred B. McKinley, Burleson, Texas, June 30, 2011; Bill Kirkpatrick (bkirktx@sbcglobal.net), e-mails to Fred B. McKinley, Burleson, Texas, June 30; July 2, 2011; Anthony "Pete" Hillin, telephone interview with Fred B. McKinley, July 29, 2011.

13. Hillin, telephone interview with McKinley.

14. Hargrove, telephone interview with McKinley; "Buna Chalks Up No. 26," Jan. 1, 1961; Moses, *Basketball Pressbook of the 41st Annual University Interscholastic League Boys' Basketball State Championship Tournament*, 26.

15. Hillin, telephone interview with McKinley (quotation). Pete Hillin went on to say that during the entire time he played on Cotton's teams, this was the only occasion he ever saw Coach express any strong verbal reaction after winning a game.

16. Moses, *Basketball Pressbook of the 41st Annual University Interscholastic League Boys' Basketball State Championship Tournament*, 26; "Buna Cougars Beat Buffs for 28th Win," *Beaumont Enterprise*, Jan. 4, 1961; "Buna Cougars Bop Woodville in Loop Fray," *Beaumont Enterprise*, Jan. 14, 1961; George Pharr, "Buna Gives Bears Short Thrill, Then Wins 61–34," *The Orange Leader*, n.d.; "Cougars Post 33rd Triumph," *Beaumont Enterprise*, Jan. 27, 1961; "Cougars Smash Wildcat Quint for 35th Win," *Beaumont Enterprise*, Feb. 4, 1961.

17. "Buna Cougars Move Nearer to Loop Title," *Beaumont Enterprise*, n.d.; George Pharr, "Bears Strike Out as Buna Rolls On," *The Orange Leader*, n.d. (quotation).

18. "Buna Posts 38th Victory Score 80–29," *Beaumont Enterprise*, Feb. 15, 1961.

19. Red Hebert, "Buna Looks Every Inch Itself, Wins 58–35," *Beaumont Enterprise*, n.d. (quotation).

20. "Buna Shoots for State in Regional Meet," n.p., n.d. (quotation).

21. Ibid. (quotation).

22. Ibid.

23. "Buna Cops Regional Title, Eyes State Show," n.p., n.d.

24. Ibid.; "Buna Shoots for State in Regional Meet," (first quotation); "Buna Rolls Into Austin With Regional Victory," n.p., n.d.; Johnny Carter (sallie.carter@yahoo.com), e-mail to Charles Breithaupt, Austin, Texas, Aug. 22, 2011 (second quotation).

25. "41st State Tournament Opens Schedule Today," *The American Statesman* [Austin], Mar. 2, 1961.

26. Ibid. (first quotation); "They've Seen a Demonstration," n.p., n.d. (second quotation).

27. "41st State Tournament Opens Schedule Today," Mar. 2, 1961; "East Texas Quintets Sight Titles," *Beaumont Enterprise*, n.d. (quotation); Moses, *Basketball Pressbook of the 41st Annual University Interscholastic League Boys' Basketball State Championship Tournament*, 25; Tommy Ayres, "Mauriceville Buna Eye Cage Scraps Today," *Beaumont Enterprise*, Mar. 2, 1961. Between 1954 and 1961, New Boston had not made an appearance in the state tournament.

28. Tommy Ayres, "Panthers, Cougars Advance," *Beaumont Enterprise*, Mar. 3, 1961 (quotation).

29. Ibid.; Scoring sheets, quarter by quarter results, Buna vs. New Boston, UIL, Mar. 2, 1961; Harold V. Ratliff, "Mighty Buna Extends Winning Streak to 42," n.p., Mar. 3, 1961.

30. Ayres, "Panthers, Cougars Advance," Mar. 3, 1961 (quotation).

31. Ibid.; Scoring sheets, Buna vs. New Boston.

32. Carlos D. Conde, "Buna Wins, but Robinson Takes It in Stride," *Beaumont Enterprise*, Mar. 4, 1961.

33. Ibid. (quotation).

34. Ibid. (quotation).

35. Moses, *Basketball Pressbook of the 41st Annual University Interscholastic League Boys' Basketball State Championship Tournament*, 24, 27.

36. Wilbanks, Texas Basketball Champs–Team Narratives; "41st State Tournament Opens Schedule Today," Mar. 2, 1961. According to the first source, Linden-Kildare defeated Dimmitt, 52–44, in the 1960 Conference-AA finals. In 1961, the Texas Sportswriters' Association named Junior Coffey as a member of both the Conference AA All-State Basketball and Football Teams.

37. "41st State Tournament Opens Schedule Today," Mar. 2, 1961 (quotation).

38. Tommy Ayres, "Cougars Take Drill Before Final Contest," *Beaumont Enterprise*, Mar. 4, 1961 (quotation).

39. CPQ, James Burke; "Negro Star All-State; Ellison, Too," n.p., n.d.

40. CPQ, Melvin Ellison; CPQ, Billy Kirkpatrick (quotation); James Simmons, telephone interview with Fred B. McKinley, July 28, 2011. In the latter interview, James "Sambo" Simmons said that the night before the Dimmitt game, his brother, Harold Simmons, the ninth grade coach at Buna, came to his room and stated that Cotton wanted to see him. At first, James thought he had done something wrong, but he realized that he had not when Robinson assigned him to guard Junior Coffey the next day. In reality, both James Simmons and Billy Kirkpatrick drew the duty, as well as other members of the Cougar team who collapsed around the big Dimmitt center to limit his scoring.

41. Tommy Ayres, "Buna Smashes Dimmitt for State AA Cage Title," *Beaumont Enterprise*, Mar. 5, 1961; Scoring sheets, minute by minute, quarter by quarter results, Buna vs. Dimmitt, UIL, Mar. 4, 1961; Scoring sheets, quarter by quarter results, Buna vs. Dimmitt, UIL, Mar. 4, 1961.

42. Ibid.

43. Ibid.

44. Ibid.

45. Ibid.

46. Ayres, "Buna Smashes Dimmitt for State AA Cage Title," Mar. 5, 1961 (quotation).

47. Ibid. (quotation).

48. Ibid.; Scoring sheets, minute by minute, quarter by quarter results, Buna vs. Dimmitt, UIL, Mar. 4, 1961; Scoring sheets, quarter by quarter results, Buna vs. Dimmitt, UIL, Mar. 4, 1961; Wilbanks, Texas Basketball Champs–Team Narratives; Tom Beard, "Houston Cops AAAA Title as Tourney Ends," *Waco Tribune-Herald*, Mar. 5, 1961.

49. George Breazeale, "Buna Prevails, 60–36; Closes Year Unbeaten," *The American-Statesman* [Austin], Mar. 5, 1961 (quotation).

50. *Tournament Schedule, Texas High School State Championships, March 2–4, 1961* (UIL, n.d.), n.p.; Wilbanks, Texas Basketball Champs–Team Narratives. During the intermission of the Conference-AAA championship game between Clear Creek (League City) and South San Antonio, the first source stated, "The Conference AA state championship and runner-up teams will assemble in the center of the court to receive team

honors. The ceremony will be broadcast. Presentation will be made by Dr. Lynn McCraw, Professor of Health and Physical Education, and a member of the State Executive Committee." According to the latter source, South San Antonio defeated Clear Creek, 67–54, to win the Conference-AAA championship. Nacogdoches, whom Buna had convincingly beaten earlier in the season, 50–39, lost to South San Antonio in the semifinals by one point, 62–61, but they went on to take the consolation trophy by besting Dumas by one, 46–45.

51. Carter, e-mail to Breithaupt (quotation); Moses, *Basketball Pressbook of the 41st Annual University Interscholastic League Boys' Basketball State Championship Tournament*, 30. According to the latter source, Clear Creek had met Madisonville three times during the regular season. Clear Creek won the first two games, but Madisonville took the third, 54–47.

52. Carter, e-mail to Breithaupt (quotation).

53. Ibid. (quotation).

54. Ibid. (quotation).

55. Tommy Ayres, "3 Area Cage Stars Placed on 'All' Team," *Beaumont Enterprise*, n.d.; "A&M Honor Cage Stars Are Named," n.p., n.d.

Chapter Fourteen

1. James E. Richardson (jim_richardson@qhr.com), e-mail to Fred B. McKinley, Burleson, Texas, June 4, 2011 (quotation); Pat Stom, telephone interview with Fred B. McKinley, Aug. 23, 2011. During this interview, Pat said that when he left school at the end of the tenth grade, he moved to Conroe. Later on, he received a letter from Coach Robinson asking him to return to the team, because he really needed a guard. This was after John Richardson hurt his knee playing football.

2. Max R. Haddick, *Boys' Basketball Pressbook of the 42nd Annual University Interscholastic League State Championship Tournament, Austin, Mar. 1, 2, and 3, 1962* (UIL, n.d.), 26.

3. Hal Reagan, "Twice Over Lightly-Buna Eyeing YMBL Test," *Beaumont Journal*, n.d. (quotation).

4. Ibid. (quotation).

5. Hal Reagan, "Milby, Buna Tower Above Field As YMBL Kicks Off," *Beaumont Journal*, Dec. 8, 1961; Joe Lee Smith, "YMBL Meet Begins Today," *Beaumont Enterprise*, n.d.

6. Jack E. Mooney, "Favored Buna Hits YMBL Semis," *Beaumont Enterprise*, Dec. 9, 1961.

7. Jack E. Mooney, "Buna Captures 5th YMBL Toga," *Beaumont Enterprise*, Dec. 10, 1961.

8. Ibid. (quotation).

9. Haddick, *Boys' Basketball Pressbook of the 42nd Annual University Interscholastic League State Championship Tournament*, 26.

10. Charles Vincent, "Cougars Roll to PA Crown, Dominate All-Star Squad," *Beaumont Journal*, Dec. 30, 1961; Untitled Article, *Beaumont Enterprise*, Dec. 30, 1961.

11. "Greenies Host Buna Tonight," *Beaumont Enterprise*, n.d.

12. CPQ, Raymond Cleveland (quotation).

13. Ibid. (quotation); Haddick, *Boys' Basketball Pressbook of the 42nd Annual University Interscholastic League State Championship Tournament*, 26.

14. "Simmons Shines in Cougar Win," *Beaumont Enterprise*, n.d.; Haddick, *Boys' Basketball Pressbook of the 42nd Annual University Interscholastic League State Championship Tournament*, 26.

15. Fred Cervelli, "Robinson Takes Buna Back Again for Fame," *The Orange Leader*, n.d. (quotation); Haddick, *Boys' Basketball Pressbook of the 42nd Annual University Interscholastic League State Championship Tournament*, 26.

16. "Buna Off and Running For More Cage Prestige," n.p., n.d. (quotation).

17. Ibid. (quotation).

18. Haddick, *Boys' Basketball Pressbook of the 42nd Annual University Interscholastic League State Championship Tournament*, 26; "Buna Annexes Regional Title," *Beaumont Enterprise*, Feb. 25, 1962.

19. "Buna Launches State Bid Tonight," *Beaumont Enterprise*, Mar. 1, 1962 (quotation); Haddick, *Boys' Basketball Pressbook of the 42nd Annual University Interscholastic League State Championship Tournament*, 27; *Tournament Schedule, Texas High School State Championships, Mar. 1–3, 1962* (UIL, n.d.), 27.

20. Orland Sims, "Cougars Win 59–48," *Beaumont Enterprise*, Mar. 2, 1962.

21. Ibid. For more information on the 1961 Donna championship football team, please visit the "Miracle at Donna" website (http://www.miracleatdonnafilm.com/aboutus.html) which provides information about the sports documentary film of the same name. Donna was trying to become the first Texas team to win championships in both football and basketball during the same year.

22. Haddick, *Boys' Basketball Pressbook of the 42nd Annual University Interscholastic League State Championship Tournament*, 25; Orland Sims, "Buna Wins Sixth Crown," *Beaumont Enterprise*, Mar. 4, 1962.

23. Ibid.

24. Sims, "Buna Wins Sixth Crown," Mar. 4, 1962 (quotation).

25. Ibid. (quotation); Scoring sheets, minute by minute, quarter by quarter results, Buna vs. Jacksboro, UIL, Mar. 3, 1962.

26. Sims, "Buna Wins Sixth Crown," Mar. 4, 1962 (quotation).

27. Ibid.; 1962 All-Tourney Teams, UIL records, n.d.; Dr. Billy Wilbanks, Texas Basketball Champs–Team Narratives (http://www.drbillywilbanks.com/basketball/teams.htm), accessed Feb. 10, 2011.

28. Sims, "Buna Wins Sixth Crown," Mar. 4, 1962 (quotation); Harold V. Ratliff, "Buna High Becomes All-Time Champion," *Beaumont Enterprise*, Mar. 5, 1962.

29. "Buna Off and Running For More Cage Prestige," n.p., n.d. (quotation).

30. Richardson, e-mail to McKinley, June 20, 2011.

31. Ibid.

Chapter Fifteen

1. *Boys' Basketball Pressbook of the 43rd Annual University Interscholastic League State Championship Tournament, Austin, Mar. 7, 8, and 9, 1963* (UIL, n.d.), 24.

2. Ibid.

3. *The Cougar, 1963*, Buna School's Yearbook (no publication data available); James E. Richardson (jim_richardson@qhr.com), e-mail to Fred B. McKinley, Burleson, Texas, June 19, 2011; *Pressbook of the 43rd Annual University Interscholastic League State Championship Tournament*, 24; CPQ, James Richardson (quotation).

4. CPQ, Richardson (quotation).

5. Ibid. (quotation).

6. Ibid. (quotation); *Pressbook of the 43rd Annual University Interscholastic League State Championship Tournament*, 24.

7. *Pressbook of the 43rd Annual University Interscholastic League State Championship*

Tournament, 24; Charles Breithaupt (cbreithaupt@uiltexas.org), e-mail to Fred B. McKinley, Burleson, Texas, June 22, 2011. According to the Buna yearbook, *The Cougar, 1960*, football returned to the school in 1959 with the hiring of Coach Fred Godwin. "This year was the first step in gradually building a full scale football program," the annual stated. "The football team of 1959–60 was composed of seventh and eighth graders. The inexperienced boys had to be taught football starting with the very fundamentals of the game. In 1962, the Cougars will enter district competition and add another feather to their athletic cap."

8. *The Buna East Texan*, Feb. 14, 1963 (quotation).

9. CPQ, Richardson (quotation).

10. Dr. Billy Wilbanks, Texas Basketball Champs–Team Narratives (http://www.dr billywilbanks.com/basketball/teams.htm), accessed Feb. 10, 2011.

11. "Buna Socks Gladewater 71–39," *Beaumont Enterprise*, Mar. 8, 1963. According to this source, Canyon beat John Foster Dulles of Missouri City by a score of 75–39.

12. Ibid. (quotation).

13. Ibid. (quotation).

14. Ibid.; Scoring sheets, quarter by quarter results, Buna vs. Gladewater, UIL, Mar. 7, 1963. For Buna, the latter source reflects John Hatch with fourteen points; Jimmy Richardson, thirteen; Pete Hillin had twenty-six; John Meaux, two; John Richardson, three; Doug Barclay, four; Wade Reese, three; Larry Hatch, two; and Herbert Ross, four. Neither Mike Barley nor James Norris scored.

15. "Robinson Isn't Like Most Guys, Displays No Emotion in Tourney—Cougars Never Get Shook," n.p., n.d. (quotation).

16. Ibid. (quotation).

17. Ibid. (quotation).

18. Richardson, e-mail to McKinley, June 20, 2011 (quotation).

19. *Pressbook of the 43rd Annual University Interscholastic League State Championship Tournament*, 22.

20. Richardson, e-mail to McKinley, June 20, 2011 (quotation).

21. *Tournament Schedule for Texas High School State Championships, Mar. 7–9, 1963* (UIL, n.d.), n.p.

22. "Buna Beats Canyon For State Flag, 47–41," *Beaumont Enterprise*, Mar. 10, 1963; Charles Breithaupt (cbreithaupt@uiltexas.org), e-mails to Fred B. McKinley, Burleson, Texas, June 19; July 31, 2011.

23. Breithaupt, e-mails to McKinley, June 19; July 31, 2011.

24. Ibid.

25. Scoring sheets, quarter by quarter results, Buna vs. Canyon, UIL, Mar. 9, 1963; Scoring sheets, minute by minute, quarter by quarter results, Buna vs. Canyon, UIL, Mar. 9, 1963; "Buna Beats Canyon For State Flag, 47–41," Mar. 10, 1963.

26. Ibid.

27. Ibid.

28. Wilbanks, Texas Basketball Champs–Team Narratives.

Chapter Sixteen

1. Larry Dean Jackson, *The Buna Offense*, e-book (no publication data available), n.p. (quotation).

2. Harold Ratliff, *Texas Boys' Basketball: A History* (Austin: UIL, 1976), 43, 44 (quotation).

3. Luke Winn, "Inside Basketball—The Hoops Ideology Report," SI.com (Nov. 17,

2008) (http://sportsillustrated.cnn.com/vault/article/web/COM1148679/2/index.htm), accessed July 7, 2011 (quotations).

4. James Burke, interview with Charles Breithaupt, Austin, Texas, Mar. 10, 2011; James Burke, letter to Fred B. McKinley, Burleson, Texas, Apr. 19, 2011 (quotation).

5. Ibid. (quotations)

6. Cotton Robinson's handwritten notes from personal collection of Charles Breithaupt (quotation).

7. Ibid. (quotation).

8. Ibid. (quotation).

9. Ibid. (quotation).

10. Ibid. (quotation).

11. Ibid. (quotation).

12. Ibid. (quotation).

13. Ibid. (quotation).

14. George Pharr, "How Does Buna Win? Robinson Gives Philosophy," *The Orange Leader*, Feb. 19, 1961.

15. Ibid. (quotation).

16. Ibid. (quotation).

17. Ibid. (quotation).

18. Ibid. (quotation).

19. Ibid. (quotation); Breithaupt, e-mail to McKinley, July 9, 2011. In the latter source, Dr. Breithaupt stated, "Coach did begin using the double post in 1958–59. He used one of the options called Double X because of the unique skills of Jimmy Cobb. This option got the ball to Cobb so he could isolate one-on-one with a defender."

20. Bill McMurray, "Fabulous Cotton Robinson Career Nearing End at Buna High," *The Buna East Texan*, Feb. 14, 1963 (quotation).

21. "Cotton Set Pace for Winning Programs," *Texas High School Hoops*, vol. 1, no. 2 (Apr. 1987 Honors Edition), 12 (quotation).

22. Ibid., 12 (quotation). Actually in the 1960–61 season, the two posts, Glen Stancil and Melvin Ellison, were six-foot-three and six-foot-one, respectively. Coach Robinson may have been thinking about Pete Hillin, one of the posts in the 1962–63 season, who was five-foot-eleven.

23. Ratliff, *Texas Boys' Basketball: A History*, 44 (quotation).

24. Ibid. (quotation).

25. Burke, interview with Breithaupt; Burke, letter to McKinley (quotation).

26. Cotton Robinson, "Half Court Pressure Defense," *Coach & Athlete*, vol. XIX, no. 4 (Dec. 1956), 24 (quotation).

27. Ibid. (quotation).

28. Ibid. (quotation).

29. Ibid., 24-25 (quotation).

30. Ibid., 25-36 (quotation).

31. Burke, interview with Breithaupt; Burke, letter to McKinley (quotation).

32. James E. Richardson (jim_richardson@qhr.com), e-mail to Fred B. McKinley, Burleson, Texas, Aug. 3, 2011 (quotation).

Chapter Seventeen

1. Mike Whitehead, "Robinson: A Coach to Cotton to," *Dallas Morning News*, Dec.

13, 1981; "Robinson of Buna High is Retiring," *Beaumont Enterprise*, Feb. 10, 1963 (quotation). According to an e-mail received from Lynda Robinson Sanford, Christi Fountain, an employee in the office of the Buna ISD Administration, verified that Cotton Robinson worked there continuously from 1948–49 through 1963–64. Payroll records for the school years of 1952–53 and 1960–61 reflect that Robinson earned a gross annual income of $3,600 in the former and $6,477 in the latter. Among Buna ISD's total of approximately thirty-seven employees in both years, he ranked third on the salary chart, following Superintendent Bob Cummings and Principal R. C. Hyden, respectively. The difference, however, between Hyden's and Robinson's salaries in 1952–53 amounted to only $150 per annum. By 1960–61, that had narrowed to just $63. Robinson remained with the school as a teacher of history and civics for one year after retiring as head basketball coach. However, he returned for one more year, 1971–72, to teach social studies in order to increase his benefits from the Teacher Retirement System of Texas. This information is also verified by Buna Junior Historians, *A History of Administration and Faculty, 1911–1989*, Vol. II, n.p. (printed internally at Buna High School, 1988–89). In another e-mail received on June 8, 2011, from Lynda Robinson Sanford, she stated that she found her father's "contract for the 1971–72 school year, and it was $9,220." *A History of Administration and Faculty, 1911–1989*, Vol. II, n.p., also reflects that Cotton Robinson served on the Buna School Board from 1966–67 through 1970–71.

2. Betty Barker and Carolyn Rauwerda, eds., *Buna Remembered: The Times* (Nederland [TX]: Cate Media, 2002), 18.

3. "Buna Coach Presented New Auto," *Beaumont Enterprise*, Apr. 26, 1962 (quotations).

4. Ibid.

5. Ibid. (quotation).

6. "'The System' Moves to Snook … and to Dallas," *Texas High School Hoops*, vol. 1, no. 2 (Apr. 1987 Honors Edition), 12; "Robinson Gets Honored Again," n.p., n.d.; Barker and Rauwerda, *Buna Remembered: The Times*, 69. According to the latter source, the Buna Chamber of Commerce presented Cotton Robinson with a community service award in 1985.

7. Mike Ramsey, "Basketball: It's Changed Since His Days," *The Orange Leader*, Feb. 25, 1973 (quotation).

8. Ibid. (quotation).

9. "A Special Section Honoring M. N. "Cotton" Robinson," *The East Texas News*, May 11, 1983; "Luncheon to Honor Robinson," *The East Texas News*, n.d.; Brochure of the Tenth Annual Installation Banquet, Apr. 7, 1983, Waco Convention Center, Waco, Texas, Texas High School Basketball Hall of Fame.

10. CPQ, Bob Ener (quotations).

11. Brochure of the Tenth Annual Installation Banquet.

12. "'The System' Moves to Snook … and to Dallas," 12 (quotation).

13. Brad McBride, "Coaching Lineage," *Beaumont Enterprise*, n.d.; Buna Junior Historians, *A History of Administration and Faculty, 1911–1989*, vol. II, n.p.; "'The System' Moves to Snook … and to Dallas," 12. In the latter source, Joel Pittman said, "I have run the Buna System for the five years I have been [head coach] at First Baptist Academy, Dallas, and with great success. To learn how to play the System, I visited Coach Robinson twice in Buna, as well as Jimmy Horn in Longview and Don Horn at Snook. Several phone calls to Coach Robinson also helped. These coaches were very generous with their time and help. I can't thank Coach Robinson enough for the im-

pact he has had on my career. He will be missed by Texas high school basketball fans."
The article went on to detail Pittman's five-year record at First Baptist Academy: 45–1
in district, 131–23 overall, district champions 1983–84–85–86–87, and state champions
1985–86–87. It should be noted, however, that the Snook Blue Jays actually accumulated the most wins and state championships of any high school basketball organization
in Texas. However, it took three different coaches to accomplish their amazing record.
In 1961–62, Jimmy Horn had been the ninth grade basketball coach at Buna, and when
he left there, he took the Buna System to Snook. He coached the Blue Jays to three state
championships in Conference B. Then he turned the program over to his brother, Don
Horn, who added two more. Later, Donnie Victorick stepped in and claimed another
five. Altogether, Snook holds the UIL record with ten state championships. For more
information about the Snook program, consult *Texas Boys' Basketball: A History* by
Harold Ratliff (Austin: UIL, 1976) and the website of Dr. Billy Wilbanks, Texas
Basketball Champions. The latter can be accessed at: http://www.texasbasketball
champs.com.

 14. Herbert Muckleroy, telephone interview with Fred B. McKinley, July 28, 2011
(quotation).

 15. Ardie Dixon, telephone interview with Fred B. McKinley, Mar. 15, 2011 (quotation).

 16. Ibid.

 17. Ibid. (quotation).

 18. Ibid.

Chapter Eighteen

 1. Harold Simmons, letter to Fred B. McKinley, Burleson, Texas, May 11, 2011.

 2. Ibid.

 3. James E. Richardson (jim_richardson@qhr.com), e-mail to Fred B. McKinley,
Burleson, Texas, Apr. 18, 2011; Mike Barley, telephone interview with Charles
Breithaupt, May 20, 2011.

 4. Barley, telephone interview with Breithaupt (quotation).

 5. Ibid.; Richardson, e-mail to McKinley.

 6. Richardson, e-mail to McKinley.

 7. Ibid.; Barley, telephone interview with Breithaupt; *The Cougar, 1964*, Buna
School's Yearbook (no publication data available).

 8. Barley, telephone interview with Breithaupt (quotation).

 9. *The Cougar, 1965*, Buna School's Yearbook (no publication data available).

 10. Wade Reese, one of Robinson's Cougars, replaced Harold Simmons as head basketball coach at Buna High School. Although Simmons coached Charles Breithaupt
while he was on the team as a player, Breithaupt later took the lessons that he learned
from Reese, Simmons—and Cotton Robinson to his coaching positions at Beaumont's
Westbrook and Hardin-Jefferson of Sour Lake, where he coached Jamey Harrison.
Harrison played on Breithaupt's 1991 Conference-AAA state championship team, the
Hawks of Hardin-Jefferson High School, and later on, he came to Buna as head basketball coach of the Cougars. A *Beaumont Enterprise* article by Brad McBride, titled
"Coaching Lineage," n.d., chronicles the Robinson succession.

 11. UIL Records, Austin, Texas.

 12. "Buna High No Longer Best in State, but Memories," *Fort Worth Star-Telegram*,
Mar. 10, 1987.

13. Ibid. (quotation).
14. Ibid. (quotation).
15. Simmons, letter to McKinley.

Epilogue

1. Lynda Robinson Sanford (dulcilynda1@hotmail.com), e-mail to Fred B. McKinley, Burleson, Texas, June 13, 2011.

2. Rusty Sowell, telephone interview with Fred B. McKinley, Nov. 28, 2010 (quotation).

3. CPQ, John Rich (quotation).

4. Sanford, e-mail to McKinley, May 12, 2011 (quotation).

5. Ibid. (quotation).

6. CPQ, Ernest Clinton "Radar" Johnson (quotation).

7. CPQ, John A. Hatch (quotation).

8. Marshall Neil Robinson, Certificate of Death, Mar. 16, 1986, State File Number 333, County of Jefferson, State of Texas; "Famous Coach Dies," *The East Texas News*, Mar. 19, 1986. In an e-mail received on May 12, 2011, Lynda Robinson Sanford wrote, "Mama [Monte Sybil Robinson] had a rare autoimmune disease called scleroderma. She was diagnosed about 1992, and during the next four years, it attacked her heart and lungs. She was in the process of being placed on the lung transplant list at Methodist Hospital in Houston when she died in 1996."

9. Carlos D. Conde, "Buna Wins, but Robinson Takes It in Stride," *Beaumont Enterprise*, Mar. 4, 1961 (quotation).

10. CPQ, James Mellard (quotation).

Glossary

While the authors do not intend the following terms to be all inclusive of those used in the sport of basketball, younger readers might find these most helpful. For additional questions about terminology, we recommend the basketball glossary which can be accessed at http://www.firstbasesports.com/basketballglossary.html.

Buna "Five"—The five members of the Buna Cougars' basketball team. Throughout *King Cotton*, the term "Five" is preceded by names of other teams to denote their specific location and/or identification.

Cage—During the early days of basketball, fences were built around the court to keep the ball in play, and they are still used in outdoor venues, such as parks. Thus, basketball gymnasiums are sometimes referred to as *cages*.

Cagers—Members of a basketball team, usually referred to as a group. See *cage* above.

Class—During the time period covered in this work, most newspaper and magazine reporters referred to *conference* designations, such as B, A, AA, AAA, and AAAA, as *classes*. For example, an article might indicate that Buna is the Class-A state champion, which is the same as saying that Buna is the Conference-A state champion. Therefore, the two terms, *conference* and *class*, are used interchangeably.

Crip Shot—The older term for a lay-up.

First Stringers—The starting five members of a basketball team, frequently referred to as *starters* or the *starting lineup*.

Full-Court Press—"An aggressive defensive strategy in which one or two players harass the ball handler in the backcourt while the rest of the team maintains a close man-to-man or zone defense." —Quote courtesy Answers.com.

Half-Court Press—"Defensive pressure applied as soon as the opposing team takes the ball into the frontcourt or across the half-court line." —Quote courtesy SuperGlossary.com.

Medicine Ball—In basketball, the large, weighted medicine ball is used in rehabilitation and strength training. Ranging between 2-25 pounds, its diameter is approximately 14 inches. By comparison, a men's regulation basketball measures 9.39 inches in diameter.

Meet—Same as *tournament*, whether during the regular season, bi-district, regional, or state level competition.

Pivot—Same as *center*. See *post* below.

Post—Refers to a player who occupies the position at *center*. At times, the *center* might also be referred to as a *pivot*. Some teams have two posts; the one nearer the goal is the *low post*, and the one on the outside is the *high post*. The Buna Cougars successfully used this two-post offensive system, which came to be called the "Buna Offense."

Quint—Five members of a basketball team. *Quintets* are, therefore, multiple basketball teams.

Scoring Sheets—Records maintained at the scoring table. These show statistical data by quarter, by player, and includes the number of fouls, field goals, free throws, and points scored.

Sixth Man—Though not a starter, the sixth man is usually the first brought in from the bench and inserted into the lineup of a basketball team.

Sudden Death—If opposing teams were still tied after two overtime periods of three minutes each, they played another period, commonly referred to as *sudden death*. The first team to score two points won the game. *Sudden death* no longer exists in high school basketball. The National Federation changed the ruling in the early 1970s. Currently, teams play four-minute overtimes until someone wins.

Tilt—Refers to any basketball game or competition on any level. Thus, these terms are used interchangeably.

Tourney—Same as *tournament*.

Bibliography

Abbreviations

UIL   University Interscholastic League of Texas, based in Austin
CPQ Completed Player Questionnaire. All completed surveys are either in Fred B. McKinley's or Charles Breithaupt's possession.

Collected Documents and Books

1920 United States Federal Census. Record for William Bryan Robinson. Year: 1920; Census Place: Justice Precinct 1, Leon, Texas; Roll: T625_1828; Page: 11A; Enumeration District: 65; Image: 664. Ancestry.com. 1920 United States Federal Census [database on-line]. Provo, UT, USA: Ancestry.com Operations Inc, 2010. Images reproduced by FamilySearch.

1943 Boys' State Basketball Tourney Records. Conference B, First Round. UIL, n.d. Copies are in authors' possession.

1955 Boys' Basketball-State Tournament Bracket. Teams and results. UIL records, n.d. Copies are in authors' possession.

1955 Boys Class 1A Final, Buna vs. Dickinson, UIL Basketball Film.

1957 Boys Class 2A Final, Buna vs. Seminole, UIL Basketball Film.

1959 Boys Class 2A Final, Buna vs. Bowie, UIL Basketball Film.

1961 Boys Class 2A Final, Buna vs. Dimmitt, UIL Basketball Film.

1962 All-Tourney Teams. UIL records, n.d. Copies are in authors' possession.

1962 Boys Class 2A Final, Buna vs. Jacksboro, UIL Basketball Film.

1963 Boys Class 2A Final, Buna vs. Canyon, UIL Basketball Film.

All-Tournament Teams. 35th Annual State Boys Basketball Tourney, 1955. Copies are in authors' possession.

Barker, Betty, and Carolyn Rauwerda, eds. *Buna Remembered: The Places*. Jasper [TX]: Jasper Printing Company, 1997.

———. *Buna Remembered: The Times*. Nederland [TX]: Cate Media, 2002.

Boys' Basketball. 1947–1948. Conference B (Tentative List). UIL, n.d.

———. 1949–1950. Conference B (Tentative List). UIL, n.d.

———. 1950–1951. Conference B (Official List). UIL, n.d.

———. 1951–1952. Conference A (Official List). UIL, n.d.

———. 1952–1953. Conference A (Official List). UIL, n.d.

———. 1953–1954. Conference A (Tentative List). UIL, n.d.

———. 1956–1957. Conference Designations and Number of Schools. UIL, n.d.

———. District Winners–1948. UIL, n.d.

———. Official List, 1948. UIL, n.d.

Boys' Basketball Pressbook of the 43rd Annual University Interscholastic League State Championship Tournament, Austin, March 7, 8, and 9, 1963. UIL, n.d.

Brochure of the Tenth Annual Installation Banquet, April 7, 1983. Waco Convention Center, Waco, Texas. Texas High School Basketball Hall of Fame.

Buna Area Historical Writers. *Buna Remembered: The People.* Jasper [TX]: Jasper Printing Company, 1999.

Buna Independent School District. Payroll Work Sheets, 1952–53, Period Ending October 31, 1952, and 1960–61, Period Ending July 31, 1961. Copies are in authors' possession.

Carter, Johnny. *The First Season: The True Story of How a Rookie Coach Took a Newly Integrated Team to a Texas State Championship.* Dallas: Brown Books, 2011.

Chalk Talk, 2006. Texas Association of Basketball Coaches. No publication data available.

Completed player questionnaire. Bill "Billy" Kirkpatrick, March 19, 2011.

———. Bobby Guy Ener, June 13, 2011.

———. Charles Simmons, June 27, 2011.

———. Delman L. Rogers, March 7, 2011.

———. Don Stanley, March 19, 2011.

———. Ernest Clinton "Radar" Johnson, April 6, 2011.

———. Herbert Ross, March 25, 2011.

———. James "Jimmy" Burke, March 19, 2011.

———. James Mellard, March 8, 2011.

———. James E. "Jimmy" Richardson, March 20, 2011.

———. Jasper C. "J. C." Smith, Jr., February 18, 2011.

———. Jerry E. Smith, March 13, 2011.

———. John A. Hatch, March 17, 2011.

———. John R. Rich, March 12, 2011.

———. Lionel A. Reese, March 25, 2011.

———. Mark Kimbrough Mosley, April 27, 2011.

———. Melvin Ellison, March 18, 2011.

———. Pat Stanley, March 18, 2011.

———. Raymond Harvey Cleveland, March 7, 2011.

———. Revis Whitmire, April 7, 2011.

———. Robert Lynn "Bull" Muckleroy, April 16, 2011.

———. Tommy G. Clark, April 1, 2011.

Constitution and Rules of The University Interscholastic League. Austin: The University of Texas, July 15, 1948–July 1, 1963.

First Annual Beaumont YMBL (Young Men's Business League) High School Basketball Tournament-1952. Listing of teams. Copies are in authors' possession.

Haddick, Max R. *Basketball Pressbook of the 42nd Annual University Interscholastic League Boys' Basketball State Championship Tournament, Austin, March 1, 2, and 3, 1962.* UIL, n.d.

Hawthorne, Bobby. *University Interscholastic League: An Illustrated History of 100 Years of Service.* Marceline [MO]: Walsworth Publishing, n.d.

Jackson, Larry Dean. *The Buna Offense* (e-book). No publication data available. A copy is in Dr. Charles Breithaupt's possession.

Moses, Roy. *Basketball Pressbook of the 37th Annual University Interscholastic League Boys' Basketball State Championship Tournament, Austin, March 7, 8, and 9, 1957*. UIL, n.d.

———. *Basketball Pressbook of the 39th Annual University Interscholastic League Boys' Basketball State Championship Tournament, Austin, March 5, 6, and 7, 1959*. UIL, n.d.

———. *Basketball Pressbook of the 41st Annual University Interscholastic League Boys' Basketball State Championship Tournament, Austin, March 2, 3, and 4, 1961*. UIL, n.d.

Permanent Record of Marshall N. Robinson [student transcript]. Sam Houston State Teachers College [now Sam Houston State University], Huntsville, Texas. Copies are in authors' possession.

Press Release, Game No. 7, March 5. UIL Tournament, 1959. Copies are in authors' possession.

Press Release, Game No. 8, March 5. UIL Tournament, 1959. Copies are in authors' possession.

Press Release, March 5, 1956. University of Texas, Sports News Service. Copies are in authors' possession.

Press Release, March 9, 1959. University of Texas, Sports News Service. Copies are in authors' possession.

Press Release, March 11, 1957. University of Texas, Sports News Service. Copies are in authors' possession.

Ratliff, Harold. *Texas Boys' Basketball: A History*. Austin: UIL, 1976.

Robinson, Marshall Neil. Birth Certificate Number 456147, filed May 25, 1942. Texas Department of Health, Bureau of Vital Statistics, County of Travis, State of Texas.

———. Certificate of Death, March 16, 1986. State File Number 333. County of Jefferson, State of Texas.

———. Handwritten notes from personal collection of Dr. Charles Breithaupt.

———. Leona High School Class Material. Copies are in authors' possession.

———. Leona High School Diploma, May 26, 1943. Copies are in authors' possession.

———. Notice of Separation from U.S. Naval Service. Number 2277, May 6, 1946. Copies are in authors' possession.

——— and Monte Sybil Smith. Marriage license, issued June 26, 1950, and recorded in volume 5, page 442 of the Marriage Records of Walker County, Texas.

Sam Houston State Teachers College. Commencement Program, August 27, 1948. Copies are in authors' possession.

Schneider, James G. *The Navy V-12 Program: Leadership for a Lifetime* [second edition]. Champaign: Marlow, 1993.

Smith, J. C. (Sr.). Score books. These fragile documents remain in the possession of J. C. Smith, Jr., Buna, Texas.

Scoring sheets. Minute by minute, quarter by quarter results. Buna vs. Bowie, UIL, March 7, 1959. Copies are in authors' possession.

———. Minute by minute, quarter by quarter results. Buna vs. Canyon, UIL, March 9, 1963. Copies are in authors' possession.

———. Minute by minute, quarter by quarter results. Buna vs. Dimmitt, UIL, March 4, 1961. Copies are in authors' possession.

———. Minute by minute, quarter by quarter results. Buna vs. Jacksboro, UIL, March 3, 1962. Copies are in authors' possession.

———. Quarter by quarter results. Buna vs. Bowie, UIL, March 7, 1959. Copies are in authors' possession.

———. Quarter by quarter results. Buna vs. Canyon, UIL, March 9, 1963. Copies are in authors' possession.

————. Quarter by quarter results. Buna vs. Clear Creek of Webster, UIL, March 7, 1957. Copies are in authors' possession.

————. Quarter by quarter results. Buna vs. Deer Park, UIL, March 1, 1956. Copies are in authors' possession.

————. Quarter by quarter results. Buna vs. Dickinson, UIL, March 5, 1955. Copies are in authors' possession.

————. Quarter by quarter results. Buna vs. Dimmitt, UIL, March 4, 1961. Copies are in authors' possession.

————. Quarter by quarter results. Buna vs. Gladewater, UIL, March 7, 1963. Copies are in authors' possession.

————. Quarter by quarter results. Buna vs. New Boston, UIL, March 2, 1961. Copies are in authors' possession.

————. Quarter by quarter results. Buna vs. Plano, UIL, March 3, 1955. Copies are in authors' possession.

————. Quarter by quarter results. Buna vs. Seminole, UIL, March 9, 1957. Copies are in authors' possession.

————. Quarter by quarter results. Buna vs. Seminole, UIL, March 5, 1959. Copies are in authors' possession.

————. Quarter by quarter results. Buna vs. Troup, UIL, March 3, 1956. Copies are in authors' possession.

Social Security Death Index [database on-line], Provo, UT, USA: Ancestry.com Operations Inc, 2010. Original data: Social Security Administration. *Social Security Death Index, Master File*. Social Security Administration.

Stevens, Traxel. *Basketball Pressbook of the 35th Annual University Interscholastic League Boys' Basketball State Championship Tournament, Austin, March 3, 4, and 5, 1955*. UIL, n.d.

————. *Basketball Pressbook of the 36th Annual University Interscholastic League Boys' Basketball State Championship Tournament, Austin, March 1, 2, and 3, 1956*. UIL, n.d.

Texas Almanac and State Industrial Guide, 1943–1944. Dallas: *Dallas Morning News*, 1944.

Texas Almanac and State Industrial Guide, 1947–1948. Dallas: *Dallas Morning News*, 1948.

Texas Birth Index, 1903–1997. Record for Janice Marie Robinson. Ancestry.com. Texas Birth Index, 1903–1997 [database on-line]. Provo, UT, USA: Ancestry.com Operations Inc, 2005. Original data: Texas Birth Index, 1903–1997. Texas: Texas Department of State Health Services. Microfiche.

————. Record for Lynda Nell Robinson. Ancestry.com. *Texas Birth Index, 1903–1997* [database on-line]. Provo, UT, USA: Ancestry.com Operations Inc, 2005. Original data: *Texas Birth Index, 1903–1997*. Texas: Texas Department of State Health Services. Microfiche.

Texas Death Index, 1903–2000 [database on-line], Provo, UT, USA: Ancestry.com Operations, Inc, 2006. Original data: Texas Department of Health. *Texas Death Indexes, 1903–2000*. Austin, TX, USA: Texas Department of Health, State Vital Statistics Unit.

The Cougar, 1950, 1951, 1952, 1953, 1954, 1955, 1956, 1957, 1958, 1959, 1960, 1961, 1962, 1963, 1964, and 1965. Buna School's Yearbook. No publication data available.

Tournament Schedule. Texas High School State Championships, March 4–6, 1943. UIL, n.d.

————. *Texas High School State Championships, March 4–6, 1954*. UIL, n.d.

————. *Texas High School State Championships, March 3–5, 1955*. UIL, n.d.

————. *Texas High School State Championships, March 1–3, 1956*. UIL, n.d.

————. *Texas High School State Championships, March 7–9, 1957*. UIL, n.d.

————. *Texas High School State Championships, March 5–7, 1959*. UIL, n.d.

————. *Texas High School State Championships, March 2–4, 1961.* UIL, n.d.
————. *Texas High School State Championships, March 1–3, 1962.* UIL, n.d.
————. *Texas High School State Championships, March 7–9, 1963.* UIL, n.d.
————. *Texas High School State Championships, March 10–12, 2011.* UIL, n.d.

Magazine and Newspaper Articles

"3 Champions Are Ousted in Playoffs." *Beaumont Enterprise*, February 26, 1958.
"20 East Texas Quintets Register For 2nd Annual Jasper Cage Tournament." *Beaumont Enterprise*, January 17, 1954.
"41st State Tournament Opens Schedule Today." N.p., March 2, 1961. Copies are in authors' possession.
"A&M Honor Cage Stars Are Named." N.p., n.d. Copies are in authors' possession.
"A Special Section Honoring M. N. "Cotton" Robinson." *The East Texas News*, May 11, 1983.
Arendale, Blackie. "Buna, Royal Purples Score Wins." *Beaumont Enterprise*, December 4, 1952.
Ayres, Tommy. "3 Area Cage Stars Placed on 'All' Team." *Beaumont Enterprise*, n.d. Copies are in authors' possession.
————. "Buna Smashes Dimmitt for State AA Cage Title." *Beaumont Enterprise*, March 5, 1961.
————. "Cougars Take Drill Before Final Contest." *Beaumont Enterprise*, March 4, 1961.
————. "Mauriceville Buna Eye Cage Scraps Today." *Beaumont Enterprise*, March 2, 1961.
————. "Panthers, Cougars Advance." *Beaumont Enterprise*, March 3, 1961.
"Basketball Scores." *Beaumont Enterprise*, February 27, 1952.
————. *Beaumont Enterprise*, March 2, 1952.
————. *Beaumont Enterprise*, February 24, 1960.
Beard, Tom. "Dusting Em Off." *Beaumont Journal*, December 10, 1959.
————. "Houston Cops AAAA Title as Tourney Ends." *Waco Tribune-Herald*, March 5, 1961.
"Bears Nose Out Buna To Take League Lead." N.p., n.d. Copies are in authors' possession.
"Belton Upsets Cougars." *Beaumont Enterprise*, February 28, 1960.
Boatner, Verne. "Sundown to Battle Sweeny for A Crown." N.p., n.d. Copies are in authors' possession.
"Boys in 1949." Group photograph and listing of Cotton Robinson's 1949 Boys' Basketball Team. *The Buna Beacon*, January 10, 1973.
Breazeale, George. "Buna Beats Bowie, Takes Fourth Title." *The American Statesman* [Austin], March 8, 1959.
————. "Buna Prevails, 60–36; Closes Year Unbeaten." *The American Statesman* [Austin], March 5, 1961.
————. "Don Stanley Hits 51 Points as Buna Wins AA Crown." *The American Statesman* [Austin], March 10, 1957.
————. "Seminole, Buna Win." N.p., n.d. Copies are in authors' possession.
Brookshire, Paul. "Buna, Huntington Capture Regional Tourney Titles." *The Bryan-College Station Eagle*, March 1, 1959.
"Buna Annexes Regional Title." *Beaumont Enterprise*, February 25, 1962.
"Buna Beats Canyon For State Flag, 47–41." *Beaumont Enterprise*, March 10, 1963.
"Buna Beats Jasper." *Beaumont Enterprise*, February 24, 1960.

"Buna Beats Lamar Redskins for YMBL Title." *Beaumont Enterprise*, December 11, 1960.

"Buna, Belton in Region Finals; Bobcats Beaten." *Beaumont Enterprise,* March 1, 1959.

"Buna Breezes as Pampa, Milby Clash in Feature." *Port Arthur News*, March 6, 1959.

"Buna Bumps Woodville's Eagles 67–37." *Beaumont Enterprise*, February 23, 1955.

"Buna Cagers Win 2 From Orangefield." *Beaumont Enterprise*, December 22, 1952.

"Buna Captures District Title." *Beaumont Enterprise*, February 14, 1959.

"Buna Chalks Up No. 26." *Beaumont Enterprise*, January 1, 1961.

"Buna Coach Presented New Auto." *Beaumont Enterprise*, April 26, 1962.

"Buna Collars Milby 52 to 45." *Beaumont Enterprise*, December 24, 1960.

"Buna Cops Regional Title, Eyes State Show." N.p., n.d. Copies are in authors' possession.

"Buna Cougars—3rd Place State Winners." *The Kirbyville Banner*, March 19, 1954.

"Buna Cougars Beat Buffs for 28th Win." *Beaumont Enterprise, January 4, 1961.*

"Buna Cougars Bop Woodville in Loop Fray." *Beaumont Enterprise,* January 14, 1961.

"Buna Cougars Move Nearer to Loop Title." *Beaumont Enterprise,* n.d. Copies are in authors' possession.

"Buna Cougars Squeeze By Yellow Jackets, 44–42." *Beaumont Enterprise,* December 1, 1960.

"Buna Defeats Kirbyville." *Beaumont Enterprise,* January 21, 1959.

"Buna Downs Port Arthur in 47–37 Go." *Beaumont Enterprise,* December 21, 1960.

"Buna Drubs French Buff Five 39–31." *Beaumont Enterprise,* December 7, 1960.

"Buna Dumps Smiley Quint Score 74–31." *Beaumont Enterprise*, January 14, 1955.

"Buna Edges Troup 46–44 For Regional Title." *Beaumont Enterprise*, February 28, 1954.

"Buna Grabs Jasper Cage Meet Crown." *Beaumont Enterprise*, January 24, 1954.

"Buna High No Longer Best in State, but Memories." *Fort Worth Star-Telegram*, March 10, 1987.

"Buna Launches State Bid Tonight." *Beaumont Enterprise*, March 1, 1962.

"Buna Leaves For Austin Meet Today." *Beaumont Enterprise*, March 3, 1954.

"Buna Massacres Dayton 85–28." *Beaumont Enterprise*, February 6, 1957.

"Buna Nudges Dickinson to Win Class A Crown." *Beaumont Enterprise*, March 6, 1955.

"Buna Off and Running For More Cage Prestige." N.p., n.d. Copies are in authors' possession.

"Buna, Orange Win Meet Openers." *Beaumont Enterprise*, n.d. Copies are in authors' possession.

"Buna Places Two Players on All-State." *Beaumont Enterprise*, March 11, 1954.

"Buna Posts 38th Victory Score 80–29." *Beaumont Enterprise*, February 15, 1961.

"Buna Quint Gains Crown on 82–43 Win." *Beaumont Enterprise*, February 6, 1954.

"Buna Quint Suffers Last-Second Loss." *Beaumont Enterprise*, February 26, 1958.

"Buna Quintet Wins 71–33." *Beaumont Enterprise*, January 14, 1953.

"Buna Raps Bears to Win 20-A Title." *Beaumont Enterprise*, February 17, 1954.

"Buna Rolls Into Austin With Regional Victory." N.p., n.d. Copies are in authors' possession.

"Buna Salutes State Champions." *The Kirbyville Banner*, March 31, 1961.

"Buna Shoots for State in Regional Meet." N.p., n.d. Copies are in authors' possession.

"Buna Slips Past Marlin to Take Regional Crown." *Beaumont Enterprise*, March 3, 1957.

"Buna Socks Gladewater 71–39." *Beaumont Enterprise*, March 8, 1963.

"Buna-Sweeny Clash Set Today As State Cage Tourney Opens." *Beaumont Enterprise*, March 4, 1954.

"Buna Sweeps Into Regional on 63–41 Win." *Beaumont Enterprise*, February 24, 1954.

"Buna Takes District: Plays Here on Friday." *The Buna East Texan*, February 14, 1963.

"Buna Takes Third Place in Class A." *Beaumont Enterprise*, n.d. Copies are in authors' possession.

"Buna Teams are Honored at Banquet." *Beaumont Enterprise*, March 25, 1959.

"Buna Victor Over Dayton by 52–39. *Beaumont Enterprise*, January 28, 1953.

"Buna Wins Division 2, BHS Cops Consolation." *Beaumont Enterprise*, December 18, 1960.

"Buna Wins Regional." *Beaumont Enterprise*, February 27, 1955.

"Buna Wins YMBL Tourney. *Beaumont Enterprise*, December 15, 1957.

"Buna's All-American." N.p., n.d. Copies are in authors' possession.

Byers, Bo. "Sweeny Ousts Buna from Tourney 74–72." *Beaumont Enterprise*, March 5, 1954.

"Cage Scores." *Beaumont Enterprise*, March 1, 1952.

"Cedar Bayou Nips Buna 40–37 To Win 20-A Title." N.p., n.d. Copies are in authors' possession.

"Cedar Bayou Places Pair on 20-A Stars." *Beaumont Enterprise*, n.d. Copies are in authors' possession.

Cervelli, Fred. "Fabulous Records of Robinson, Hyden Make Buna Basketball Paradise." *The Orange Leader*, February 19, 1961.

———. "Robinson Takes Buna Back Again for Fame." *The Orange Leader*, n.d. Copies are in authors' possession.

"Champion Cagers Advertise Two Winners: Hargrove Station and Humble Products." *Humble Sales Lubricator*, January 27, 1949.

"Champs from the Past." *The Buna Beacon*, August 14, 2002.

"Coach-of-the-Year, 1957–1958." N.p., n.d. Copies are in authors' possession.

Conde, Carlos D. "Buna Wins, but Robinson Takes It in Stride." *Beaumont Enterprise*, March 4, 1961.

"Cotton Set Pace for Winning Programs." *Texas High School Hoops*, vol. 1, no. 2 (April 1987 Honors Edition).

"Cougars Nip Purples in 49–46 Contest." *Beaumont Enterprise*, November 27, 1960.

"Cougars Post 33rd Triumph." *Beaumont Enterprise*, January 27, 1961.

"Cougars Smash Wildcat Quint for 35th Win." *Beaumont Enterprise*, February 4, 1961.

"District 62-B Champions." *Beaumont Enterprise*, n.d. Copies are in authors' possession.

"District Basketball Tournament To Be Held Here Saturday." *Leon County News*, January 14, 1943.

"Dragons Down Purples, Buna Wins in Tourney." *Beaumont Enterprise*, December 17, 1960.

"East Texas Quintets Sight Titles." *Beaumont Enterprise*, n.d. Copies are in authors' possession.

"East Texas Quints Play In Regionals Saturday." *Beaumont Enterprise*, n.d. Copies are in authors' possession.

"East Texas Teams Set For [Bi-District] Games." *Beaumont Enterprise*, n.d. Copies are in authors' possession.

"Famous Coach Dies." *The East Texas News*, March 19, 1986.

"French and Buna Favored in State Cage Tourney." *Beaumont Enterprise*, n.d. Copies are in authors' possession.

Galiano, Julian. "Robinson Reflects on Top Cage Mark at Buna." N.p., n.d. Copies are in authors' possession.

"Greenies Host Buna Tonight." *Beaumont Enterprise*, n.d. Copies are in authors' possession.

Hebert, Red. "6 East Texas Champs Seek Bi-District Wins in Area Cage Action." *Beaumont Enterprise*, February 23, 1960.

———. "Buna Looks Every Inch Itself, Wins 58–35." *Beaumont Enterprise*, n.d. Copies are in authors' possession.

Hill, Kirk. "Smiley Wins Title, 58–42, Pampa, Henrietta, Buna, Huntington, Champions." *Houston Post*, March 8, 1959.

Holt, Corlis. "Buna Gains 23rd Win." *Port Arthur News*, n.d. Copies are in authors' possession.

———. "Buna Sinks Jackets, 41–39, in Overtime for News Title." *Port Arthur News*, n.d. Copies are in authors' possession.

"Jasper Meet Fetes Teams and Players." *Beaumont Enterprise*, January 25, 1954.

"Just a Memory." *The Buna Beacon*, January 10, 1973.

Lee, Ray. "Buna Tops Buffs 61–49." *Beaumont Enterprise*, December 14, 1952.

"Leona Basketball Star Enlists in U.S. Navy." *Leon County News*, March 18, 1943.

"Leona Lions Will Play In Regional Tourney Saturday." *Leon County News*, February 25, 1943.

"Leona Lions Win Regional Basketball Championship." *Leon County News*, March 4, 1943.

"Leona Wins First District Tourney." *Leon County News*, January 28, 1943.

"Luncheon to Honor Robinson." *The East Texas News*, n.d. Copies are in authors' possession.

McBride, Brad. "Coaching Lineage." *Beaumont Enterprise*, n.d. Copies are in authors' possession.

McMurray, Bill. "Fabulous Cotton Robinson Career Nearing End at Buna High." *The Buna East Texan*, February 14, 1963.

"Milby Bumps Lamar 54–42 For YMBL Crown." *Beaumont Enterprise*, December 6, 1953.

Mooney, Jack E. "Buna Captures 5th YMBL Toga." *Beaumont Enterprise*, December 10, 1961.

———. "Favored Buna Hits YMBL Semis." *Beaumont Enterprise*, December 9, 1961.

"Negro Star All-State; Ellison, Too." N.p., n.d. Copies are in authors' possession.

Osius, Bob. "Mellard Leads Buna Past Plano." *Beaumont Enterprise*, March 4, 1955.

Pharr, George. "Bears Strike Out as Buna Rolls On." *The Orange Leader*, n.d. Copies are in authors' possession.

———. "Buna Gives Bears Short Thrill, Then Wins 61–34." *The Orange Leader*, n.d. Copies are in authors' possession.

———. "How Does Buna Win? Robinson Gives Philosophy." *The Orange Leader*, February 19, 1961.

Photo of Cotton Robinson, flanked by Pat and Don Stanley, with accompanying article that discusses the 64-game winning streak. N.p., n.d. Copies are in authors' possession.

"Prep Survivors Eye Regional Play." *Port Arthur News*, February 26, 1958.

Price, Bob. "Buna Outlasts Deer Park by 55–39." *Beaumont Enterprise*, March 2, 1956.

———. "Buna Wins State A Title." *Beaumont Enterprise*, March 4, 1956.

Ramsey, Mike. "Basketball: It's Changed Since His Days." *The Orange Leader*, February 25, 1973.

Ratliff, Harold V. "Buna High Becomes All-Time Champion." *Beaumont Enterprise*, March 5, 1962.

———. "Mighty Buna Extends Winning Streak to 42." N.p., March 3, 1961. Copies are in authors' possession.

Reagan, Hal. "Gift Shots 'Killing' Buna-Saw it Coming." *Beaumont Journal*, n.d. Copies are in authors' possession.

———. "Lamar, Buna Expected to Collide for YMBL Championship Tonight." *Beaumont Journal*, December 10, 1960.

———. "Milby, Buna Tower Above Field As YMBL Kicks Off." *Beaumont Journal*, December 8, 1961.

———. "Twice Over Lightly—Buna Eyeing YMBL Test." *Beaumont Journal*, n.d. Copies are in authors' possession.

"Regional Basketball Champions." *Leon County News*, March 11, 1943.

Robinson, Cotton. "Half Court Pressure Defense." *Coach & Athlete*, vol. XIX, no. 4 (Dec. 1956).

"Robinson Gets Honored Again." N.p., n.d. Copies are in authors' possession.

"Robinson Isn't Like Most Guys, Displays No Emotion in Tourney-Cougars Never Get Shook." N.p., n.d. Copies are in authors' possession.

"Robinson of Buna High is Retiring." *Beaumont Enterprise*, February 10, 1963.

"Rusk, Pineland Advance, Buna Takes Upset." *The Jasper Newsboy*, February 27, 1958.

"SHS Cagers Edge SFA Jacks, 62–57." *The Houstonian* [Sam Houston State Teachers College], February 7, 1947.

Schmidt, Hunter. "Buna Blasts Clear Creek 64–40 to Enter Finals." *Beaumont Enterprise*, March 8, 1957.

———. "Don Stanley Sets New Record as Buna Hits Seminole for Flag." *Beaumont Enterprise*, March 10, 1957.

"Schoolboy Action Opens Thursday." *Port Arthur News*. March 4, 1958.

"Second District Basketball Meet Here Saturday." *Leon County News*, February 4, 1943.

"Simmons Shines in Cougar Win." *Beaumont Enterprise*, n.d. Copies are in authors' possession.

Sims, Orland. "Buna Wins Sixth Crown." *Beaumont Enterprise*, March 4, 1962.

———. "Cougars Win 59–48." *Beaumont Enterprise*, March 2, 1962.

———. "Sweeny, Sundown 'A' Victors." N.p., n.d. Copies are in authors' possession.

Smith, Joe Lee. "YMBL Meet Begins Today." *Beaumont Enterprise*, n.d. Copies are in authors' possession.

Smith, Perry. "Buna Captures State AA Title." *Beaumont Enterprise*, March 8, 1959.

———. "Buna Slashes Seminole 60–42." *Beaumont Enterprise*, March 6, 1959.

———. "Cougar Rally in 4th Beats Bowie 53–48." *Beaumont Enterprise*, March 8, 1959.

———. "Cougars Must Stop Thompson." *Beaumont Enterprise*, March 6, 1959.

———. "State Cage Meet Starts Today." *Beaumont Enterprise*, March 5, 1959.

"'The System' Moves to Snook … and to Dallas." *Texas High School Hoops*, vol. 1, no. 2 (April 1987 Honors Edition).

"They've Seen a Demonstration." N.p., n.d. Copies are in authors' possession.

"Top High School Stars, Texas." *Dell Sports Magazine*, February 1960.

"Tourney Picks Play Openers." N.p., n.d. Copies are in authors' possession.

"Town Supper to Fete Cotton." *The Buna East Texan*, April 25, 1963.

"Two Favorites Ousted Quickly." N.p., n.d. Copies are in authors' possession.

Untitled Article. *Beaumont Enterprise,* December 30, 1961. Copies are in authors' possession.

Vincent, Charles. "Cougars Roll to PA Crown, Dominate All-Star Squad." *Beaumont Journal*, December 30, 1961.

Weekley, Bob. "Buna Lands Stancil and Ellison on All-District." N.p., n.d. Copies are in authors' possession.

"Westbrook Cobb Named to All-State." *Beaumont Enterprise*, n.d. Copies are in authors' possession.

Whitehead, Mike. "Robinson: A Coach to Cotton to." *Dallas Morning News*, December 13, 1981.

"Wide-Open YMBL Meet Rushes toward Saturday Night Title Tilts." *Beaumont Journal*, December 14, 1957.

Wilbanks, Dr. Billy. "The Unforgettable Tiger Basketball Team of 1960." *The Belton Journal*, January 4, 2001.

"Winners Enter State Cage Meet." *Beaumont Enterprise*, February 25, 1952.

Letters, E-Mails, and Memoranda

Barbara Kievit-Mason (lib_bak@shsu.edu), e-mails to Fred B. McKinley, Burleson, Texas, February 18; March 30, 2011.

Bill Kirkpatrick (bkirktx@sbcglobal.net), e-mails to Fred B. McKinley, Burleson, Texas, June 30; July 2, 2011.

Cade Sirmans (ctsirmans1126@gmail.com), e-mail to Fred B. McKinley, Burleson, Texas, February 15, 2011.

Charles Breithaupt (cbreithaupt@uiltexas.org), e-mails to Fred B. McKinley, Burleson, Texas, February 14, 20, 21; March 18; April 18, 19, 24; May 23; June 19, 22, 27; July 9, 31, 2011.

Cindy D. Menard (cdm2796@louisiana.edu), e-mails to Fred B. McKinley, Burleson, Texas, February 14, 17, 2011.

Don Muckleroy (dcmuckleroy@bunaisd.net), e-mail to Fred B. McKinley, Burleson, Texas, June 9, 2011.

Dot Smith (dotsmith419@sbcglobal.net), e-mail to Fred B. McKinley, Burleson, Texas, March 21, 2011.

Harold Simmons, letter to Fred B. McKinley, Burleson, Texas, May 11, 2011.

I. Bruce Turner (bturner@louisiana.edu), e-mails to Fred B. McKinley, Burleson, Texas, February 22; March 2, 3, 2011.

J. C. Smith (jakesmith2836@sbcglobal.net), e-mails to Fred B. McKinley, Burleson, Texas, February 19, 20, 21; April 14, 24; May 2; July 25, 2011.

James Burke, letter to Fred B. McKinley, Burleson, Texas, April 19, 2011.

_____ (jburke@cmaaccess.com), e-mails to Fred B. McKinley, Burleson, Texas, June 30; July 8, 2011.

James Mellard (jsmellard@aol.com), e-mails to Fred B. McKinley, Burleson, Texas, May 10; August 13, 2011.

James E. Richardson (jim_richardson@qhr.com), e-mails to Fred B. McKinley, Burleson, Texas, April 18; June 19, 20; August 3, 2011.

Johnny Carter (sallie.carter@yahoo.com), e-mail to Charles Breithaupt, Austin, Texas, August 22, 2011.

Lewine Foster (lewinefoster@sbcglobal.net), e-mail to Fred B. McKinley, Burleson, Texas, April 2, 2011.

Lynda Robinson Sanford (dulcilynda1@hotmail.com), e-mails to Fred B. McKinley, Burleson, Texas, February 11, 13, 15; April 4, 5, 11; May 1, 2, 4, 12; June 8, 13, 2011.

Lyndall Robinson Hale, letter to Lynda and Butch Sanford, Buna, Texas, February 19, 2010.

Matt Lucas, Director of Communications, Deer Park (Texas) Independent School District (mlucas@dpisd.org), e-mail to Fred B. McKinley, Burleson, Texas, April 22, 2011.

Phil Rogers, (progersland@aol.com), e-mail to Fred B. McKinley, Burleson, Texas, March 9, 2011.

Rhea H. Williams, State Athletic Director, letters to Mr. O. E. Greathouse of the Oak Motel, January 24; February 27, 1956.

Robbie Muckleroy (robjoy87@ktc.com), e-mail to Fred B. McKinley, Burleson, Texas, July 16, 2011.

Robbie Thomas (rthomas@centerville.k12.tx.us), e-mail to Fred B. McKinley, Burleson, Texas, February 14, 2011.

Robert Lynn "Bull" Muckleroy (tee4bull8214@sbcglobal.net), e-mails to Fred B. McKinley, Burleson, Texas, May 1, 2, 10, 2011.

Sandra Uselton (sku002@shsu.edu), e-mail to Fred B. McKinley, Burleson, Texas, February 15, 2011.

Interviews

Barclay, Doug. Telephone interview with Fred B. McKinley, August 22, 2011.

Barley, Mike. Telephone interview with Charles Breithaupt, May 20, 2011.

Battise, Edwin. Telephone interview with Fred B. McKinley, July 28, 2011.

Black, Janice Robinson. Telephone interview with Fred B. McKinley, June 30, 2011.

Booker, Odis. Interview with Fred B. McKinley and Larry Gerald, March 25, 2011, Buna, Texas.

Buckner, Jerry Lynn. Telephone interview with Fred B. McKinley, August 13, 2011.

Burke, James. Interview with Charles Breithaupt, March 10, 2011, Austin, Texas.

———. Telephone interview with Fred B. McKinley, May 12, 2011.

Cobb, Kenneth. Telephone interview with Fred B. McKinley, August 2, 2011.

Cummings, Robert Dale. Telephone interview with Fred B. McKinley, August 10, 2011.

DeVore, Richard. Telephone interview with Fred B. McKinley, August 12, 2011.

Dixon, Ardie. Telephone interview with Fred B. McKinley, March 15, 2011.

Ener, Bobby. Telephone interviews with Fred B. McKinley, February 22; April 27, 2011.

Fletcher, Coy. Telephone interview with Fred B. McKinley, August 15, 2011.

Foster, Thomas. Telephone interview with Fred B. McKinley, April 29, 2011.

Gibson, Macarthur. Telephone interview with Fred B. McKinley, August 14, 2011.

Goins, Jerry. Telephone interview with Fred B. McKinley, August 8, 2011.

Guillory, Charles. Telephone interview with Fred B. McKinley, August 12, 2011.

Hargrove, Robert. Telephone interview with Fred B. McKinley, February 9, 2011.

Hillin, Anthony "Pete." Telephone interview with Fred B. McKinley, July 29, 2011.

Hillin, Helene. Telephone interview with Fred B. McKinley, July 9, 2011.

Hyden, Geraldine. Interview with Fred B. McKinley and Larry Gerald, March 24, 2011, Buna, Texas.

———. Telephone interview with Fred B. McKinley, February 15, 2011.

Johnson, Benny. Telephone interview with Fred B. McKinley, August 16, 2011.

Johnson, Clinton "Radar." Telephone interview with Fred B. McKinley, July 15, 2011.

Jones, George. Telephone interview with Fred B. McKinley, August 13, 2011.

Knight, Jo Nell. Telephone interview with Fred B. McKinley, August 15, 2011.

Lindsey, Charles. Telephone interview with Fred B. McKinley, August 12, 2011.

McFarland, R. C. Telephone interview with Fred B. McKinley, August 3, 2011.

McHugh, John. Telephone interview with Fred B. McKinley, August 12, 2011.

Meaux, John "Nickie." Telephone interview with Fred B. McKinley, August 22, 2011.

Mellard, James. Telephone interview with Fred B. McKinley, February 10, 2011.

Muckleroy, Herbert. Telephone interview with Fred B. McKinley, July 28, 2011.

O'Keefe, J. D. Telephone interview with Fred B. McKinley, August 13, 2011.

Pierce, Lillian Robinson. Telephone interview with Fred B. McKinley, June 1, 2011.

Reese, Dwaine. Telephone interview with Fred B. McKinley, February 20, 2011.

Reese, Lionel. Telephone interviews with Fred B. McKinley, February 20, 25, 27; May 12, 19, 2011.

Rich, John. Telephone interviews with Fred B. McKinley, February 26; July 15, 2011.

Rogers, Delman. Telephone interview with Fred B. McKinley, March 7, 2011.

Rogers, Phil. Telephone interview with Fred B. McKinley, February 19, 2011.

Rogers, Victor. Telephone interview with Fred B. McKinley, August 5, 2011.

Ross, Herbert. Telephone interview with Fred B. McKinley, February 17, 2011.

Sanford, Lynda Robinson. Interview with Fred B. McKinley and Larry Gerald, March 26, 1911, Buna, Texas.

Sheppard, Johnny and Nelda. Telephone interview with Fred B. McKinley, May 5, 2011.

Simmons, Bobby. Telephone interview with Fred B. McKinley, August 15, 2011.

Simmons, Charles. Telephone interview with Fred B. McKinley, June 14, 2011.

Simmons, James. Telephone interview with Fred B. McKinley, July 28, 2011.

Simmons, Kay Cobb. Telephone interview with Fred B. McKinley, June 14, 2011.

Simmons, Richard Charles. Telephone interview with Fred B. McKinley, August 16, 2011.

Smith, Jasper "J. C." Telephone interviews with Fred B. McKinley, February 17; March 15, 2011.

Smith, Jerry. Telephone interview with Fred B. McKinley, February 25, 2011.

Smith, Joan. Telephone interview with Fred B. McKinley, July 27, 2011.

Sowell, Rusty. Telephone interview with Fred B. McKinley, November 28, 2010.

Stancil, Glen. Telephone interview with Fred B. McKinley, August 14, 2011.

Stanley, Don. Interview with Fred B. McKinley and Larry Gerald, March 24, 2011, Buna, Texas.

———. Telephone interview with Fred B. McKinley, February 24, 2011.

Stanley, Jerryl. Telephone interview with Fred B. McKinley, August 14, 2011.

Stanley, Pat. Interview with Fred B. McKinley and Larry Gerald, March 24, 2011, Buna, Texas.

———. Telephone interview with Fred B. McKinley, February 22, 2011.

Stom, Pat. Telephone interview with Fred B. McKinley, August 23, 2011.

Stratton, Bobby. Telephone interview with Fred B. McKinley, July 28, 2011.

Swearingen, Jackie. Telephone interview with Fred B. McKinley, July 27, 2011.

Swearingen, Paul. Telephone interview with Fred B. McKinley, August 3, 2011.

Walters, Peggy. Telephone interview with Fred B. McKinley, August 3, 2011.

Walters, Thomas Richard. Telephone interview with Fred B. McKinley, August 7, 2011.

Westbrook, Charles. Telephone interview with Fred B. McKinley, August 15, 2011.

Westbrook, Thomas E. Telephone interview with Fred B. McKinley, March 5, 2011.

Whitehead, Peggy. Telephone interview with Fred B. McKinley, August 3, 2011.

Withers, James "Blackie." Telephone interview with Fred B. McKinley, July 18, 2011.

Withers, William. Telephone interviews with Fred B. McKinley, February 17; April 4; July 24, 2011.

Unpublished Sources

Buna Junior Historians. *A History of Administration and Faculty, 1911–1989, Vol. II.* Printed internally at Buna High School, 1988–89.

———. *Buna High School—A Sports History: Vol. I.* Printed internally by Office Duplication Practices Class, Buna High School, 1987–88.

Web Sources

Ancestry.com. *Social Security Death Index* [database on-line]. Provo, UT, USA: Ancestry. com Operations Inc, 2010. Original data: Social Security Administration. *Social Security Death Index, Master File.* Social Security Administration.

"Baby Galvez Resort Brought Visitors From All Over Texas." *The Silsbee Bee Sesquicecentennial, 2008* (http://issuu.com/gdickert/docs/silsbee_bee_sesquicentennial), accessed May 5, 2011.

Buna Independent School District's website (http://www.bunaisd.net/campuses), accessed March 7, 2011.

"Casey at the Bat by Ernest Thayer." *Baseball Almanac* (http://www.baseball-almanac.com/poetry/po_case.shtml), accessed May 14, 2011.

Class (Conference) Champions, 1940–70. Prairie View Interscholastic League Basketball Records (http://www2.uiltexas.org/athletics/archives/basketball/pvil_records.html), accessed September 1, 2011.

"Real 'Hoosiers' Better Story than the Movie's?" Apr. 3, 2010. CBS News.com (http://www.cbsnews.com/stories/2010/04/03/earlyshow/saturday/main6360209.shtm), accessed March 13, 2011.

Smith, Aaron. "Top Five Basketball Dynasties of All Time," (http://www.associated content.com/article/1387540/top_five_basketball_dynasties_of_all.html), accessed March 2, 2011.

Snyder, Brent. "Buna." BeaumontEnterprise.com (http://www.beaumontenterprise.com/default/article/Buna-748121.php), accessed March 1, 2011.

Wilbanks, Dr. Billy. Coaches with Most State Championships-Boys (http://www.drbilly wilbanks.com/basketball/misc.html#coaches), accessed June 5, 2011.

———. Texas Basketball Champions (http://www.texasbasketballchamps.com), accessed March 9, 2011.

———. Texas Basketball Champs–Team Narratives (http://www.drbillywilbanks.com/ basketball/teams.htm), accessed February 10, 2011.

Winn, Luke. "Inside Basketball-The Hoops Ideology Report." SI.com (Nov. 17, 2008) (http://sportsillustrated.cnn.com/vault/article/web/COM1148679/2/index.htm), accessed July 7, 2011.

Wood, Dylan. "LEONA, TX." *Handbook of Texas Online* (http://www.tshaonline.org/handbook/online/articles/hll38), accessed March 15, 2011.

Wooster, Robert. "BUNA, TX." *Handbook of Texas Online* (http://www.tshaonline.org/handbook/online/articles/hjb22), accessed March 4, 2011.

Authors' Personal Reflections

In 1954, soon after the East Texas Pulp and Paper Company (Eastex) opened in Evadale, my dad got a job there, and just across the Neches River in Silsbee, he rented an apartment. Mom and I left our San Augustine County home and joined him in early 1955. Later that summer, we moved to Buna and into our two-bedroom house in the Sheppard Subdivision built recently by Tom Barker and his son, Eugene, whom everyone called "Buck."

We were surprised to learn that most of our new neighbors came from Louisiana. Bobby Breithaupt, who'd lived in the Pelican state while working for the International Paper Company in Natchez, Mississippi, was now at Eastex, along with other new hires, Lionel Turner, Leroy Mitchell, Dub Wendell, Ed Mabrey, and Leo "Buster" Patterson, all ex-employees of the paper company in Elizabeth, near Oakdale. Because all of them had also bought in the same subdivision as we did, we laughingly called the place "Little Oakdale."

When I first enrolled in the fall of 1955 as a student in Buna Junior High, I was in the eighth grade. It didn't take long until I began to hear about this game of basketball, and how important it was to the community. Ad nauseam, I heard my classmates comment about how the boys' high school basketball team almost won their division in 1954, and at the finish of the 1955 season, just this past March, the Cougars came home with a Conference A state championship trophy.

"We have a good coach," they said, "and we'll probably go back next year and win again."

At first, I thought the comments too boastful, especially when one student said that the school calendar had the days for the upcoming March already blocked out for a holiday, so that many as possible could attend the state tournament in Austin.

They asked if I played basketball.

"No," I responded. "In Chinquapin, where I'm from, we didn't play anything besides softball, that is, unless you include the game of marbles."

"What about football?" I countered.

"No, we don't play that," another student answered, "and we haven't for quite a while."

I wanted to know why, but I never got a straight answer.

A year later, at the urging of several buddies, I tried out for the ninth-grade basketball team. Coach Harold Simmons exhibited patience beyond all reason, teaching a new recruit how to hold a ball, how to dribble, how to shoot, and about the time the season concluded, I was getting the hang of it. I was not good, mind you, but better.

Before school was out, Mr. Simmons advised us that if we wanted to try out for the varsity team, coached by Cotton Robinson, we should report about ten days into the summer break. So, I gathered along with other members of my class, all former teammates—and timidly walked onto the floor with Jimmy Cobb, Charles Simmons, Jerry Goins, Dan Stancil, William Withers, Paul Swearingen, Bull Muckleroy, and Herman Davis. Each of these veterans had been on the Conference-AA state championship team of the previous season, and in their presence, I was awestruck.

About two weeks later, unfortunately, my interest in making the team began to wane. I went to Coach Robinson and informed him of my decision to leave. He asked if I had given this serious thought, and could he talk me out of it.

I answered, "My mind's made up."

He responded first with a huge grin, and then his demeanor turned serious. "Fred, you'll regret this decision," he said. "But if you quit now, there's only one way to come back."

"And that is?"

"It's simple. All you have to do is stand under the goal, jump, and touch the rim."

"Is that all?"

"Yep," he said, "but that's not an easy thing to do." With the short exchange at end, I nodded and left his office.

As it turned out, Coach was right on all counts. I did regret my decision, and I was never able to touch the rim of a basketball goal, no matter how many times I attempted it, or inches in height were added to my skinny frame.

But this was not the end of my relationship with Cotton Robinson. One morning after geography class, he asked me to come by later and talk to him. I had no idea why, but I did as directed. To my surprise, he proposed that I go to work at his and Monte Sybil's drive-in, similar to a Dairy Queen, across from the school and on the corner of the street that ran beside his house and Highway 62. What's more, the benefits included a salary of fifty cents an hour and all the hamburgers, malts, and other snacks that I could possibly consume. I accepted what was then a generous offer for a student, and stayed there for about two years.

After obtaining a degree from Lamar State College of Technology (now Lamar University) in Beaumont, Texas, I returned to Buna High to teach civics (political science) and every history course offered by the school's curriculum. Cotton had since retired and left the high school basketball coaching duties to Harold Simmons.

During that year, which was to be the first and last of my teaching career, I talked to Cotton many times, and I even bought a life insurance policy from him. When the spring semester ended, I returned to Beaumont, life took control, and I never saw him again. That's another of my regrets.

In 2009, Rusty Sowell, a friend of mine who served as student manager on the 1962–63 Buna boys' state championship team, advised me that Larry Hatch, a member of that year's squad, had often said that someone should write a book about Mr. Robinson. Rusty asked me to think about it, and I agreed.

Frankly, I doubted being able to find enough source material to do justice to the topic. Nevertheless, I contacted Dr. Charles Breithaupt, Executive Director of the University Interscholastic League in Austin, and inquired about holdings that might aid my research.

Charles, the son of Melba and Bobby Breithaupt, dear friends of my family, said that he had once given consideration to writing a comparable book, but he had never found the time. It took only a few minutes of conversation to convince the two of us that we should pool our resources and begin the collaboration which led to this finished work.

—FRED B. MCKINLEY
Burleson, Texas

My childhood home was sandwiched between our church and the high school in Buna, Texas. The front door to the gymnasium was less than 100 yards from our house, and the back door to the church was less than 50. In fact, I left a furrowed path through the preacher's backyard on my way to the gym. In youth, I got a heavy dose of the two Bs: Bible and basketball. In many ways, I probably had an unhealthy dose of the latter.

No doubt that interest was piqued because of the enormous success of the Buna Cougars, our high school basketball team. Led by legendary coach M. N. "Cotton" Robinson, the Cougars won seven state championships between 1955–1963. I was a witness to a large number of those victories. And I was hooked.

My parents originally lived in the "Little Oakdale" subdivision of Buna as referred to by Fred. My dad worked shift work at the paper mill, and he scheduled his long weekends and vacation around basketball tournaments.

As my parents carted me to game after game, I became very aware of the Buna legacy and the prevailing notion that Cotton Robinson was "king" of the Cougar dynasty. I started elementary school in 1960, the year of Buna's fifth state championship. Only a first grader, I was already a Ph.D. in all things Buna basketball.

When my own playing career began in fourth grade in the old Buna log gym, I became quite aware of the fact that it wasn't as easy as Coach Robinson and the Cougars made it out to be. We finished fourth in the church league. I am not sure how our coach, Mike Husbands, tolerated us, but he did so for the next five years.

The junior high teams I played on were highly successful. We lost only four games in three years. Coach David Stark and our ninth-grade coach, Noah Boyette, always had great teams, and we were no exception. They taught us how to win and how to act. We thought we would easily be able to carry on the great Cougar basketball tradition. But not so fast.

We lost the district championship, a one-point heartbreaker to Newton in my sophomore year, but this was only the beginning of sheer agony. Because of a racial divide in my junior year, our team was left with only six players, all small, all slow, white guys. Too much could be made of the fact that every African-American player left the Buna program during that season. While there were some undercurrents of displeasure from the black players about the direction of the program, in my opinion this was simply a misunderstanding, blown out of proportion.

One of our starters, who happened to be black, refused to comply with the coach's guidance, and either quit or was dismissed from the team. His brother, another starter, quit in protest, and by the end of the next day, every African-American player on both the junior varsity and freshman teams dropped out of the program. Some were coerced into quitting, including two of my good friends, Leo Brown and Jackie Renfro. We ended that 1970–71 season with only three wins, and my senior year was not much better. While we improved to an eight-win season, this was a far cry from state title aspirations.

There were several other factors that caused the downturn in our fortunes. First, we flat out weren't very talented. Secondly, we weren't very committed, and thirdly, other teams had caught and passed Buna in the sport of basketball. And, too, the times, they were a-changing.

Cotton Robinson had a great impact on my own coaching career. Even though he was not my high school coach, I spent as much time as possible listening to him and asking questions. I pored over the films of the Buna state championship games, and I based the foundation of my coaching principles on what I had learned from the Robinson philosophy.

Making it to the state tournament for the first time in my coaching career in 1984 with my Hardin-Jefferson team was a tremendous professional accomplishment. I remember vividly a phone call that I received from Coach Robinson, congratulating me on our win in the regional finals and wishing me luck at state. That was a great thrill.

In 1991 when my Hardin-Jefferson Hawks' team won the Conference-AAA state championship, I thought a great deal about the legacy of Cotton Robinson, for on my team, I had a six-foot-four forward named Jeff Burke. Thirty years to the day earlier, Jeff's father, Jimmy, was the point guard for Buna's state title team. It felt as if Coach Robinson had his hand on our shoulders.

While he has been gone from the game for nearly half a century, his contributions to the game and his mark on the sport are apparent at almost every level. The Buna System fashioned by him is still utilized by coaches today. But none have come close to matching his phenomenal records.

—CHARLES BREITHAUPT
Georgetown, Texas

Index

The Authors

Fred B. McKinley, a native of Beaumont, received a B.A. in government (1964) from Lamar State College of Technology and an M.A. in history (1987) from Lamar University. In 1964, he returned to Buna to teach high school social studies for one year. Thereafter, he embarked on a long and distinguished career in the credit industry before joining the Louisiana Department of Justice, in which he served as a supervisory criminal investigator in the Attorney General's office, before retiring in 1999. In the interim, he also attended Louisiana State University, where he obtained a law enforcement certification (1995).

He is the author of three other books, including *Chinqua Where? The Spirit of Rural America, 1947–1955*; *Devil's Pocket, a Novel*; *A Plea for Justice: the Timothy Cole Story*; and co-author of another with Greg Riley titled *Black Gold to Bluegrass: From the Oil Fields of Texas to Spindletop Farm of Kentucky*. McKinley, a contributor of numerous articles to national magazines and other professional publications, continues to write and lecture on various subjects that relate to his works. He and his wife, Dottie, currently reside in Burleson, Texas.

Dr. Charles Breithaupt was named by the University of Texas as Executive Director of the University Interscholastic League in 2009 after fourteen years as UIL Director of Athletics. He is the seventh Executive Director in the 100-year history of the organization. The UIL governs extracurricular activities for over 1,400 high schools with nearly two million participants. He also serves as Associate Vice President for the Division of Diversity and Community Engagement at UT.

A graduate of Buna High School, he earned both his bachelor's and master's degrees from Lamar University. He completed his doctorate at the University of Texas in Austin.

He was a head basketball coach for fourteen years and amassed a record of 392–92, an 81 percent winning ratio. His teams won ten district championships, advanced to the regional tournament five times and to the state tournament twice. His 1984 team finished as state runner-up, and his 1991 team won the Conference-AAA state championship with a 37–1 record. He was named coach of the year nine times and state coach of the year by the Texas Association of Basketball Coaches (TABC) in 1991.

He served as president of the TABC in 1989–90. Thereafter, he was inducted into the Texas High School Basketball Hall of Fame in 2003 and the Texas High School Coaches Hall of Honor in 2005.

Nationally, Dr. Breithaupt serves on the Board of Directors for the National Federation of State High School Associations, and he has also served on the NFHS Basketball Rules Committee. He and his wife, Debbie, currently reside in Georgetown, Texas.